Ramblings of a
Lowcountry Game Warden

RAMBLINGS OF A LOWCOUNTRY GAME WARDEN

A Memoir

Ben McC. Moïse

The University of South Carolina Press

© 2008 University of South Carolina

Cloth edition published by the University of South Carolina Press, 2008
Paperback edition published in Columbia, South Carolina,
by the University of South Carolina Press, 2009

www.sc.edu/uscpress

Manufactured in the United States of America

18 17 16 15 14 13 12 11 10 09   10 9 8 7 6 5 4 3 2 1

The Library of Congress has cataloged the cloth edition as follows:

Moïse, Ben McC.
  Ramblings of a lowcountry game warden : a memoir / Ben McC. Moïse.
      p. cm.
  ISBN 978-1-57003-728-3 (cloth : alk. paper)
  1. Moïse, Ben McC. 2. Game wardens—South Carolina—Biography.
  3. South Carolina—Description and travel. I. Title.
SK354.M65A3 2008
363.28—dc22
  [B]   2007033326

ISBN 978-1-57003-881-5 (pbk)

To Anne, Melissa, and Sarah

Contents

Illustrations

Foreword

The year was 1996, and my wife, Martha, and I were attending the South-eastern Wildlife Exposition in Charleston. I serve on the board for this wonderful organization and never miss an event. One of the exhibitors we met that year was Danie Malan, a hunting outfitter from South Africa. After a short visit we booked our fifth African safari with him.

Danie invited us to join him at a local friend's home the following Saturday night for a lowcountry feast highlighted by an oyster roast. Debating the invitation, I casually mentioned it to a friend who was a Charlestonian. He immediately proceeded to question my epicurean discriminatory abilities as well as my cerebral competence. How could I even consider not attending? This, he elaborated, was a highly coveted invitation to all that is divine in coastal culinary delights. I accepted forthwith, and there I met our hosts, Ben Moïse and his lovely bride, Anne. My friend did not exaggerate the righteousness of this sumptuous repast, and for ten years I have not missed this annual event, invitation or not.

Much more was born of that first meeting than the consumption of brown whiskey and delightful delicacies from the tidewater. Ben and I became fast friends. It was obvious that we had a lot in common. We were the same age and had both produced two children with wonderful southern ladies who by the grace of God have remained with us. We both enjoy good cigars, clear elixir produced under lunar light, and old musty hunting and history books. Canine companions and homes full of hunting memorabilia are additional shared traits.

But there was one marked difference. Ben was a game warden, and I spent my life, at least in my younger days, looking over my shoulder for the likes of him. Although my record is clean through all these years, I was always nervous about the multitude of regulations by which I had to be careful to abide. Because I have served on many conservation boards, including the advisory board to the Georgia Department of Natural Resources, it would never have worked for me to shoot an early duck or keep an undersized fish. My wife said that I just had a guilty conscience.

Ben Moïse, however, was not just a conservation officer, he was a game warden of renown, undeniably the most famous to ever inhabit the tidal estuaries and broad spartina flats of South Carolina. On hearing a strange sound in the night, many a duck hunter, crabber, or fisherman has called out, "Ben, is that you Ben?" And often it was. Emerging from the black of night or through sheets of rain, Ben would appear in his thirteen-foot Boston Whaler or his small johnboat. He spent twenty-four years bringing game-law violators to justice and fighting governmental-political bureaucracy, which too often is deleterious to the cause. Like a pit bull when he was hot on the trail of a lawbreaker or trying one in court, he never let go.

Any conservation officer will, by retirement time, have ample fireside stories to tell. But one of Ben's repute will have volumes. So after a little encouragement from me and other friends—and an inward desire to do so anyway—Ben has now spent countless hours recording his memoirs. For all who enjoy the outdoors and its array of wild critters, this book will be a great read. However, for coastal South Carolinians it will be a must read. After all some of you may now become infamous.

Ben's preparation for a career in law enforcement was substantial. He attended Carlisle Military School, the Citadel, the University of South Carolina, and Webster College and served four years in the United States Coast Guard. His book quickly takes the reader through his decision to become a game warden and the ensuing hurdles he faced to make his dream come true.

Most of Ben's "ramblings" are divided into categories, including shrimpers, dove hunters, crabbers, night hunters, dope smugglers, duck hunters, and the like. In each he relates adventures featuring hair-raising, life-threatening experiences as well as peculiar personalities and coastal characters that defy belief. There are also many misadventures, and here Ben pulls no punches. In ample detail he describes some of his slightly humorous mistakes and absolutely hilarious bad luck. "Murphy's Law," which took place with his daughter Sarah, had me laughing so hard that Martha snatched the manuscript from me to read it.

With some of the lowcountry culture who didn't mind pushing the legal envelope, Ben developed a reputation of being ruthless and without mercy. With some who deserved it, this will ring loud and true. But in fact there was a soft heart when amnesty was prudent. Such was the case with the group of feeble old men hunting marsh hens or the youngster who killed an illegal pintail on his first duck hunt with his father. Ben often went far beyond required limits to avoid penalizing some and even helped them with their future outdoor endeavors.

Ben Moïse didn't limit his career experiences as a conservation officer to just chasing bad guys. He made presentations to educational groups and conservation societies. He received many awards and much recognition for his dedicated service and achievements, including the Order of the Palmetto, South Carolina's highest civilian recognition.

When Ben officially retired on January 20, 2002, he was in his boat, just off Matthew's Canal late in the afternoon. As the sun set in the west, so did one of the finest careers in conservation come to an end. It left a sizable gap in the "thin green line," one that will be hard to fill. But many of his amazing experiences are now recorded here for everyone to enjoy. It's one of those books you will read quickly while experiencing a complete range of emotions. You will not put it down.

Dr. Lloyd Newberry

Acknowledgments

I am truly grateful to the watermen, hunters, and sports fishermen of the lowcountry for providing a career's worth of stories. My appreciation extends to family, friends, and colleagues who sat with me in various circles around campfires, kitchen tables, and boardroom tables and told me I should write a book. Those sentiments also apply to friends who read portions of the slowly emerging manuscript and offered encouragement and valuable perspective.

Thanks beyond measure go to my bride, Anne, who was an ever-present force in spirit, if not in person, on each page of this book. The warm, nurturing home I returned to after every patrol was an anchor of stability and reality in a sometimes-chaotic and unreal career. In the creation of this book, she not only listened patiently to my readings of countless passages at all hours of the day and night, but she also reviewed each and every page with an eye for the fatal syntactical fluctuations that frequently beset my narratives and dispensed sage advice on how to bring them back to life.

I am indebted to my daughter Melissa, who made me a grandfather, for sorting several decades' worth of old slides and photographs and scanning them onto a computer disc. All the photographs in this book are from my personal collection. Also welcome was the timely assistance of my younger daughter, Sarah, who frequently came to my rescue by helping me navigate through the briar patch of word processing, of which she is the unexcelled master.

I am sincerely grateful to my friend Dr. Lloyd Newberry, a sporting author and senior editor of *Sporting Classics*. Despite being involved in the completion of his third book—he graciously read my manuscript and wrote the foreword.

Finally I would like to acknowledge my appreciation of the South Carolina Department of Natural Resources, which provided the bailiwick from which these stories spring.

Charleston to Beaufort—60 miles

WMA: Wildlife Management Area
ACE: Ashepoo-Combahee-Edisto

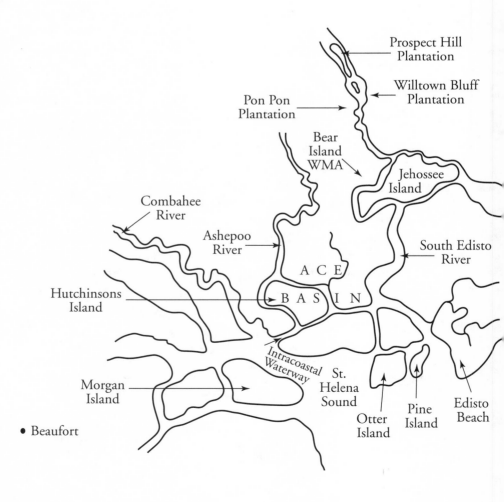

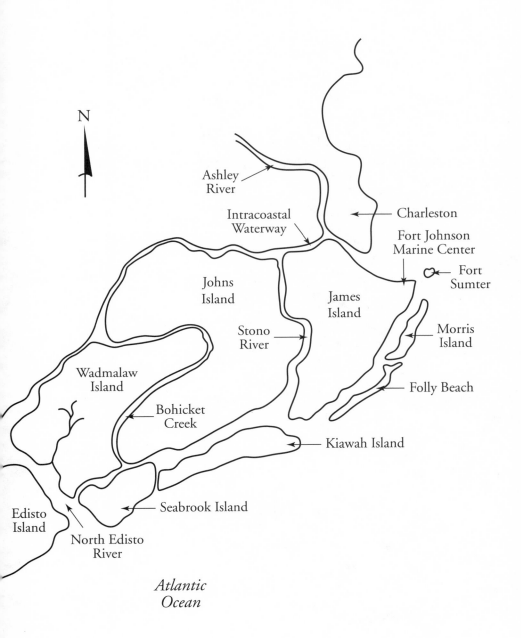

N

Ashley
River

Intracoastal
Waterway

Charleston

Fort Johnson
Marine Center

Fort
Sumter

Johns
Island

James
Island

Morris
Island

Stono
River

Wadmalaw
Island

Folly Beach

Bohicket
Creek

Kiawah Island

Seabrook Island

Edisto
Island

North Edisto
River

*Atlantic
Ocean*

Map by Judy Burress

CHARLESTON TO GEORGETOWN—65 MILES

Francis Marion
National Forest

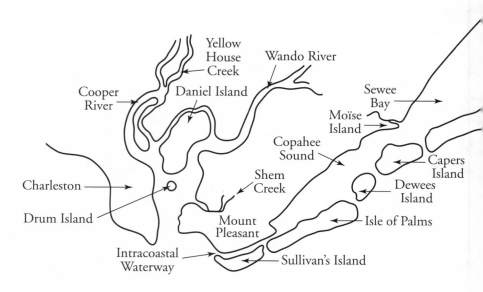

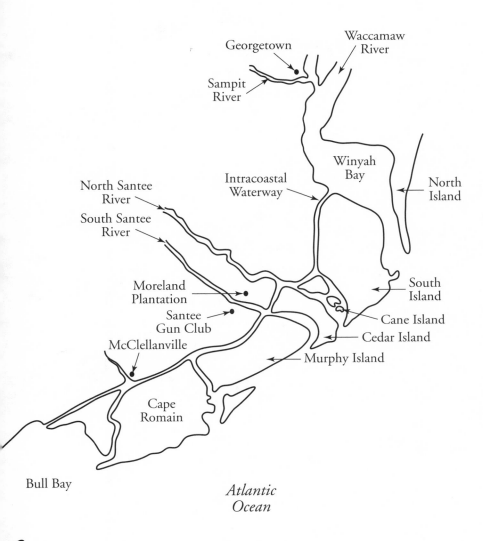

Georgetown

Waccamaw
River

Sampit
River

Winyah
Bay

North Santee
River

Intracoastal
Waterway

North
Island

South Santee
River

Moreland
Plantation

South
Island

Santee
Gun Club

Cane Island

McClellanville

Cedar Island

Murphy Island

Cape
Romain

Bull Bay

*Atlantic
Ocean*

Bull Island

Ramblings of a
Lowcountry Game Warden

Introduction

This memoir describes my adventures and sometimes misadventures during almost twenty-five years of wildlife-enforcement work in the South Carolina lowcountry. In that quarter century I was eyewitness to many dramatic changes not only in the coastal marshscape but also in public attitudes and governmental policies that determined the direction of our state's resource-protection efforts.

The lowcountry is a land of curious contradictions. There are vast reaches of tranquil swamps, spacious stretches of marshlands, and wooded barrier islands that stand side by side with populous cities and insurgent suburban development, whose visible manifestations include docks, roads, and traffic —elements that persistently chisel away at the quality of open spaces and the wildlife that inhabits them.

Most of those changes I was powerless to contain, but enforcing regulations protecting what was left was one thing I could contribute. The poacher operates in remote areas, the nether reaches of marshes and swamps, places with few witnesses. It required a great deal more than just a passing familiarity with the topography to understand such locales and to patrol them effectively.

Some have described my pursuit of violators as "driven." I would rather describe my labors as "strongly motivated" by my deep respect for the fragile diversity of our coastal resources and my desire to protect them from the depredations of an assorted lot of culprits hell-bent on harming them. Those remote locales became my "office" in all seasons, in all states of the weather, and at all hours of the day and night.

I shared that huge estuarine environment with a cast of characters whose temperaments and points of view covered an almost unimaginable span of human behavior. The following stories reveal a broad range of interventions with those characters. Some did not exactly go my way, but I believe that I prevailed more often than not. In any event each encounter was a learning experience, teaching me tolerance, humility, patience, and persistence. Many of the incidents were not without humorous elements.

In a few stories the names of misdemeanants have been omitted to spare them further embarrassment. All the included names and incidents are matters of public record.

Someone recently asked me if writing tickets was really my main "thing," and I had to admit frankly, without a whole lot of soul-searching, that it was.

A coastal marsh-scape, my "office"

Doing what I did best, writing a ticket

I was sure in the knowledge that a ticket conveyed the message that the bearer should be more careful and attentive to the values of good sportsmanship embodied in words of the law. The law's function is to articulate society's moral condemnation of certain behavior. Some people need to be reminded every now and then that there are consequences attendant on bad behavior. I always felt good about what I did—and what all game wardens do—protecting our state's natural resources and helping to ensure that everyone can continue to share and enjoy those resources.

If there is a moral to be found in any of these stories, it is "if you dance to the music, you had better be prepared to pay the piper." That is the personal perspective I bring to the field of outdoor writing. There is much to be enjoyed in the lowcountry by taking the time to savor the experience and by respecting others who might be trying to do the same.

Becoming a game warden was a defining moment for me. I cannot imagine any other occupation that would have been as rewarding or have generated as much personal satisfaction. Besides, would you be reading a book about my life as a shoe salesman? I am thankful that I had the opportunity to make my mark as a member of South Carolina's "thin green line."

"Mudflat Moïse"

I came on the job in June of 1978, three years after my initial application. After successfully passing a written state-merit-system exam and a physical-agility test, I sat for an interview with two district captains and the chief of the Law Enforcement and Boating Division at the Columbia headquarters.

At that time I was one course away from completing my long-awaited undergraduate degree at the University of South Carolina. I had served for four years in the United States Coast Guard, mostly right in the Charleston area, and had already run through a series of careers that included newspaper writing, house painting, stevedoring on the Charleston waterfront, and operating four different businesses: two catering companies, a tape-recorded tour-guide company, and a tourist-brochure distribution service along the South Carolina coast.

Although I would hardly call it an obsession, I had pretty much wanted to be a game warden since my first encounter with one back in the mid-1950s. Every afternoon while delivering newspapers by bicycle in rural Sumter County, I stopped by a small country store along my route (a forerunner of the 7-Eleven), owned by G. A. Thompson, a delightful and gregarious old gentleman. There I had the opportunity to listen to the adventures of a game warden who routinely arrived about the same time I did. Without fail he would buy a cold bottle of Coca-Cola, which he called a "dope," and a cellophane bag of salted peanuts. After taking a hefty swig of Coke, he would pour the peanuts and a sleeve of BC Powder into the bottle. There was no end to the stories he told as he variously shook, swigged, and chewed that amazing concoction.

He wore a khaki uniform and a brown fedora and carried a blue steel revolver in a leather holster on his belt. I was suitably impressed. He was the only uniformed person I was acquainted with other than the sheriff's deputies who guarded the stripe-clad chain gang that worked along the county highways. (I met the sheriff, I. Byrd Parnell, in person one time during an unfortunate episode involving the midnight acquisition of some watermelons, but that is another story.)

My family and I lived on my grandfather's farm, about two miles out of Sumter at the junction of Brewington Road and Highway 401. The family called it Ingleside. The house we lived in, the circa 1790 Heriot-Moïse House, is on the National Register of Historic Places. The farm had acres of cultivated fields and gardens, a pecan orchard and grapevine, a large barn, numerous outbuildings, a swimming pool, and the main attraction for me, Rocky Bluff Swamp, which was located across Brewington Road at the end of the holly-tree avenue in front of the house.

It was my daily playground. In the tree-shaded confines of the section of Rocky Bluff Swamp that extended between Highway 15 and Highway 401, I explored, camped, hunted, and trapped. I traversed it day or night from end to end and side to side, usually without even getting my feet wet. My hideouts were everywhere. My mother described me as a swamp rat.

I became infamous for the "swamp things" that I brought to school (when I bothered to attend). They wreaked havoc among the old-maid teachers and female students. Following a few noteworthy episodes, I was made to promise not to bring any more large spiders or snakes of any size to class, regardless of whether they were poisonous or not, at penalty of expulsion and a good whipping by the principal. My father backed up the school by promises of more to come at home if I caused any more disturbances. My mother was heard to say that I was not an easy boy to raise.

Probably because of my legendary show-and-tell episodes in school, in 1958, when I was fifteen years old, the Sumter County Fish and Game Association sponsored my attendance at the Wildlife Conservation Camp in Cheraw, South Carolina. It was one of those "Saul on the road to Damascus" experiences, for there I found my true calling.

There were wildlife classes and daily field trips to study indigenous flora and fauna, and the people there actually liked snakes. I came to know Gordon Brown, the Wildlife Department photographer, who took me under his wing and showed me how to observe nature with a keen eye for even the smallest details. I was not only enchanted by the extra attention but also excited to see and understand things I had previously noticed just casually. It gave me an altogether new perspective. Here were experiences and things worth preserving. I became even more firmly convinced that I wanted to be a game warden and work in the woods.

At that time I did not have a proper regard for academic achievement. My mother and father saw fit to remove me from my carefree, barefoot existence and send me to Carlisle Military School in Bamberg, South Carolina, to focus my attention on more scholarly matters. My father said that he sent me to Carlisle to study map reading since I seemed, more often than not, to stray unerringly down the primrose path. Electroshock therapy could not have applied as much of a jolt. I got to wear a uniform, but it was not the one I had in mind. Three years at Carlisle Military School, three years at the Citadel, a two-year interval at the University of South Carolina, and four years in the Coast Guard—followed by numerous intervening career moves —provided distractions from my earlier ambition to be a game warden. The

Conservation officer's shoulder patch and badge before the Wildlife and Marine Resources Department was renamed the Department of Natural Resources in 1993

desire remained, however, and I thought about it in those existential reveries when I had time to ponder the limitless possibilities of being.

Somehow—and for the life of me I cannot remember what specifically precipitated it—I decided in 1975 to apply to the South Carolina Wildlife Department for a conservation officer's (game warden's) job. Periodic calls to the personnel office in Columbia for several years after my initial contact yielded pretty much the same response: "There are no openings in Charleston County."

Believing there to be no likelihood of change in that forecast for the foreseeable future, I decided to pursue another avenue of adventure. Having investigated job opportunities with the United States Military Sealift Command and gone through the lengthy application and security-clearance process, I was offered a billet as storekeeper aboard one of their ships. Days before I was to report to Bayonne, New Jersey, to have a physical, fill out additional paperwork, and be assigned to the ship, I got a phone call from the personnel office at the Wildlife Department asking if I was still interested in a job with them.

I was one of several applicants for three Charleston County openings. One of the positions was in District Nine, which was then called the Coastal Environmental Enforcement District. The other two positions were in the boating division and in District Five, which handled fresh-water fish and game laws in Charleston County. One of the other applicants was Betty Jean McCaskill, a petite and attractive young lady, who was hired for the District Five opening as the first female conservation officer in South Carolina.

By the time of the interview with the chief of the Wildlife Department Law Enforcement Division and two district captains, I had already completed the state-merit-system examination. I had also appeared with other applicants at the Criminal Justice Academy in Columbia, where I was required to run, walk, or crawl the distance of one mile within a measured length of time and pick up and carry a twenty-five-horsepower outboard engine between sawhorses set around fifty feet apart. Those little exercises were called a physical-agility test.

At the time I was living on Sullivan's Island, just outside of Charleston. Not too long after the interview, I had a surprise visit from Sergeant Earl Driggers, the leader of the Charleston County District Nine unit. He gave me the good news that I had been hired and that I was to go with him to Columbia in several days to obtain uniforms and equipment as well as a patrol car.

The headquarters office was then in Dutch Plaza. There I was issued all the accoutrements for a conservation officer: long- and short-sleeve gray cotton shirts, a clip-on green tie, green polyester dress trousers, a lattice-weave-patterned ranger belt, briar-proof pants, an L.L. Bean goose-down "Warden's Parka," black oxford shoes, green leather boots, caps, a pair of handcuffs with belt case, a dash-mounted blue light, and a stainless-steel model 66 Smith & Wesson .357 Magnum pistol. Later that afternoon, I was issued a 1969 Plymouth patrol car with a driver's side spotlight and a mobile radio with a large whip antenna.

Between equipment issues I appeared before the director of the Law Enforcement and Boating Division for the first of six monthly interviews during my probationary period. Pat Ryan, the director, was regarded as somewhat of an "éminence grise." A former Marine, he was not big on small talk. He usually got right to the point, had his say; then the interview was over.

I had much to think about during the long drive back to Sullivan's Island in my newly acquired patrol car. I was proud of it even though it was nine years old, had more than one hundred thousand miles on it, and was soon to become a maintenance nightmare. I remember thinking, "What in the hell have you gotten yourself into now?" Then I adjusted the rear-view mirror so I could see the long whip antenna swooping back in the wind and listened with great interest all the way back to Charleston to the frequent radio calls blaring from the Wildlife Department radio. I was happy. I was at long last a game warden, making just over nine thousand dollars a year. How in the world was I going to spend that much money?

The next morning, decked out in my brand-new uniform, I drove over to the marine center at Fort Johnson on James Island, where the District Nine headquarters was located. I was given a daily-activity report book, issued a book of summonses (tickets), and informed that I had been assigned to the Georgetown unit, which covered the coast from Sullivan's Island to Little River at the South Carolina–North Carolina line. This included the coast of northern Charleston County and Georgetown and Horry counties.

I was assigned to work with Corporal Buster Fort, whose home over-looked the Intracoastal Waterway bordering Buck Hall Landing near Awendaw. It was about twenty miles from my house on Sullivan's Island to Fort's house and more than forty miles from my house to the Georgetown unit office. I reported to Fort's home that same afternoon to begin learning the ropes before entering the police academy.

Officer Fort was small of stature and slightly portly. He had a reputation for being persistent and thorough. He chewed Red Man tobacco, smoked cigars, and had an intimate knowledge of the myriad creeks, bays, and sounds that intersected the vast marsh between the Santee Delta and Capers Island. He was also well acquainted with the people who worked there.

It seemed that most of the officers then chewed tobacco, a pernicious habit that I soon acquired. Officer Fort could spit right out of his car window while running down the highway. I used a bottle or cup as a receptacle, being unable to attain sufficient velocity to project any great distance. I did observe that the whole driver's side of his car, from front door to rear bumper, was covered by a large brown streak. In a few places the chrome around the windows had been eaten away by the tobacco juice. At least he could project it out the window. The presence of full spit cups in several of my vehicles had grievous consequences over the years.

Fort set our patrol schedules. Most of the time we patrolled during the day, launching his seventeen-foot Glassmaster at either Buck Hall Landing or the McClellanville boat ramp. I quickly learned that the coastal marshes held many surprises in the form of shallow flats or shell banks just beneath the surface. When I got my own patrol boat, I found operating a boat is a completely different experience than being a passenger in one.

After I launched forth on my own, I think I went aground on each and every flat and shell rake at least once. My talent for wearing down propellers to the hub was legendary. One of the outboard repair shops in Mount Pleasant had a row of my truncated props mounted on the wall. At one time I was known as "Mudflat Moïse." I think Captain Ed McTeer had one particularly noteworthy example that he used as a paperweight on his desk. I was not issued any expensive stainless-steel props until the row of damaged aluminum props had substantially ceased growing.

Despite his familiarity with the area, even Officer Fort occasionally strayed out of the channels. One night we were on a night patrol in Cape Romain Harbor, a large bay behind Cape Island, searching for illegal shrimp-trawling activity. We came out of the mouth of Casino Creek and headed diagonally across the bay to a point called the Cowpens. A deep channel runs across and intersects with another deep channel behind Cape Island. That was a restricted area where trawling was prohibited. Though trawling there at any time was regarded as a serious violation of the law, it was a favorite "dragging" spot for violators.

It was a dark night, and visibility was next to nil with only a few distant lights on the mainland to give one any orientation. We got across to the

Cowpens dock and sat for several hours just listening. All we heard was the surf breaking on the other side of Cape Island and the frequent slap of our hands as we swatted representatives of Cape Romain's legendary mosquito swarms.

Around one in the morning Fort concluded the patrol and headed back across to the mouth of Casino Creek. I assumed that he knew where he was going, and the thought that we would run aground never entered my mind until the boat suddenly lurched upward. All forward motion ceased; the engine roared; the propeller started spinning mud and shell over the back of the boat.

Illumination from a flashlight quickly revealed that we were in the marsh grass, perched atop a shell bank with the tide rapidly receding. We had missed the mouth of the creek about twenty yards to port. We jumped out of the boat and tried to turn the bow around but to no avail. Glassmasters were just too heavy to pick up and move.

There was one hour until low tide and five or six more hours until there would be enough water to refloat the boat. Among his great store of equipment Buster always kept several army-surplus mosquito nets in a bag under the seat. We unfolded the boat seats to form a sort of bed and arranged the netting over us.

A goodly number of pesky little beasts either found tiny holes to enter or crawled under the net. Those that managed to escape our frequent swattings feasted royally on an ever-diminishing supply of our blood. The morning light revealed what appeared to be clusters of grapes hanging inside the netting: hundreds of mosquitoes, each gorged like a tick.

We were hungry, thirsty, and tired after a fitful night with the constant drone of mosquitoes. It also was extremely boring just to sit there high and dry and watch the tide come in. At least we didn't suffer the indignity of hearing the distant throb of an outboard engine towing a try net across the bay behind us.

Sunrise came as a welcome sight, and around eight thirty in the morning we heard the sound of a plane flying high over the marsh. As it approached, we recognized it as one of the Wildlife Department airplanes. Spotting us perched atop our shell bank, the plane made a looping turn and started a rapid descent directly toward us.

Fort clicked on the walkie-talkie, which he had turned off to conserve battery power, and called for the plane. The voice of Sergeant Eugene Pluto, our unit supervisor, came back and said, "Is that really you, Buster?" As the plane swooped low over us and began circling to come back, Sergeant Pluto heckled Officer Fort about his navigational dilemma. The second swoop was lower and the heckling grew more strident.

Officer Fort's patience, which was already pretty well worn, was ebbing just about as fast as the tide had left us the night before. He stood up on the bow of the boat, drew his pistol, and said over the walkie-talkie, "If you come over me one more time like that, I'm going to shoot you down!"

As it was preparing for its third dive, the plane suddenly flared off and left the area. We were finally able to push the boat off the bank and made our way back across the cape to McClellanville, muddy, sweaty, hungry, thirsty, tired, bug bit, and glad to be back. That episode was fodder for derision from our fellow officers for months to come.

We spent a lot of time checking crabbers, oyster pickers, and clammers. The first ticket I ever wrote was to Mose Weston for possession of undersize blue crabs. Crabs, then as now, had to be at least five inches across the back from point to point to be legal. After I checked his baskets, I found Mr. Weston to be in violation. I wrote the ticket and imposed the standard twenty-five-dollar bond, which in most instances was the amount of the fine if the facts were clear and the defendant was found guilty.

The magistrate in McClellanville was the honorable Tom Dukes, a delightful and hardworking gentleman, who operated Bull Bay Seafood. Sometimes court was held wherever he happened to be, in his office, on the dock, or down in the hold of a trawler.

When we entered the judge's office for Mr. Weston's bench trial, the judge's secretary, Mossy, told us that the judge was down on the dock. We went looking for him and called around for him a few times before we heard, "I'm over here; come on down."

He was in the hold of one of his shrimp boats washing out the old ice. After we boarded the trawler and joined him below, I informed Judge Dukes of the purpose of the visit, whereupon he knocked on the bulkhead with his knuckle and announced, "Court's in session!"

I enumerated the facts of the case, which were not in dispute. Mr. Weston admitted that he had small crabs, "but not too many." Judge Dukes instructed Mr. Weston to find his secretary and give her ten dollars for the fine. As Mr. Weston climbed the ladder to leave, the judge tugged on my sleeve, indicating that he wanted me to stay. He offered me his hand and said, "Tom Dukes, Mr. Moïse. I'm glad to see you working here. I hope you stick around and do a good job." He continued, "Mr. Moïse I'm just a country judge and I dispense country justice. I grew up with these people, and I know what they can afford to pay. They have wives and children at home to feed, and they work hard for what little they make. I hope you don't have a problem with that?"

Even though I was filled with enthusiasm for protecting our resources and never got cynical about it, I understood early on that in the courtroom the judge rules. Only much later in my career were lawyers regularly appointed as magistrates. Then the courtroom atmosphere became much more formal. I always thought, at that level of the judicial process, "country justice" was just fine.

I quickly learned that, to be effective in protecting the resources, I had to establish a sound professional rapport with the magistrates. Each had his own peculiarities and perspectives, but they all had one thing in common and that was a strong preference for sound, reasonable, uncontroversial cases. They didn't want to hear what I thought about a case; they wanted the law and the facts. If a person was issued a whole string of tickets related to the same stop, magistrates tended to get the impression that the individual was being picked on—unless, of course, there were particularly aggravating circumstances. The best rule I discovered about the courtroom experience was that the only opinion that counted was the judge's.

Over the years I got to know most of the magistrates in Charleston County. I kept them informed of new resource laws and why they had been enacted, giving them some background for when the time came to try violators of those laws. I also visited the federal courthouse and relayed the same information to the federal judges. They seemed to appreciate being informed.

I regarded the courtroom experience as an educational process and the magistrates as teachers of responsibility. During a trial the specific words of the law were read. The defendant's actions in violating the law were described. The judge took all the facts into consideration and made a judgment. If the judge's decision went against me and the defendant was found not guilty, then I learned from the experience and took appropriate corrective measures to strengthen my case when approaching a similar incident later.

If the judgment went against the defendant and he was found guilty, a fine was imposed to discourage further illegal activity, or—in the terms of modern law-enforcement philosophy—to encourage voluntary compliance with the law. That lofty ideal often fell well shy of the goal, as certain defendants seemed to reappear in court time and time again. In later years, with the advent of the point system, habitual offenders lost their licenses to engage in commercial fishing or to hunt or fish recreationally.

Officer Fort and I covered a lot of territory, and—over the days, weeks, and months that followed—I learned much about the laws and the watermen who had to abide by them. Practical experience was soon supplemented by academic training. I was assigned a date to go to the South Carolina Criminal Justice Academy in Columbia for the thirteen-week basic police training required of all law-enforcement officers in the state. There our classes included constitutional law with an emphasis on search and seizure and interrogation (Fourth and Fifth Amendment rights), self-defense, report writing (especially valuable, considering all the paperwork we had to do), gathering and protecting evidence, shooting, and driving.

Every morning we arose early and attended a physical-training class, after which we returned to our rooms and got ready for breakfast. The cooks and much of the maintenance staff were trusties from the state prison bordering the academy grounds. The food was generally good although it was tough on people who were trying to limit their cholesterol intake.

We watched lots of training films depicting the variety of law-enforcement encounters to which we were likely to be exposed. The many "Shoot, Don't Shoot" films constantly drove home the message that law-enforcement work occasionally demanded split-second decisions meaning the difference between life and death for somebody.

On the firing range we shot for hours round after round at human-profile targets set at varying distances, until our faults were corrected and our shooting techniques improved. It was my observation that the state's criminal element would be perfectly safe from serious injury from some of my fellow law-enforcement officers. In a few cases officers to the right and left of poor shooters on the firing line shot a few rounds into their targets for them so they could pass the firearms-qualification test.

The driving range was a real adventure. There we worked on the techniques of automobile stops, elements of self-defense, and a variety of law-enforcement problems that involved the preservation of evidence and capture and arrest of culprits. Perhaps the most hair-raising part of the driving-range experience was defensive driving. In these exercises the trainee, with an instructor as a passenger, drove through a course bordered by close-set orange traffic cones. The straightaways were demanding enough, but going into a relatively tight right-hand curve at sixty miles an hour between cones set not four feet off either side of the car was truly challenging. In

With Belle I on patrol in Price Inlet between Bull and Capers islands

these turns the trainee was absolutely forbidden to employ the brake pedal and had to run through full throttle. On some of the courses we had to back through and make turnarounds, maneuvers that required steady hands and feet.

Every time we knocked down cones during these exercises, we had to stop, get out of the car, and reset them. I can't recall any rollovers or accidents on the driving range, but there were some close calls. Some trainees wiped out entire rows of the cones. The academy instructors knocked themselves out coming up with scenarios that tested our imaginations and with practical applications of the lessons we were supposed to be learning in class.

Back then we were able to go home every weekend. I think the word was out in that part of Columbia that on Friday afternoon between four and five, one risked life and limb anywhere near the academy on Broad River Road as trainees decamped and fanned out for their homes throughout the state.

After graduation I settled into a fairly steady routine of riding with Buster around the Cape Romain marshes, checking crabbers at the landing or the loading dock of the McClellanville Crab Company, and occasionally going to court to settle cases.

My first boat was a 1967 thirteen-foot Boston Whaler hull that had been sitting on the ground behind the Port Royal office for three or four years. When I went to pick it up, it was filled with leaves and dirt and even had several small trees growing in it. Along with this venerable "planter," I was also assigned a well-used, forty-horse-power, long-shaft Evinrude outboard motor.

I gathered all the parts from opposite ends of the district, carried them to the Time Out outboard-repair shop in Mount Pleasant, and placed them under the able care of mechanic Louis Legare, who over the years performed heroic emergency repairs to several issues of outboard motors. A new console was installed; the motor was mounted on the transom; and I was issued a brand-new trailer. Now we were cooking!

Murphy's Law

There were days when everything that could go wrong did. One outing brought Murphy's Law into full fruition. I remember it all too well. It was the proverbial frosty morning late in the duck season. The Maybanks had invited me to stop by the old house on Jehossee Island on the Edisto River to have breakfast after my morning patrol. I asked my younger daughter, Sarah, then barely a teenager, to come along on the patrol that morning, after which we would join the Maybanks.

On numerous occasions I had enjoyed the culinary talents of their cook, John Brown, whose breakfasts were the stuff of memory. Mr. Brown was a man of many talents. In addition to owning his own contracting business in Charleston, he was the Maybank family factotum, serving variously as automobile driver, boat operator, children's nurse, and cook extraordinaire.

During the duck season I kept my ancient johnboat almost permanently attached to the patrol car. I had not seen the floorboard or the seat in the back of the car for months. I had gear for every possible contingency and temperature range. The pile also included a considerable array of duck-hunting disguises, including camouflage outfits, decoys, and duck calls. My strategy was to look like a duck hunter so I could sit in my boat and observe nearby blinds without arousing suspicion. I would even occasionally shoot at a passing duck. Every now and then I would actually hit one, adding to the realism of my subterfuge.

I woke Sarah hours before sunrise and headed for the Jehossee landing on Dahoo Creek. In the roughly forty-five minute trip from Charleston to the landing, I regaled Sarah with various scenarios of what we were likely to encounter. Every time I took people on the duck patrol, I was careful to let them know what to expect in advance, since once we launched and got into position, there could be no talking.

I was busy running my mouth as we turned off the main dirt road on Grove Plantation, heading down to the landing. It was one of those pitch-black nights when one could see only what was directly in front of the head-lights.

My attention, normally devoted to negotiating the narrow road in the darkness, was distracted by my conversation with Sarah, and somehow I missed the small road that turned off to the right and ran along a fence line down to the landing. I noticed this lapse when the road I was on became narrower and narrower, almost disappearing in a dense grove of planted pine trees. At that point there was absolutely no place to turn around, especially with the trailer attached. Backing up was out of the question because of the limited visibility and the fact that there was a fairly deep ditch on one side.

I got out of the car, detached the trailer, and began pushing it around to get it off the center of the road headed in the opposite direction. At that point I noticed one of the trailer tires had gone flat, adding greatly to the difficulty of moving it. After completing that maneuver, I then began the tedious and lengthy task of turning the car completely around on the narrow road without getting it in the ditch. With the car finally turned around, I drove just past the trailer and refastened it to the ball hitch. By the time we got to the landing the tire had come completely off the rim, a problem I figured I would attend to after the duck patrol. Sarah, being learned in the tales told by Uncle Remus, acted like ole Brer Fox ("lay low and ain't say nuttin").

I turned around in the small parking lot and backed the boat down to the ramp. I got out, shined a light down toward the water, and saw that it was a little lower than half tide and going out. I stowed some gear in the boat and then slowly backed down the ramp, careful of the sheer drop-off at the end of the concrete ramp. Despite my attention the tireless wheel rim ran off the end. The trailer dropped suddenly to one side, and the water came poring in over the transom of the boat. I continued backing to level the boat, and then the other wheel fell over the edge.

I had to get in the flooded boat, start it up, pull the plug out, and run up and down the creek for a few minutes to drain all the water out of it. I came back to the landing, tied the bow line to an old piling, and got in the car to pull the trailer up. The trailer wouldn't budge. The frame was right down on the ramp and the wheels were jammed behind the broken end, which was completely under water. Needless to say my pressure gauge was considerably elevated by that time, but I stoutly resisted the temptation to indulge in a good pressure-releasing cussin' fit. As for Sarah, she just continued to lay low.

I backed the trailer a little further down the ramp, got out, grabbed the frame, lifted the good wheel side, and dragged it over where the wheel was sitting just above the broken edge of the ramp. I got back in the car and with a mighty surge managed to get the trailer up the ramp. I noticed that the collision of the tireless rim with the concrete ramp had managed to flatten the rim out at the point of impact, a condition that caused a distinct gash as I towed it across the grassy parking area.

When we went down to the boat, I noticed in the beam of my flashlight that I had apparently carried the plug with me after I had tied it up, and— owing to my lengthy exertions in extracting the trailer from the ramp— the boat had once more taken on a considerable quantity of Dahoo Creek water.

After running the boat up and down the creek once again to drain out the water, I approached the landing to retrieve Sarah, who was waiting there patiently in the dark and who was, no doubt, wondering if I worked this hard launching the boat every morning. We ran a short distance out of Dahoo Creek into the Edisto River and down a little further, where we entered Fish Creek, which winds through the marsh on the western side of Jehossee Island.

Amid all the clamor back at the landing, I had already heard the distant sounds of outboard motors running in the river. As we got well into Fish Creek, I spotted the light of a blinded-up boat ahead of us. As we passed by, I could see that there was only one person in the boat. I slowed as we drove around his set of decoys, continued some distance away from him and steered the boat into a narrow side drain. I pulled the engine up and turned the boat around with my push pole. After turning off my lights, I pushed the boat back just far enough to look down the creek toward the other boat.

I slapped the surface of the water off the bow with the oar six or eight times to make it sound as though I were putting out decoys. Sarah and I then sat and quietly waited for legal shooting time to arrive. A full ten minutes before that moment, our man began firing at passing wood ducks. I stood on the bow to get a better look and saw him only a moment later dropping one and then another. I didn't see whether he had hit any with his

Cartoonist Bill Thompson's poster of me with Belle I. Copies were auctioned at Ducks Unlimited events and filled in with the violation of the buyer's choice.

first shots, but I did see him drop a third and a fourth, which—for wood ducks—made two over the limit.

I stepped to the back of the boat with the push pole in hand, stuck it over the stern, and leaned on it. The boat did not budge. The tide had left us high and dry. I got Sarah in the back of the boat with me to lighten the bow, and pushed with all my might, sinking the push pole about five feet into the pluff mud. What little forward movement I succeeded in gaining only served in pushing up a wall of mud in front of the boat.

I got my radio out of my boat box to summon another officer who I knew was working several miles up the river, thinking I could ask him to come over and make the apprehension. The radio battery was stone dead. Shortly after realizing that dilemma, I began to hear this eerie muffled moaning sound emanating from the direction of my daughter, who apparently could stand it no longer and was quaking from hysterical laughter with her head buried in the depths of her parka.

Not seeing anything one bit funny, I went back to the front of the boat with the oar in hand, scooped the pile of mud off to the side, and returned to the stern. Using the oar as a lever against the outside of the transom, I began to wedge the boat forward over the mud. I had already come out of my warm outfit, as I was sweating profusely.

I made agonizingly slow progress but finally managed to reach the mouth of the drain at the somewhat deeper main creek. Just about at the point where I was home free, the handle of the oar broke in half. More muffled squealing and hissing came from that headless insulated coat. It had almost taken on the tones of a steady rattling moan, with intermittent gasps for breath.

By that time I was light years ahead of anything resembling mere exasperation. I left the stump of my oar sticking up in the mud, wildly flung the handle out into the marsh, and grabbed the then very muddy push pole and continued my tortured journey down the creek toward the culprit, who was by then picking up his decoys.

When I finally got into some deep water, let the engine down and pushed the starter, but it wouldn't crank. After a few minutes of that, I pulled the engine back up and resumed poling. I got close enough to call breathlessly over to the hunter and tell him who I was and that I wanted to check him before he left.

He waited as I approached his boat, and I told him that I wanted to see his ducks. He produced two woody drakes. I told him that I had seen him drop two more than that and that I wanted to search his boat. Well, I combed that boat from bow to stern. I made him take off his waders. I looked through his decoy bag. I looked through his boat box. There were only the two wood ducks, and those were the only ones he would admit to shooting. I could tell that any professional demeanor that I possessed was fading fast, and I sent him on his way forgetting even to check his gun and license or write him a ticket for the violation of shooting before legal hours.

The tide was still too low to get into House Creek at Jehossee, just a short distance down the river from the mouth of Fish Creek. On low tide House Creek becomes impassable with a profusion of stumps and water-logged trees. Several more attempts to start the engine failed, and I wound up poling all the way back to the landing, fortunately aided by an incoming tide.

Since my trailer was useless and the tide was still low enough that the drop-off at the ramp was exposed, the only thing to do was to detach my trailer and hook on to one of the other trailers parked there at the landing. I knew the owner and was confident that he wouldn't mind. I carefully backed it down to the point of the drop-off and pulled the winch cable down to the bow eye of the boat.

There was a pretty stiff current moving across the end of the ramp, and I had tied the bow line of the boat to the trailer frame to hold it in place. I pulled the bow of the boat up at a steep angle to rest on the trailer skids, and began to winch the boat out of the water. I had just untied the bow line and was about to flip it back into the boat when the winch cable snapped, sending the boat stern-first into the water. As a result of the backward motion, I saw my push pole slide down the back of the boat into the water and go floating off with the tide. I was unable to retrieve it since the boat wouldn't run.

Sarah was sitting in the car, having reverted to her Brer Fox routine out of sheer exhaustion. At any rate, by now normal conversation was simply impossible because every time she looked over at me she broke out in un-controllable laughter, scarcely able to catch her breath.

I got one of my big tobacco cups out of the car and bailed the water out of the boat. Then I cut the winch hook off the end of the broken cable and refastened it along what seemed to be a sounder section. By this time the tide had come up a little further, and I didn't have so far to lift the bow of the boat onto the trailer skids. I never let go of that bow line either. After removing the gas tanks to lighten the boat, I successfully winched it onto the borrowed trailer and pulled it up the ramp. I tied the stern of the boat to a utility pole, pulled the trailer out from beneath the boat, and left it sitting there on the grass.

I reattached the borrowed trailer to the proper vehicle, wrote a note, which I put on the windshield of Jack Maybank's car, apologizing for missing breakfast and headed back to Charleston. I came back that afternoon with a new tire and rim. Sarah never again accompanied me on a duck patrol.

Hen Hunting in the Salt Marsh

The arrival of the winds of autumn brings forth the "marsh hen tides" and ushers in the hunting season for the elusive clapper rail, an inhabitant of the salt marsh commonly known as the *marsh hen* or *mud hen*. When coupled with the effects of a north-easterly wind, this tide provides the most ideal conditions for hunting hens, for the birds are no longer hidden in the depths and shadows of the marsh grass. The hunt is chiefly a waterborne quest, but some hunters disembark from their boats to walk the small hummocks and the fringes of marsh islands exposed above the high tides to flush out the birds.

The marsh-hen tides really cast a dramatic appearance over the marshscape between the barrier islands and the mainland. With a little bit of wind the water could get up so high that only the very tips of the marsh grass were visible. There would be one vast sheet of water, with only a tall fringe of grass marking the borders of the myriad small creeks and the hummocks and marsh islands visible above the surface.

The two-part season usually begins near mid-September and concludes near mid-December. The seasons are fixed to take advantage of the occurrence of as many high tides as possible. Regularly occurring "spring tides" come usually twice a month on the full moon and the new moon when the earth, the sun, and the moon are in a line, an astronomical event called a *syzygy*, my favorite Scrabble word. Really high tides, seven feet or better, occur every year and a half when the moon comes closest in its orbit to the earth in the new-moon phase. That phenomenon is called a *proxigean spring tide.*

Marsh-hen hunters demonstrating the violation of "taking rails while under motor power"

Regulated by the federal migratory-bird laws, marsh-hen hunting has a few restrictions. The hunter must have a state license as well as a free federal Harvest Information Program permit. There is a fifteen-bird limit. Repeating shotguns must be plugged to hold no more than three shells. No birds may be taken while the boat is in motion from the effects of motor power. It is also prohibited to use motor power to drive or concentrate marsh hens into a small area for shooting. That is the offense called *rallying*.

The last two restrictions have caused many hen hunters to come to grief. I recall few hen patrols where I did not see at least one boatload of hunters careening headlong through the marsh grass, firing away at birds fleeing their approach. That violation was common not just among run-of-the-mill game hogs, of whom there would be few expectations of sportsmanship, but also among such exalted sorts as lawyers, doctors, preachers, and law-enforcement officers. One lawyer happened to be an assistant solicitor, and one law-enforcement officer was a deputy sheriff. The preacher was a Holiness cleric, who was in no way forgiving or repentant on the morning when I took all his birds and handed him several $250 tickets. I have observed many hen hunters who suddenly tire of poling their boats, let their engines down, and go to running. I found that it was often only a matter of time before the hunter became an offender.

During my hen patrols I loved to take along people who had previously expressed interest in coming with me when I was out working. I also took new game wardens out from time to time on training patrols. Usually I took them to one of the small hummocks that dotted the salt marsh, where we could stand up without being obvious. I handed them my binoculars and described to them what a running violation looked like.

In my descriptive narrative, I would usually say that they would likely see someone standing up in the forward part of the boat with a gun in his hands and someone sitting down in the back running the boat. I said that they should be able to observe a bow wake and possibly hear some engine noise, which was audible at great distances in the crisp fall air. All those elements—coupled with the sight and sound of gunshots—constituted the offense of "taking rails while under motor power." Every person in the boat would be issued a ticket.

My guests or trainees could see everything unfolding and generally became excited to see violations happening right in front of their eyes. At length I had to take the binoculars back and view a violation myself before we stepped back in the boat and headed out to intercept the culprits. Sometimes we saw two boats running hens in the same area and had to choose which one to catch first, usually the closer. In such circumstances we dashed over to the first boat, checked their guns quickly, took their licenses, and told them to sit tight as we pursued the other boat.

One morning while viewing the hunting scene from the edge of a hummock, I observed in the far distance what appeared to be an eighteen-foot white fiberglass boat launching from a small dirt landing on Copahee Sound. I idly assumed that they were heading out to go fishing. My attention was diverted to several other boats running in the opposite direction in the marsh, when to my complete astonishment I saw that white boat come around in front of me and run across the flooded flats, with the people in it firing broadsides at every flushing bird. Peering though the binoculars, I could see that there were four people in the boat.

The only time they slowed down was to circle around and scoop up dead birds with a dip net. I stared intently at this activity for a few minutes longer, long enough to observe everyone in the boat taking a shot. I jumped in my johnboat and made a beeline toward them. They must have seen me coming because everyone suddenly sat down as the boat veered and headed out toward the waterway. Since they had around seventy-five more horse-power than I did, I was trailing at some distance. Their lead evaporated as their propeller became gradually befouled with marsh grass, and they slowed to a crawl as I closed the gap between us.

The only things that outnumbered the dead birds lying on their deck—which included one white egret and one bittern—were the beer cans. The welcome mat was definitely not out as I pulled alongside and asked to see their guns and their licenses. Two of the four were using unplugged shot-guns. In addition to tickets for those violations, each person on board was cited for shooting rails while under motor power.

At first no one would admit shooting the nongame bittern and the egret. I threatened to write up all of them, saying that they all were in constructive possession of the birds, but then one of the men took the blame. He was issued a separate ticket for each of the illegal birds, in addition to the charges that he shared with his fellow shooters. All their birds were seized and, except for the egret and bittern, were taken to Jenkins Orphanage in Charleston, often the repository of confiscated game. Following one noteworthy morning of apprehending violators I turned over ninety-seven marsh hens to the orphanage staff. That season the staff tired of cleaning all the birds brought to them, and I began giving some to several Roman Catholic priests around Charleston.

On one hen patrol fairly early in my career, I saw, while sweeping the marsh scene through my binoculars, several johnboats slowly running around the little creeks behind Goat Island. The people in the boats never stood up, but I could hear their engines running and the reports of their guns. When I finally caught up with them, I found that most of the men in each boat were in their late seventies. Several were even older than that.

They explained that they went out only a couple of times a season and had been doing so for almost thirty years and that they cleaned and cooked their birds at their camp on the end of Goat Island. One of them told me that none of them was physically able to stand up and pole a boat through the marsh. It was pretty obvious that they probably would not be up to such exertions.

Everything else checked out. They all had the gratis hunting licenses granted to state residents at reaching sixty-five. They all had rusty old single-barreled smoke poles, and they had only around thirty birds among the six of them. I could tell that they were nervous at the prospect of getting ticketed, and one old gentleman opined openly that this might be their last hen hunt.

I could sense, in light of their age and infirmities, that this situation ought to be handled with some delicacy. I calmed their apprehension by telling them that I was not going to write them a ticket, but I warned them that I was not the only game warden who patrolled that area. In a somewhat convoluted effort to maintain their ancient hen-hunting tradition, I asked them before their next hen hunt, to call me to see if I was going to be patrolling the area.

When that happened, I would ask them to mount a long cane pole bearing an orange streamer on the stern of each johnboat, so that I would not waste a lot of time staring at them through my binoculars. I made a further request that they not take more than four birds each, which was as much as they said they could eat. I also continued to remind them that I was not the only warden who checked that area. I think they hunted only one more season after that initial encounter.

Occasionally I would have an opportunity to do a little hen hunting myself. I would drive my boat up to the windward edge of a hummock and send the dog out to flush them out of the thick growth. Both my Boykin spaniels—as well as Woo, my younger daughter's Jack Russell—were particularly good flushing dogs. I would stand on the bow of my boat and drop any birds that took to wing, but most of them would run to the water and go swimming off barely visible above the surface of the water, especially on a windy day. Even though it was not illegal to shoot them on the water, there would have been little sport to it. Little Woo was even good at water retrieves, but she would sneeze a few times and lick the mud to get the taste out of her mouth after she returned with a bird.

Much earlier I used to step off the boat, walk around, and flush them up myself, but I found that I had to be constantly alert for the presence of paper-wasp nests, some covered with hundreds of large red wasps. In my boot-clad sloshing across one little hummock, I was stung by a wasp just at the top of my boot and bitten on my upper arm by some unidentified poisonous spider. My foot became so swollen that I had to cut the laces off my boot in order to pull it off, and I had to go to a doctor for a shot for the spider bite.

If the tide were particularly high, it would not be uncommon to see as many as a dozen or more cotton rats, which are indigenous to the marsh, festooned around the tops of the shrubs like furry ornaments. One time I stepped on an enormous brass-colored spottail bass that was up in the weeds feeding on marsh snails. At that surprise I think I cleared the entire length of the hummock in a single bound.

Hunting marsh hens is an ideal situation in which to teach children shooting skills in the field. Everything is done at a fairly slow pace and in uncrowded spaces. The shooter can generally spot the birds on the water before they take flight, and they usually fly level with the marsh, affording shooters, with a little practice, ample opportunities for success. My older daughter, Melissa, had her first hunting experience in the marshes of Gray Bay between Capers Island and the mainland north of Mount Pleasant while on a marsh hen patrol with me.

For many years a number of black men who lived near the marsh front off Copahee and Hamlin Sound, as well as several on Sewee Road, took hunters out in small bateaux and poled them around the marsh, which was the old-fashioned way to go hen hunting. I encountered them early in my career, but they all eventually became too old, and the next generation did not embrace the tradition. One of the last was King Saul Jackson of Awendaw, who also "scratched" for clams during the shellfish season and sold them to dealers in McClellanville.

It was not uncommon back then for the hunter to take both his own limit and the limit of the man who was doing the poling. It required a long time staring through the binoculars to observe a hunter taking more than his fifteen birds. Often the hunters inclined to do that would fall afoul of the law when I checked them and discovered that their guide had no hunting license. Either the guide got a ticket for not having a license, or the hunter got a ticket for taking over the limit.

I found that sometimes I had to study carefully some of the boats that were gliding through the grass. One day I saw a canoe with two people standing up in it, one holding a gun and the other holding a push pole. Since that is the right and proper way to hunt, I would normally scope right on past them to find what else was going on, but my binoculars lingered on them just long enough for me to see that the man holding the pole did not appear to be using it. Further observation revealed that he was using it to steer the canoe, not propel it.

As I watched with mounting interest, I saw the man in front drop a few hens and the man in the rear steer the canoe around to pick up the birds. I could neither see nor hear any sign of an engine running. After watching their activity for around twenty minutes, I could stand it no longer and motored over to check them out. As I was approaching them from behind, I saw that they were both sitting down and that the canoe continued in steady motion from no direct action on the part of its occupants that I could see.

When I came alongside I recognized the one sitting up front, who had been doing all the shooting. As greetings were exchanged, I asked to see his gun as well as their licenses. I could clearly see that there was no sign of an outboard engine, but I did spot a car battery attached to cables that disappeared underneath a burlap bag draped over the starboard side. When I asked if they would show me what was under the bag, the man in the back reluctantly pulled it aside, revealing a small electric motor.

Without another word ever being spoken, I filled out and handed each of them a ticket along with his license. Then I reached into their canoe and took all the marsh hens. I started my engine, backed away, and left them sitting there to ponder the eternal verities.

One blustery morning just after launching my johnboat at the Isle of Palms Marina to commence a marsh-hen patrol, I noticed four college-age boys arriving at the top of the ramp with a trailered bow-rider fiberglass boat. As I was walking back from parking my car and trailer, I noticed that they had a German shorthaired pointer along, and I saw one of them put three gun cases into the boat.

When I walked over to chat, they told me that they were going out marsh-hen hunting and asked if I knew of any good spots. I informed them it would be difficult to pole a boat that big with four people in it and suggested that they might want to walk the hummocks scattered around the marsh. I said they could get out and walk up the birds or use their dog to flush them up as they stayed in the boat. They thanked me for the advice, and I left for the gas dock to get fuel for my boat.

I topped off the two six-gallon tanks I had aboard and spoke with Otto Marten, the dock master, for a few moments. Just as I was leaving the marina, I heard a barrage of gunfire coming from up the waterway. Heading around the bend in the stretch leading to Dewees Inlet, I spotted a boat pulled up on the shell bank on the left side of the waterway.

As I got closer, I could see that it was the boat belonging to the boys I had spoken to earlier, and I could see them walking atop the washed oyster shells lining the bank. Three of them had guns and the dog was running back and forth. As I pulled up onto the bank near them, I asked how they were doing.

One of them said excitedly that they had just shot a whole load of marsh hens, a statement I found highly unusual, because I had never even seen one of them on any of the shell banks bordering the waterway, let alone a flock of them. I walked over to where the dog appeared to be busily fetching birds

Semipalmated sandpipers shot in the mistaken belief that they were marsh hens

from the edge of the marsh, and my jaw dropped when I saw a mounting pile of semipalmated sandpipers, a tiny little bird bearing scant resemblance to the much larger clapper rail.

The dog eventually brought back eighteen of them and deposited them in front its proud owner. I know I was probably sputtering incoherently, but at length I recovered sufficiently to blurt out that those were not marsh hens. I had seen practically every species of marsh bird in the bags of neophyte hen hunters but never such an egregious enormity. I could tell that they honestly didn't know what a marsh hen looked like. As the interview progressed, it was revealed that none of them could recall ever having seen a marsh hen.

Resisting an urge to wreak vengeance in the form of a separate ticket for each of the dead sandpipers, I decided instead to use the experience as an educational opportunity. I explained to the boys that the sandpipers were a protected nongame migratory bird and told them that I was going to write each of them one ticket.

I then told them to follow me in their boat over to a hummock further up the waterway. It was a spot where I had always found birds. I pulled up on a shell bank near the hummock, and they pulled up right alongside me.

As we were walking toward the nearby clump of trees, I explained to them what marsh hens looked like, adding that they fly low and slow over the water when flushed and that they are easy to hit.

I sent Belle ahead of me as I loaded my old double-barreled, twelve-gauge Stevens and walked rapidly into the foliage. One hen flushed over to my right. Two shots rang out to no effect. I had just reloaded when another hen flushed over to my left. Two more shots, no dead bird. I could clearly detect audible murmurings among the assemblage behind me, but I persevered.

A double took to wing practically right at my feet, and with another two-shot volley, I did manage to bag one of them, which Belle dutifully retrieved. I figured, rather than risk further humiliation, I would let this one example stand for identification purposes, and I brought it over to the boys, who seemed scarcely able to contain their amusement over my shooting demonstration. They could see that I was not smiling.

I passed it around so they could identify it. They had already been witness to what marsh hens looked like in flight, even if they were a little faster than I had earlier described. I explained that, when the wind was blowing, sometimes it made the birds a little more difficult to hit.

I departed with them holding a ticket each, as well as one dead marsh hen, and—I hoped—a clearer understanding of what they were looking for. When we got back together in court several weeks later, it took a lot of talking for the judge not to lock up the lot of them after seeing that frozen pile of tiny bodies I had brought along as evidence.

I discovered the annual Edisto Island Hen Hunt quite by accident. I had been visiting an acquaintance who operated a wholesale-sporting-goods warehouse when I saw a pile of green baseball caps emblazoned with "Fourteenth Annual Edisto Island Hen Hunt." An employee was sitting at a machine busily printing more hats to fill the order. I asked my acquaintance if he knew anything about the event, and he claimed that he didn't. I glanced at the order form hanging on a nearby clipboard and made a mental note of the fact that the hats were to be picked up in two days. I also arranged to purchase two of the hats for myself.

A quick consultation of the tide charts revealed that the coming Saturday morning had ideal tidal conditions for hunting marsh hens. I called a fellow game warden, Sergeant Herman Crosby Jr., and told him what I had found. He reported that he had known about the annual hunt for years but sometimes did not know the date when it would be held. We arranged to meet early Saturday morning. We had agreed that it would be a good idea to wear plain clothes along with those green caps.

Officer Crosby and I motored out on a steadily rising tide and found a place next to a tree line to observe the large expanse of marsh extending out behind Edisto Beach. We didn't have to wait long before we saw johnboats and larger contrivances streaming through the marsh. Most that we observed seem to settle down, cut off their engines, and break out their poles, but we did spot a few that had their motors running half cocked up while a man stood up on the rear seat holding a pole in his hands and working the tiller with his feet.

One of those boats seemed to us to exhibit an awful lot of firepower. In an effort to observe more closely, we decided to go out and get in among the hunters. We slowly motored through the flooded marsh with Officer Crosby standing on the bow. He periodically fired his pistol into the water, just to add a little noise to the subterfuge. We got within a hundred yards of a couple of the boats we suspected were running hens. When we could clearly see forward motion of the boats with the engines down and hear shots fired, we knew we had a case and maneuvered over to intercept them.

Because of the hats we were wearing, they never suspected a thing, even as we came right up to them. One of the hunters we checked that morning was using an unplugged seven-shot pistol-grip pump shotgun, and he unloaded the gun on every hen that flew up. He apparently liked burning powder as much as we liked "burning him a new one."

I found out later that the hen hunt initially began as a gathering of a few friends, "the boys," as an opportunity to get out and do some hunting, a little cooking, and maybe even a little swilling. It was so successful that more and more people were invited every year, and it had turned into an annual event. With so many people it eventually became a competition, complete with a "Calcutta," a game of chance where hunting teams are auctioned off among the participants with the pot going to the "owner" of the first team back with the limit. The annual Edisto Island Hen Hunt has now completely evolved into an eating and swilling event. The few who leave the warmth and camaraderie of the gathering to go forth into the marsh are now regarded with some suspicion.

I had Coy Johnston, the South Carolina regional director of Ducks Unlimited, along on another patrol in the same area some years later. We had initially been patrolling the marshes behind Otter and Pine islands and had found no hunting activity in the area. We had heard shots fired from the marsh across the South Edisto River and decided to go over to investigate.

We finally located the source of the shooting and found a place to hide behind a tall fringe of grass bordering a small creek. Mr. Johnston was looking through the binoculars and reported that he saw three people in a white fiberglass skiff. He said they were definitely running and called out each shot. I took the binoculars, recorded a few more shots, and decided that the time was right to go over and make introductions.

When we came up to them, I immediately saw that I had something of a dilemma on my hands. One of the people in the boat was a man I knew, who had been badly injured in a fire that had left him sightless. He recognized my voice, and we chatted amiably for a while before I informed them of my earlier observations and that the nature of the violation required me to cite all in the boat. All the while I was trying to figure out how in the world I was going to handle this situation and how it would wash in court for me to be prosecuting a blind man for a hunting violation.

In a sudden revelatory moment I figured out a lesser-included violation for which I could write them a warning, the offense of "rallying rails." News of my giving even a warning ticket to a blind man spread like wildfire throughout the region. Many idle gossips considered my act an indicator of just how big an SOB I was, as well as evidence of my being mean enough to write my own mother a ticket. They obviously didn't know Momma. Some weeks later when I was in Magistrate Richard Wood's court in Green Pond, the judge told me that he had heard about the incident from at least four different people and remarked that he thought writing them warnings instead of bringing them to his court was a very good decision indeed.

Marsh hens have been maligned as table fare. I have not found that to be the case, but I have tasted some that were badly cooked. The old men on Goat Island skinned their birds, keeping the livers and gizzards and stewing all in rich bacon-fat gravy along with carrots, onions, and various and sundry seasonings. When this stew was served over rice, they said, "It was as good as it gets."

Porky Rhodes, the renowned manager of Gaylord Donnelly's Ashepoo Plantation, and his wife used to soak their birds overnight in cold, slightly briny water. Then they dredged the birds in seasoned flour and fried them like chicken. I had them cooked that way on many memorable occasions and thought that they were quite delicious. I think many people confuse what they perceive as the gamey taste of wild animals with a taste resulting from poorly preserved or processed animals.

Watermen and the Lowcountry Scene

I was quite pleased when my first patrol boat, the thirteen-foot Boston Whaler, was rigged out and ready to hit the water. Its small size and shallow draft allowed me to explore the myriad small creeks and shallow sounds in my appointed territory, which was then the Charleston Harbor estuary and the vast reaches of marsh and beach extending up to the North Santee River.

The thirteen-foot Whaler and the fifteen-foot version I was issued later were ideal creek boats, easy to keep clean and easy to get in and out of. The latter was important during my exploratory period because, when I ran aground, I had to get out of the boat to shove it off mud flats and shell tops. My encounters with those submerged obstructions occurred with alarming frequency. Some days it seemed I spent more time out of the boat than in it, pushing and shoving rather than running. If I could fit the boat in a creek, I went in. It never ceased to amaze me how far up some of those little creeks, gutters, or drains the clam diggers or oyster pickers would go, especially if they were up to no good.

Some of the smaller creeks were too shallow to enter during low tide or had bars or shell rakes that guarded their entrances, so I had to time my exploration of them according to the tide. I found that I could discover more about what is going on in an area by turning my engine off and drifting with the current or pulling up on the bank to sit quietly and listen. In the open expanses of the marsh, particularly during the winter months, I

Oystermen on the Chechessee River waiting to unload their day's harvest

could hear sounds for miles. In the quietness I began to separate the man-made sounds from the natural ones and locate their positions out in the marsh.

The hollow thud of clams hitting the bottom of a bucket and the clink of a culling iron knocking apart cluster oysters were distinctive and soon became familiar sounds. A working knowledge, a mental map, of the length, depth, and turns of the small watercourses gave me a pretty good idea of the location in the marsh where those sounds originated and how to approach them.

Very often an investigation required a lengthy slog across the pluff-mud marsh, which is distinctly an acquired skill, usually accompanied by the periodic impaction or loss of boots that required extensive excavation to re-cover. Both walking and frequent excavations had to be done with as little noise as possible to avoid alerting the poachers. Sometimes it was devilishly difficult to muffle those awful sucking noises as I extracted my boots from the clinging ooze.

More often than not in the course of such exertions, I became covered with mud to the point of being unrecognizable as anything even beginning to resemble a law-enforcement official. Occasionally it required a lengthy explanation to convince the person I was interviewing that I was really a game warden and not a fellow poacher encroaching on his territory. Display of the "gold," which sometimes I had to polish off with a handkerchief, and a smudged ticket book were always sufficient authentication.

As important as learning the landscape was becoming acquainted with the watermen who worked in the creeks and marshes. Most of them were good hardworking men. There were even a few women who occasionally "scratched" clams on the banks or served as "strikers" aboard crab boats or shrimp trawlers. Of the many people who earned a living working on the water, there were a few who chose to stray from the straight and narrow, which kept us game wardens in business.

Commercial fishermen have a huge number of laws that regulate their activities. From the instant they step into a boat, they have to comply with the boat-registration and outboard-engine titling laws. They also have to

Bagging shell oysters on Little Bull Island, Price Inlet

have the requisite equipment on board to comply with boating-safety laws. They are required to have a commercial license for their boat and a license on their person for any regulated activity in which they are involved.

If they are harvesting shellfish, they have to have a permit to harvest oysters or clams from private leases or from state banks or bottoms. They have to have "land and sell permits" that entitle them to sell their catch to a licensed wholesaler. They also have to comply with a host of Department of Health and Environmental Control shellfish laws that regulate everything from the structuring of boat decks for drainage to the tagging of the harvested shellfish to identify the area, date, and time of harvest. Stringent laws prohibit gathering shellfish at night or in areas off limits because of pollution.

Knowing and understanding all these laws is difficult. Game wardens had regular meetings and received official legal updates to keep them familiar with the laws, especially any that might have been recently enacted. Few of the watermen I knew suffered from being overeducated. A good many had never finished high school. A few of them may have had problems voluntarily complying with the law, but they generally knew what the law was. Some of those unschooled watermen could give an unsuspecting game warden an "education" any day of the week.

The laws that regulate crabbing, gill nets, and shrimping are just as numerous. Back in the early 1980s there were no restrictions on recreational fishing. There were no recreational salt-water-fishing licenses, no size limits, and no creel limits.

A new officer had much to learn. I quickly discovered that I had to observe and remember every single detail of the surrounding scene when I encountered and interviewed a person suspected of violating the law. I also learned to remember every nuance of the conversation during the encounter. These were essential components of the state's case when it got to court. A suspect's tone of voice and his attitude at the time of apprehension could be clues to what you would face before the magistrate. I also learned that I had to watch what I said because I would hear it again in court. Some of those seemingly ignorant old watermen sent me back to school time after time on the importance of remembering details.

To be considered fair and evenhanded was an important element in gaining the trust and respect of those watermen. Early in my career we did not have warning tickets. The only discretionary judgment that came into play at the moment of the encounter was whether there were sufficient facts for a citation to be written and whether I would issue one. If I had one scintilla of doubt, I did not write a ticket.

I learned that it was important for me not to speak or make inquiry of another waterman's activities. If they thought I would put other people's business in the street, they would not trust me to preserve confidential information. The grapevine in the commercial-fishing business is extensive. It doesn't take long for word to get out about how an officer conducts himself. Those in the business know who is working in the "river" and whether he is honest, fair, and inclined to be helpful.

Getting to know the watermen was sometimes not easy. Most were always a little guarded, if not downright suspicious, at my arrival alongside their boats or on the banks or flats where they were at work. It was little wonder, since any infraction of the many regulations they had to follow could cost them their day's harvest and a day out of work going to court, in addition to a stiff fine. Once I became acquainted with them, I could pretty well figure out who needed to be checked frequently and who required less scrutiny.

In the early days, before the Wildlife Department came under the Federal Fair Labor Standards Act, which dictated how many hours a month an officer could work, it was not uncommon for me to be in the boat for days at a time, particularly if I was trying to get to the bottom of some ongoing problem. Back then we got only one weekend off a month and another three days during the week. Fifteen- or sixteen-hour days were not uncommon.

I spent a lot of time checking landings at various times of the night and day and at various stages of the tide to see who was out. Sometimes those inclined to violate would be dropped off at one landing and picked up at another, so the presence or absence of vehicles and trailers in a parking lot might not tell the full story of what was going on out in the water.

Since I was out in it all the time, I became attuned to the weather. I learned that high winds and lightning storms were no deterrent to hard-core violators, particularly shrimpers and duck hunters. Seasons, market prices, tidal stages, phases of the moon, days of the week, and weather always had to be taken into consideration when I was determining the likelihood of a particular type of violation occurring and where I should go to find it.

The old metaphor about the new broom sweeping clean is appropriate in describing the large number of cases new officers tended to make—compared to some of the older officers, whose zeal for writing tickets may have mellowed with time. A new officer's entry into the field was generally somewhat unsettling to the established order. The watermen might have become used to the previous officer's way of scheduling his patrols, what he looked for, and what they thought they could get away with. The watermen seemed to be particularly keen on sensing anything that became "routine" in an officer's schedule and often adjusted their own schedules accordingly.

I sensed a lot of official ambivalence regarding whether the number of tickets an officer issued was a validation of his hard work. I was never ambivalent about it at all. My personal and professional mission was to catch people violating the law, write them tickets, and bring them to court for their infractions.

If I wrote a lot of tickets that was, in my way of thinking, proof that there were lots of violators out there who needed to be caught. I always felt strongly that the enforcement of regulations was one of the most important elements of any realistic conservation effort. History certainly reflects the fact that effective regulation of the use and protection of wildlife is one of the oldest of conservation concepts.

New officers tend to be more thorough and by the book in their approach to enforcing the law, and I certainly was no different. I started out by writing huge numbers of tickets. Many calls went in to the district office, to the Columbia office, or to local politicians from the affected parties, who were complaining that they could not earn a living because that blankety-blank Ben "Meese" was writing them all these tickets.

The good thing was that the facts that established their guilt were not essentially in dispute. They complained of the cruelty of having to pay all those fines. They said they could not get any work done because, every time they turned around, there I was writing them a ticket. It just never seemed to occur to some of them that, if they did not violate the law, their problems would go away. Needless to say their complaints were tantamount to a testimonial to my fieldwork, and my unit sergeant and captain seemed to be quite pleased.

Sometimes it is difficult to walk that fine line between lecturing a violator and trying to explain to him how he came to be issued a citation and what he should do to avoid a future occurrence. There was also a distinct separation between being confrontational and being assertive.

A crabber offended by the receipt of numerous tickets sent word by another crabber that one day I was going to wind up on the bottom of the harbor with a cinder block tied around my neck. In an effort to be helpful, I sent him by parcel post—at great personal expense—a cinder block with a short length of line and a note requesting that he make an appointment to show me just how he envisioned my descent into the briny deep to occur. I learned early to deal with threats head-on even though I knew that they posed little real danger. It was usually just a case of the boys blowing off steam.

It wasn't long before I experienced the effects of political influence on the outcome of cases coming before the magistrate. Usually this took the form of a phone call to a judge asking for consideration or "help" for a friend who had fallen afoul of the law. A few were so bold and indiscreet as to write letters to magistrates on House or Senate stationery requesting their "help" in a particular case.

The Magwood family of Mount Pleasant and Little Bull Island at Price Inlet had been in the seafood business for generations and were veritable icons of the Shem Creek shrimp-trawler fleet. Captain Clarence A. "Junior" Magwood and two of his brothers, Andrew and Dan, had been in the commercial fishing business since they were teenagers. Dan and Captain Junior trained their children, Wayne, Scotty, and Dee, to carry on the family tradition.

Andrew Magwood, captain of the shrimp trawler Hope, *on the dock at Little Bull Island, Price Inlet. After the shrimp season was over, he harvested oysters and clams from the Magwood lease behind Bull and Capers islands.*

Captain Junior was a community figure who was almost impossible to pin a ticket on, mainly because he knew everybody, and everybody seemed to know him. My last case with him involved his possession of a quantity of illegal undersized conchs (whelks). The legal size limit had been changed legislatively at least two times in about three years to accommodate the demands of the beneficiaries of this seasonal trawling activity.

Over the years, as most of the larger legal conchs had been harvested, the size of the conchs the trawlers were catching became smaller, creating more work in grading them just from the sheer numbers required to fill a bushel bag. In response conch fishermen brought pressure on the Department of Natural Resources to make the size limit accommodate what they were catching, instead of their changing their practices to accommodate to a size limit. One amendment to the law even allowed a 5 percent tolerance in the number of illegal conchs harvested. That meant that the number of undersized conchs had to exceed 5 percent of the total catch for a fisherman to be liable to prosecution for possession of undersized conchs.

When grading conchs, I began by choosing a random sample of the bags stacked on the deck of the trawler or on the dock. I emptied the bags, counted the total, and then graded every single one of them with a measuring device. The legal ones went in one pile, undersized ones in another.

Boarding Captain Junior's trawler, *Skipper and Wayne,* at the dock one day, I began grading the bags of conchs with him hovering over my shoulder, closely scrutinizing the process. He periodically directed me to make sure that the ones with broken points (the tip end of the conch) were not being counted against him. Sometimes the brittle tip ends of the conch shells break off as they are dumped from the nets or shoveled into the bags. Even giving him the benefit of the doubt on the marginal ones with fractured tips, I could see that a huge number of his conchs were clearly undersized.

I wrote him a ticket for possession of undersized conchs amid a veritable torrent of invective, of which he was the unexcelled master. I never expected him to be happy over getting a ticket, and on no occasion was I ever disappointed. I handed him the paperwork, climbed over the rail into my boat, and beat it up the creek. I could still hear him loudly cussing about "dope heads and game wardens" all the way up near the Shem Creek bridge, even over the noise of the traffic.

Several days later I got a call from the magistrate, who said that several politicians had called in behalf of Captain Junior Magwood and inquired if there was anything that could be done to "help" him. After a brief discussion the decision was made not to prosecute the case, and it was quietly settled with a not guilty verdict.

Despite all Captain Junior's idiosyncrasies—or perhaps even because of them—he and I developed a strong regard for each other and maintained a friendly relationship as long as he lived. Of the many colorful personalities that inhabited the waterfront, Captain Junior was one of the most memorable.

The lowcountry panorama was remarkably different in the late 1970s from the way it is today. Although over the years I worked along the entire South Carolina coastline, both inshore and offshore, I chiefly patrolled the waters between Charleston and the North Santee River. In the 1970s not many houses were visible on the "back beach" of Sullivan's Island or on the marsh side of the mainland from Mount Pleasant all the way to the South Santee River.

Wild Dunes, a major development on the Isle of Palms north of Charleston, had not yet begun its burgeoning growth. Everything from Forty-first Street eastward was undeveloped and densely vegetated. Where the Forty-first Street Marina is presently located was then only a dirt ramp that ran through a high sand bluff bordering Morgan Creek. It was operated by Colonel H. R. "Woody" Faison, a flight instructor, who also ran the Isle of Palms airstrip that stretched out for a distance along the waterway just west of the ramp. The road leading to the East Cooper Airport is named for him.

If I saw the colonel's car as I was passing by on the waterway, I occasionally pulled over to the bank bordering the airstrip, tied the boat up to a limb, and walked across the runway to his small office. Usually, if he were not busy, he would take me up for a short flight around my territory. On one flight, as we were lifting off and making a banking turn over the end of Goat Island, I saw a boat in Hamlin Creek on the first bend off the waterway. Its occupant was in the act of using a pair of tongs in a public area that was never open for commercial shell fishing.

Tongs are a regulated implement used for hand harvesting clams and oysters in deep water. They are a scissorlike apparatus made of opposing basket scoops attached to ten- to fourteen-foot hinged handles. As the handles are vigorously opened and closed, toothed projections on the lower leading edge of each scoop dig and scrape the bottom for clams and single oysters. The catch is retrieved by bringing the handles together and lifting the scoop to the surface, where the contents are dumped on the deck of the boat. It is back-breaking work.

I asked the colonel to circle around and land. I exited the still idling airplane, ran across the runway, and jumped back into my boat. We had not been in the air three minutes. Just as I turned off the waterway into Hamlin Creek, I saw the boat pulling up to one of the docks on the backside of Goat Island. I came alongside him, tied my boat to his, and proceeded to give his boat a thorough inspection.

I knew the offending clammer from previous law-enforcement encounters. He was clearly not pleased to see me. I checked his shellfish licenses and permits. He had only two full sacks of clams in his boat, neither of which was tagged, also a violation. He swore that those bags were all he had, that he had gotten them in a legally permitted area some distance away, and that he had just come to tie up and take a rest; but I knew differently.

I was immediately curious about why he had tied up to this particular dock. I was familiar with its owner and knew that he had a reputation for being a violator. As the clammer waited in his boat, I walked a short distance toward the head of the dock and spotted a pile of bagged clams partially hidden behind a stand of saw palmettos. They also were untagged.

Since I had not seen him put the clams there and had found him in possession of only the two bags in the boat, I did not ticket him for the hidden clams—although I did seize them for being untagged. I also seized the two bags in his possession and wrote him tickets for harvesting shellfish without an area permit and failure to tag his bagged shellfish. I scattered the seized clams in a small creek some distance up the waterway. Occasionally I revealed to watermen who were down on their luck the location of one or another of the several small creeks where I had dumped contraband clams.

There was another dirt ramp on the east end of Sullivan's Island at Breech Inlet, near the former site of the old Gline's Seafood Restaurant. Adjacent to the ramp were a bait stand and a small store that sold cold beverages and snacks. Jimmy Wear, the former chief of police of Sullivan's Island, ran it for a time. Wear always had something on the grill or ready to be grilled. It was a convivial gathering spot that attracted a large number of Wear's sociable family and friends. His little store was where I first met Belle, my beautiful Boykin spaniel, who was then only a tiny puppy and who became my constant companion on land and water.

The only marina along that portion of the waterway that sold gasoline was Kathy's Marina at Toler's Cove near the Ben Sawyer Bridge. They also had a dirt ramp just off the waterway. An Asian lady who worked at the small marina store made smoked jerky and smoked fish. Toler's sold a few

Two sets of long-handled tongs used to harvest clams in deep water. This method requires a strong back.

fishing supplies and had a regular following who hung around drinking beer and engaging in deep philosophical conversations.

I was fueling up my boat there one Saturday morning when a ragged bow-rider boat loaded with some of the most unattractive people I've ever seen pulled in and tied up just in front of me. A grossly obese woman with bad teeth asked me if I was a game warden. I replied that I was. She asked me if it would be against the law for her to be topless. I responded that I was not familiar with any specific state law prohibiting such a thing, but that I thought she might fall afoul of some municipal ordinance. Then she asked, "Does that mean you wouldn't write me a ticket?" As I was saying, "No, Ma 'am," she whipped off her halter-top revealing her enormous, pendulous, tattoo-adorned ninnies and hissed gleefully through her snags at my obvious discomfort.

Further up the waterway only a few houses could be seen in the otherwise unbroken tree line across the marsh from Copahee Sound. The old red-roofed Porcher house at Porcher Bluff, an old house near Moore's Landing, the Munn's settlement, the Methodist camp landing, Buck Hall, and Shellmore were among the few visible signs of civilization on that stretch of mainland between the Sullivan's Island causeway and McClellanville.

On the barrier island side of the waterway, from Forty-first Street on the Isle of Palms, all the way to South Island, there were even fewer signs of human encroachment. There was only the power line that crossed Dewees, Capers, and Price inlets, providing electricity to a few houses on Dewees Island, the ranger's camp on Capers, and at its terminus the Dominick House on Bull Island.

Bull Island is at the western end of the twenty-mile-long, 66,267-acre, Cape Romain Wildlife Refuge, which consists of an assortment of barrier islands and a wide expanse of salt marsh. Twenty-eight thousand acres of the refuge was included in the National Wilderness Preservation System in 1975. Just after I began patrolling the area in 1978, the U.S. Fish and Wildlife Service released a pair of endangered red wolves on Bull Island to determine if they would breed and prosper in that environment. I loved to sit in my boat near the Bull Bay end of the island and listen to them howl at the rising moon.

Stretching eastward from Bull Island was Bull Bay, Cape Romain, Murphy island, and Cedar Island, all uninhabited. Murphy and Cedar islands were part of the Santee Coastal Reserve Waterfowl Management Area and were, for the most part, old impounded rice fields that remained from the time when rice was grown in the lowcountry. Both had some ridges of high land out near the oceanfront, and Murphy Island had some scattered ruins of old slave settlements and summerhouses.

In November 2006, at a Nature Conservancy event on the Santee Delta at Rochelle Plantation, I had occasion to listen to its owner, Pierre Manigault, and Mike Prevost, manager of the Sewee to Santee unit of the Nature Conservancy, address the gathering about that long stretch of protected coastline. They explained that it was recognized in 1986 as a United Nations Educational, Scientific and Cultural Organization (UNESCO) Biosphere Reserve.

The roughly 309,000-acre Carolinian–South Atlantic Biosphere Reserve is a mosaic of terrestrial, coastal, and marine ecological systems. Its designation as a biosphere reserve is an important recognition of its uniqueness and value not only to the state but also to the nation and the world. I could not have been prouder; they were talking about what had been my "office."

Those vast stretches of tidelands may appear to be a barren landscape to the untrained eye seeing them at sea level, but after spending a little time exploring the endless winding watercourses that laced the coastal marshes, I came to appreciate their awesome beauty. I got to see the dramatic changes in color as the seasons progressed, experienced the spectacular sunrises and sunsets, and learned firsthand the terrifying fury of lightning storms. It was nature up close and personal. Most of the time I had it all to myself, along with Belle, of course.

Until the mid-1980s there was relatively little boat traffic northward of Capers Inlet, except for the commercial fishermen, a few recreational fishermen, and the semi-annual parade of migrating "snowbirds" in the waterway. I kept an eye on Capers Island, which was managed as a Heritage Trust Preserve by the Wildlife Department. I often walked the three-mile length of it from one end to the other, making sure that there were no signs of prohibited activity.

I remember walking along the back of the island late one spring, leaning over to pass under a clump of low palmettos, and coming face to face with one of the biggest, blackest cottonmouth water moccasins I have ever seen. I went from forward motion to a crow-hop leap backward in a millisecond, and I think my heart made a few giant leaps itself. The most dangerous things on the island, however, were its insects: redbugs, ticks, and mosquitoes. People who ventured unprepared through the interior of the island were likely to emerge as hosts to hundreds of deeply imbedded bugs, a painful reminder of their failure to apply bug spray. I was so reminded following one foray with an itchy infestation of several hundred red bugs. Talk about misery!

When I walked the front beach early in the morning, hundreds of animal tracks were visible in the sand. Raccoon tracks were probably the most common, followed by those of deer and frequently red wolves, which nightly swam Price Inlet to catch a few of those fat Capers Island raccoons.

The myriad inlets, bays, sounds, and creeks in that long stretch maintained a thriving community of watermen who derived their livelihood from the bounty of the marsh. Over the years I probably ran across most of them, some in the remotest backwaters, neck deep in pluff mud feeling for clams, others operating every imaginable description of watercraft in their daily quests for oysters, clams, crabs, shrimp, and fish.

Ike Coakley, a waterman who lived on the Copahee marsh front of the Six Mile community in Mount Pleasant

At rare intervals, when I had the time, I tried my hand alongside the clammers and oyster pickers or onboard one of the small shrimp trawlers or crab boats. I invariably came away with a keen sense of appreciation for the physical exertion such work required and the long hours that they devoted to it.

A substantial portion of the African American community of McClellanville and Awendaw derived their livelihood from the seafood business. Twenty years ago a number of watermen were the third or forth generation in their families to grow up around and earn their living from the surrounding marshes. They worked as crabbers or shell fishermen, as strikers on the shrimp boats, pickers at the crab factory, or day laborers on the docks. It was a rigorous type of labor whose financial rewards were scant. Few young men consider entering the seafood business today, and McClellanville's commercial-fishing waterfront is rapidly succumbing to residential development. Some of the watermen were completely charming, including Ike Coakley, "Shy" and John Manigault, and Henry Hutchinson—all of Six Mile, a community south of McClellanville and north of Mount Pleasant, bordering on Copahee Sound and Gray Bay.

Ike Coakley's wife was one of the sweetgrass-basket makers who sold her craft in North Mount Pleasant along Highway 17. One of the better-known basket makers is Mary Manigault, who in 1984 was recognized for her craft by the National Endowment of the Arts. The baskets are constructed of coils of native sweet grass and long-leaf-pine needles that are sewn with strips of palmetto fronds. This craft represents one of the oldest West African art forms in America.

Ike Coakley and his wife supported a house full of grandchildren and nieces and nephews. Mr. Coakley, like many of the men in his community, frequently went out in the sound to pick oysters and clams. He had a reputation for picking good-quality oysters.

Ike Coakley and John Manigault were helpful to me over the years; carrying me around in their boats and showing me around the marsh. They were reliable and discreet sources of information when they believed I needed to know it, some of which took the form of obtuse hints that on a particular night around the time of half tide might be a good time to look around in a certain creek across the sound. What I was likely to find, if I was diligent enough, was an unlicensed, unmarked gill net stretched across a creek from bank to bank.

Tales of the Net Patrol

On patrols around the lowcountry waterways I regularly encountered five different kinds of nets: cast nets, recreational shrimp seines, stop nets, gill nets, and channel nets. A channel net is a large baglike contrivance that resembles the nets used on shrimp trawlers. The difference is in how they are used. Channel nets are stationary, and trawl nets are towed behind a boat. The throat of a channel net is kept open by two ten-to-fourteen-foot-long poles attached to the top and bottom line of the net on either side of the opening. Each side of the net is attached to an anchor by means of a bridle constructed of heavy polypropylene line fastened to the top and bottom of the poles and extending out a hundred feet or more. The tail end of the channel net is usually anchored to hold the bag pointed in the direction of the ebb tide. A channel net uses the force of the tide to sweep shrimp through the wide panels into the tail bag, where they are trapped by the current.

To fish the channel net, the fisherman uses nearby landmarks to locate the position of the tail-bag line at the end of the net. A grapnel, a three- or four-tined hook, is dragged back and forth until the tail-bag line is snagged and pulled up to the level of the boat. As this line is pulled to the surface, the tension, like a tight collar, chokes off the throat of the bag containing the shrimp. As the tail bag comes to the surface of the water alongside the boat, the netter uses clawed metal net hooks to grab the mesh and pull the tail bag over the gunwales into the boat. The end of the bag is then untied much the same as the tail bag in a trawl net, and the shrimp are emptied onto the deck of the boat. From the moment they first hook the tail-bag line, some fishermen can have a channel net in and out of the boat in fewer than five minutes.

The use of these nets is strictly regulated, and licenses are issued for a limited number of channel nets each year. They are usually reissued year after year to the same netters, who retain their licenses with the provision that they do not violate any of the net laws. In the lowcountry just about all channel netters are from Georgetown.

Most of the channel netters were tough hardworking people. Many held daytime jobs in the construction business or at the paper mill or steel mill in Georgetown. Some were dyed-in-the-wool watermen who also seasonally crabbed, trawled for shrimp, netted for shad, and gathered clams and oysters. For some reason the channel-net fishery also attracted a number of inveterate violators.

The violators I faced regarded getting caught as just part of the cost of doing business. Even though they were breaking the law, they expected to be treated fairly. If they had even an inkling that a game warden was trying to bluff them, they would go to the wall with him, lawyers, jury trials, and all.

The illegal netters were difficult to catch in the act because their apparatus was totally hidden underwater, and they typically worked it in the darkness of night. There were a number of ways they could be caught, however. On several occasions the tides acted in my favor. Sometimes during periods of unusually low tides, the tops of the poles holding the net open would become visible above the surface, where either I would discover them or someone else would find them and make a phone call. Another time, during a period of extremely high tides, a number of crab pots were set adrift by the strong currents and became entangled in the leading edge of a submerged channel net, resulting in one of those "you ought to see this" phone calls from the crabber.

The netters occasionally came to grief through a combination of brazenness and bad luck. Once I was crossing the old Cooper River Bridge, towing my fifteen-foot Boston Whaler, when I noticed a bateau with three people standing up in it, one of whom had just thrown something into the water. I quickly sped over the first span and turned into the pull-off in the dip between the two spans. I got out my binoculars and witnessed, to my complete astonishment, a channel net breaking the surface of the river, right there in broad daylight.

Jumping back into my car, I drove at break-neck speed into Charleston and then back around over the Pearman bridge into Mount Pleasant. As I

Channel netters taking up their net anchors after being caught with illegally set nets under the old Cooper River bridges

passed over the Cooper River, I saw that the net was completely in the boat and they appeared to be in the act of unfastening it from the anchors. I hurried over to Remleys Point Landing and hovered there out of sight just outside the entrance to the parking lot. Soon after I arrived, I saw the bateau approach the landing and quickly drive up onto the awaiting trailer that had remained down on the ramp. As soon as the truck towing the boat appeared at the top of the ramp, I cut it off, blue lights flashing and siren wailing.

After informing them that they were under arrest for setting a channel net in a restricted area, I proceeded to inspect their boat. I observed that the net was full of live shrimp, that the tail bag was still tied, and that there was an equal amount of loose shrimp on the bottom of the boat under the net, which was strong evidence that they had probably fished another net before pulling the one they had in the boat.

They were still a little rattled over my sudden, noisy arrival. I informed them that I had seen them taking the net up by the bridge and that I knew they had another one set nearby, an allegation they vehemently denied. I wrote them the appropriate tickets and sent them on their way, minus their boat, trailer, net, and shrimp. I called for some help to tow everything over to the Fort Johnson compound on James Island. When that was taken care of, I launched my boat from the ramp and towed a heavy stainless-steel hook up and down the edge of the channel from just upstream of the bridge to the mouth of Molasses Creek, where I found the second net.

This same crowd was caught a year later, also in broad daylight, again working a net right off Molasses Creek in the Wando River. During a bonding procedure where seizures are involved, the defendant could post a certain amount of money, depending on the value of his boat, and retain possession. Provisions could also be made for offenders to buy back their nets. I disapproved of this practice, which was eventually discontinued. These particular offenders bonded out their boat and net in cash on the spot, as well as paying the bonds on the several charges, more than twenty-five hundred dollars in all.

Once, during a particularly busy spate of apprehensions, I had more than seven thousand dollars in cash bonds in a cigar box in the trunk of my patrol car. If the policy was to make some quick money for the state, the bond transactions might be a good deal; however, the policy was not good for the resource. I am sure that most of the time those nets were set right back in an illegal area on the same night.

Another channel-net case that didn't turn out so well taught the hard-learned lesson that sometimes too many witnesses for the prosecution may not be a good thing. I had found a channel net with one end fastened to an Intracoastal Waterway marker piling in Wappoo Cut just above where the James Island connector bridge is now located. I got together with other officers in my unit to come up with a plan to observe activity in the vicinity of the net.

One officer was in the catch vehicle and was assigned to watch the Wappoo Cut Landing from the McLeod Plantation property just opposite the boat ramp. Two officers took a position on the shell bank about seventy yards away from where the net was set. Another officer was on the fire escape behind the rice mill at the City Marina to watch for any activity at the marina boat ramp, and two other officers were in a boat in the anchorage between the Coast Guard base and the City Marina to check for any boat movement from the harbor side. They were anchored in a position to see straight up Wappoo Cut. The weather was ideal, but it was a very dark night.

I was assigned the Wappoo Landing site. We were all in radio communication. We knew within about forty-five minutes when the netters would likely appear. Approximately twenty minutes before low tide, a truck and trailered boat arrived in the landing parking lot. Two men wearing yellow rain bibs and white rubber boots launched the boat and departed into the darkness toward the harbor. A third member of the group remained in the truck at the landing with the trailer still in the water on the ramp. I notified the others of their arrival and that they were heading in their direction, running without lights. Everyone was tuned in and looking in the same direction.

The officers hidden behind the shell bank reported that they could see the boat coming. Looking straight across from their viewpoint there was not a lot of backlighting. It was almost low tide, and the bank loomed darkly on the other side of the creek. The officers reported that they could tell the occupants of the boat were on the net. The net boat's engine was idling, and the officers could hear bumps and splashes coming from the location, but they couldn't make out a lot of detail.

Peering through binoculars, the officer on the fire escape said he could just barely see the boat but couldn't tell anything about what the occupants were doing. The officers in the anchorage reported they could see nothing. They were to remain in position until after the netters left and pick up the officers from the shell bank.

In a short time the netters had taken up the entire rig and were heading back to the landing. I saw them coming. The truck had remained on the ramp. As the boat approached the lights at the ramp, I could see the big net piled up on the deck. Continuing to report events as they happened, I backed out of my position opposite the landing and started over to Folly Road. By the time I got across the Wappoo Cut Bridge I could see their truck and boat receding in the distance up near South Windermere Shopping Center. They certainly were not observing the posted speed limits. Apparently something had spooked them. Perhaps it was all our radio traffic. I finally put the blue light on them just as they passed Lockwood Boulevard.

After they were stopped, they could not be convinced that they had been observed working the net and claimed they were bringing it from down south. I pointed out all the live shrimp still flipping around in the net and informed them that they were under arrest. In a blaze of blue lights and sirens, the officer who had been perched high up on the fire escape arrived. We directed the netters to pull over into a nearby parking lot, where we unhooked their boat trailer and attached it to the officer's patrol car.

About twenty minutes later the other four officers arrived, and we proceeded to issue tickets for offenses including "setting a channel net in a restricted area," "failure to mark channel net," "setting a channel net without a license," and "operating a boat at night without running lights" to each of the men.

Somehow or another, the netters' sense of fair play was offended because we made the stop on the highway, not on the water or at the landing, and they were not absolutely convinced that we saw them over the net. They came to court with attorney Bob Lumpkin of Georgetown, the hometown of the defendants, and asked for a jury trial. With six officers to testify as witnesses, we figured this case was going to be a no-brainer. We had the net. We had the boat. We had the shrimp.

Well Mr. Lumpkin ate us alive. Every officer testified to what he saw. None of the officers could testify that he could identify any of the fishermen or the boat at the time they were working the net. I could give a description only of the boat that left and returned to the landing. I certainly could not identify the faces of the people in the boat until after I had made the stop downtown. He cross-examined each officer about details such as how far he was away from where the net was supposed to be and what was the time when he observed a boat in the water at night where the net was supposed to be.

He reiterated to the jury what a dark night it was and that no officer could say for sure that they saw his clients working that net. He also pointed out small but significant discrepancies in the testimony of each officer; small differences in estimated distances and time intervals. Each of us could feel the cold crust of egg forming on our faces. We had not done our homework. It was becoming acutely embarrassing.

In his summation Mr. Lumpkin held his cupped hands out in a figurative scales of justice and ran down the testimony, with one hand (the acquittal hand) getting lower and lower as he recounted each minute discrepancy. He concluded by stating the obvious; the arresting officers could not even agree among themselves as to what they saw and when they saw it; therefore his clients should be given the benefit of doubt and found not guilty.

It was a persuasive argument. Despite our testimony, the jury found all three defendants not guilty of all the channel-net charges. However, to our complete astonishment, the jury did find the operator of the boat guilty of operating a boat at night without running lights. At least it was not a complete loss. We all learned the valuable lesson not to take any evidentiary matters for granted and the supreme importance of proper preparation before trial.

Another antic of some of the members of the channel-net crowd was staking one of their nets across the outside of a rice-field water-control structure, or trunk, pulling the boards that regulated the water level inside and causing all the water to drain out through the net. In the fall, such impoundments generally contained large quantities of shrimp, fish, and crabs, many of which were swept into the nets in the rush of the outflow. The drainage of hundreds of acres of flooded impoundments during the duck season created enormous problems for the landowner.

Some people fell afoul of the channel-net laws by using recreational shrimp seines to block off a creek. It was legal to hand pull up to a forty-foot-wide, one-half-inch-mesh pocket seine in the salt-marsh creeks along the coast. It was a popular method of shrimping, and many people I knew had their secret creeks and holes where they would carry only a trusted few who swore they would never come back; oaths that—I might add from my observations—were frequently broken. If a person's spot were to remain a real secret, he had to go there with a cast net by himself.

A Wando River crabber called me and reported he thought someone was regularly "dragging" in a small creek above Beresford Creek on the Cainhoy side of the river. *Dragging* was the colloquial term for towing a shrimp-trawl net. He reported that he thought it was going on in broad daylight. Trawling in closed waters was a serious violation that carried a steep fines and resulted in the seizure of boat, motor, equipment, and catch. I thought this report was unusual because most people who trawled illegally did it under cover of darkness.

I entered the small creek early the next day, just before high tide, prepared to spend some time there. I followed the creek until it became fairly narrow. Arching over the stream were the branches of a huge live oak. I tied the boat to one of its low limbs and climbed onto the high bank. I found a comfortable place to sit and gazed at the tide coming in. That area of the river was then completely undeveloped, and there were no houses visible along the distant tree line. It was a tranquil scene.

After several hours things began to get exciting. In the distance, I saw a boat with two occupants entering the mouth of the creek from the river. Once they got into the marsh-lined creek, all I could see through the binoculars was their heads as they drove up the winding creek. I was beginning to become a little apprehensive, thinking they might come all the way to where I was sitting. But finally I heard the boat slow down and come to idle. They were then about two hundred yards away.

I could hear thumping noises and the rattle of chains. My plan was to let them get the net under tow so that the noise of their motor would mask any noise from mine. I was going to run slowly and quietly from up the creek and then rush them. The rattling and thumping went on for around ten minutes. I could occasionally see the tops of their heads bobbing above the marsh grass, and I continued to hear their motor idling. Then I was astonished to hear their motor suddenly come up to speed as they exited the creek, much faster than would have been possible if they were dragging a net.

I watched them leave the creek and enter the river heading toward Charleston. At that moment I could not imagine what they could have been doing. I jumped in my boat, headed down the creek, and soon discovered the source of all the carrying on. They had set a forty-foot bag seine completely across the creek from bank to bank and were using it, in effect, as a small channel net.

After examining that contrivance, I motored back to my lookout position and waited. This was going to be a good case, and I was really getting excited about the catch. My plan was to get in my boat when I saw them enter the mouth of the creek and quietly pole down stream since their idling engine would not mask the sound of mine cranking up. I really hated getting into chases, not to mention the fact that the net was set between them and me.

Three or four hours passed before I saw them reenter the creek from the river. Since the tide was much lower, I could hear only the sound of their motor once they got into the marsh. I heard them slow down and then come to an idle. I figured they had arrived at the net. I began silently poling my boat toward the scene of the crime.

Rounding a bend in the creek, I came upon them as they were taking up the net. Imagine my surprise to find a longtime friend and his father, both from downtown Charleston, with that net in their hands. They knew that they had been caught red-handed and appeared embarrassed. I had to deal with that ambivalent feeling that comes with a mixture of the letdown following the excitement at the moment of the catch and the immediate realization that I had to write my friends some pretty serious tickets. It was the sort of situation and feelings I experienced many times during my career.

Most of the people I caught violating knew what they were doing and generally were good at what they did. Even though they were never happy at being caught, I rarely had any arguments from them except in the courtroom.

There was a family who lived on Sullivan's Island, who fished a type of net known as a *stop net*. Several of the stop nets they used were close to three hundred feet long and constructed of heavy cotton twine.

Their net was weighted on the bottom and was set during the high tide parallel to and at some distance removed from the shoreline. They paid out the net over the side of the boat and set stakes at intervals to hold the top of the net out of the water as the tide receded. The extreme ends of the net were bent toward the edge of the marsh so everything inside the net would be trapped.

They set their stop nets in areas that went completely dry at low tide, when they would walk behind the net and gather the stranded fish in baskets. I had seen baskets full of whiting, trout, spottail bass, flounder, spot, and croaker stacked on their boat and destined for local markets.

Theirs was a legal licensed fishery, but there were rules. The regulation they seemed to have a hard time understanding was the prohibition against blocking off more than one half the width of a watercourse, such as a navigable creek or a bay. Most frequently they set their nets along the Mount Pleasant shoreline, along the waterway just behind Sullivan's Island, and occasionally further north in Copahee Sound.

I didn't get too excited about the net extending in front of several small sloughs or drains but they thought that they could block off the entire mouth of the much larger slough between the Ben Sawyer Bridge and the spoil area west of it. They also blocked the whole drainage on the other side of the spoil area by stretching their net completely across the mouth of the creek. This was a pretty tough crowd who had been used to doing things their way for quite a while. They were not inclined to change.

I patiently explained the law to them and showed them on a chart areas where they could legally stretch out the full length of their nets without violating. They were adamant that they had set their nets for years in the places where I told them they were in violation and were going to continue to do so. Several of them were known to brandish weaponry if they felt their constitutional right to do as they pleased was being infringed.

I preferred educating them on the applicable laws to writing a ticket and seizing that long heavy net. After repeated warnings, I resolved to write them up but to leave them with the net. I figured that a few trips to the magistrate would eventually discourage them. They had to work pretty hard for the fish they sold, and the fines would eventually add up.

The magistrate was unsympathetic to their constitutional arguments. On my recommendation he gave them a severe fine, one that got their attention. They were very angry and discoursed at length on my ancestry, but the fine had the desired effect. I never caught them in a violation again.

In my first two decades with the Wildlife Department, it was not uncommon to run into four or five gill nets a week. They could be set in just about any body of water, inshore or offshore. They ranged from small fifty to seventy-five footers to some that were more than fourteen hundred feet for use offshore. Most were monofilament, but there were still some heavy cotton twine nets used in the sturgeon fishery.

The longer offshore nets were chiefly used during the shad season, and they could be generally found in the ocean ranging from the Winyah Bay jetties down to the South Edisto. During the shad season shorter gill nets were anchored in permanent "sets" in most of the state's rivers. They were typically marked by a signboard nailed to a tree giving the name and license number of the set holder. There were sections of the South Santee, North Santee, Black, Pee Dee, Waccamaw, and Edisto rivers where I had to thread slowly and carefully around the gill nets stretching from the bank toward the center of the river. Untangling one of them from my propeller was always a nightmare, not only from the labor involved but the cussing I had to endure from the net owner.

Shad fishermen also use drift nets, which can be as long as a football field. A drift net usually carried a lot more floats than a set net and had large metal rings as weights on the foot of the net. Drift fishermen rapidly paid out their nets over the sides of their boats and occasionally went from end to end of the net pulling it tight athwart the current. A rapidly bobbing float announced the presence of a fish caught in the netting. They continued to fish the net until they got to the end of the drift, took it up, and set it out again further upstream.

There was also a recreational component of the drift fishery, particularly along the Edisto and Santee rivers. Throughout the shad season several groups of men from Orangeburg, Rowesville, Charleston, and Georgetown got together on weekend evenings at various landings. They set up tables, lights, coolers, stoves, grills, and chairs along the riverbank.

Depending on the crowd, they launched two or more boats from the landing and ran upstream, where they set the drift nets. A net was fished as it and the boats floated downstream in the current, their bobbing corks indicating periodic successes. The boatmen carried the still-jumping shad to the assembly area, where the fish went the length of a processing line, being scaled, filleted, and having their roes removed.

That activity went on until an ample amount of shad and shad roe was obtained. Then the fires were stoked, and the cooking began. On the menu one would typically find grits, fried sausage, scrambled eggs, fried shad roe wrapped with bacon, fried breaded shad fillets, hush puppies, and sweet iced tea—all served buffet style. I was privileged to sit around a number of riverside campfires over the years, enjoying the hospitality, fellowship, and good cooking of several groups who maintained that tradition.

The shad fishery was subject to a host of regulatory and reporting requirements. Net fishermen were not allowed to set a net across more than one half the width of any watercourse. There were several areas in some of the rivers where the width became constricted; some of the perennial violators went to such places in the darkness of night and set a net across the complete span of the river. If the netters heard a boat coming, they unfastened one end of the net and let it fold back with the current. One of the strategies I employed to catch them was killing the engine well upstream and drifting in the current with the engine down. When the boat stopped dead in the middle of the river with the engine caught in the float line of a net, I figured I had a violator nearby.

The law required shad nets set offshore to be taken up by noon on Saturday, and they could not be reset until noon on Monday, a restriction frequently ignored by some of the fishermen. They often used the excuse that it was too rough to get out and take up their nets, and sometimes that was true. In an effort to be fair, I told them that if it was too rough to go out, to call the wildlife hot line when they got back to land and ask the operator to relay their message to me.

Midday one Saturday I was drifting offshore of the east end of Bull Island near several sets of nets, when I got a radio call from the dispatcher in Columbia, who said a shad fisherman had left a message that it was too rough for him to go offshore. While it wasn't exactly glass smooth, I was out there in a thirteen-foot Boston Whaler. I responded to the dispatcher with the usual "ten-four, Columbia." Then I brought out my brand-new, sharp, hawk-bill limb pruners and began taking in one of several long shad nets set in the area.

Most of the time, if I had a colleague along, we took up the sand anchors at each end of the net, and when the net was free, we pulled it over the bow of the boat, carefully removing the shad and any bycatch. On this occasion I was alone and knew I had a lot of work ahead of me; I began cutting away the anchor lines from the net.

As I pulled the webbing over the bow, I twisted around in the mesh every fish I came to, cut it out of the net, and pitched it overboard, leaving a huge gap in the panel of the net. I also cut off the bricks from the bottom

Sturgeon and shad caught in legally set gill nets off the Charleston jetties. This sturgeon was among the last caught before it became illegal to harvest them.

of the net, which served as additional anchors to hold the net upright in the water column. I neatly folded the net back and forth in front of the console. As I took each net aboard, I stuffed it into in an oyster bag.

On Monday afternoon—following the pattern of many violators over the years—after these shad fishermen had gone out to work their nets and discovered they were missing, I was the first one they called. I told them I had their nets, and they could come over to Fort Johnson to pick them up, after receiving a ticket and posting the required bond for each net.

When they arrived, I brought out the oyster bags containing the nets. When they asked where the anchors and weights were, I told them that they were still on the bottom of the ocean. They paid the bonds and departed sulking and muttering. The next day, after they stretched out their nets to rerig them, the phone lines to the Charleston and Columbia offices heated up. I explained to the Columbia office, my supervisors, one member of the

South Carolina House of Representatives, and two Wildlife Department Commissioners that the shad netters had deliberately lied about the sea conditions and that I had been patrolling offshore alone.

That seemed to satisfy them, although the Columbia office crowd, never losing an opportunity to be supercilious, scolded me for working by myself. From then on, most nets were taken up over the weekend unless there was a bona fide raging storm that prevented the netters from venturing offshore.

The shad fishermen were often their own worst enemies. Sometimes they set their nets offshore of Bull Island, part of the Cape Romain National Wildlife Refuge, and off Sullivan's Island and Folly Beach, popular beaches with the serious conservation crowd.

If the weather had been rough and the fishermen had not tended their nets, there would be a lot of dead and decomposing fish caught in their nets, which attracted small scavenging fish. These would in turn attract sea ducks and cormorants that also became entangled in the mesh and drowned. When the fishermen returned to work their nets, they extracted the dead birds from the webbing and pitched them overboard. The carcasses drifted up on the beaches in shoals causing a great stir among the environmental folk, who made their concerns known in the halls of the General Assembly. Eventually gill nets were outlawed in inshore waters except for the larger mesh nets allowed during the shad season. The lengthy offshore sets were banned completely. There remains a large seasonal drift fishery in the Santee and Waccamaw rivers, which have the width and depth to accommodate the larger mesh nets.

Early in my career there was an active sturgeon fishery in South Carolina, mainly in the Georgetown area. The season ran from March to October. The sturgeon nets, also a form of gill net, were constructed of heavy cotton twine, and the mesh could not be smaller than ten inches square. The offshore sets were typically found near the Winyah Bay or Charleston jetties or offshore of Cape Romain, and they were set in all the rivers of the state.

It was not uncommon in the early 1980s to see rows of huge sturgeon carcasses that had been hauled up on North Island at the entrance to Winyah Bay, where they had been carved up for their roe and their meat. Sturgeon meat and caviar formed a thriving seasonal part of the local seafood business that was largely centered around Rene Cathou's fish house on the Sampit River in Georgetown.

One afternoon I was offshore with Conservation Officer Craig Whitfield, in the forty-one-foot patrol boat *Wildlife 1,* looking for illegal nets set off Cape Romain. The weather was blustery and the water frothy, conditions that limited our ability to spot the floats marking the position of submerged nets. We were running along at a good clip, parallel to the shoreline but well outside the shoals, when the boat suddenly slowed and came to a total stop. We had "T-boned" an unseen sturgeon net. Officer Whitfield quickly pulled back the throttles and took the boat out of gear. Fortunately the east wind was off our bow, and we drifted back off the net without fouling the propellers or the rudders. Running over these long nets was a constant danger, especially when operating at night.

Our worst nightmare was finding an illegal net and having to haul it on board. They were heavy and difficult to manage, leaving our hands cold and our fingers blistered and bleeding. It got particularly hairy pulling them in over the stern to windward. We would be standing knee deep in nets, bricks, anchors, and sometimes large rotten sturgeon—or, even worse, a live sturgeon that had to be cut out of the net and released—all the while hanging on for dear life in a lurching boat.

Before it became illegal to set gill nets in inshore waters there used to be quite a substantial recreational gill-net fishery. Recreational nets were required to be licensed. They could not exceed forty feet in length or have a mesh size smaller than three and a half inches. The biggest violation associated with the use of the small gill nets was stringing them across more than half the width of the watercourse in which they were set. Whole creek drainages were sometimes blocked off with nets that caught everything leaving on the outgoing tide.

Once I was hauling my trailered boat along the main road onto the Isle of Palms and noticed a line of cork floats that extended all the way across Hamlin Creek. I didn't see a boat near it as I drove by, but I rushed down to the dirt landing at Forty-first Street, launched my boat, and quickly ran down the waterway to where I had seen the floats. As I rounded the bend, I saw a small boat with three men in it. One man was standing in the front of the boat just beginning to haul in the net.

When I arrived alongside, I explained that their net had been set illegally and asked to see some identification and the net license. One of the men, Alton Buck, produced a license for one net, but I could see there were at least three separate nets tied together. I asked him to finish taking up his nets and to pitch any fish overboard. Issuing Mr. Buck a ticket for setting a net across the full width of Hamlin Creek, I explained that I was going to take the nets and hold them until after the trial.

When I got to the trial, my first gill-net case, it got ugly in a hurry. When the judge, Paul Foster of Mount Pleasant, asked Mr. Buck how he pled to the charge, he replied "not guilty." He told the judge that at no time had his net been set across the creek. I told the judge that I had seen Mr. Buck's nets stretched from bank to bank as I was driving by, not fifty yards away, and that it was absolutely clear to me that the nets had been illegally set.

Judge Foster looked me in the eye and firmly said, without even asking the first question, that I could not possibly have seen what I said I saw and immediately brought his gavel down while saying "not guilty." At the time I didn't know Judge Foster well and had little courtroom experience. We became friends over the ensuing years, but at that moment the judge seemed blatantly hostile toward my case and seemed to be accusing me of lying about what I had seen. He demanded that I take immediate steps to return the seized nets.

I waited until court was over, went into the judge's office hat in hand, and politely asked what was going on. He said, "Mr. Moïse, everybody has friends. That man you wrote the ticket to is one of my best friends. We grew up together." I told him that I had no problem with that line of thought but that the case might have been settled without humiliating me in front of a courtroom full of people.

In time we worked out little signals that the judge wanted a defendant to be "helped" or that I wanted the defendant to be shown no mercy. On the rare occasions when we signaled each other on the same defendant, we had a quick conference in the judge's office to work things out.

While out on the duck patrol during the winter, I used to find gill nets set in the small creeks off the North and South Santee rivers. One morning before daylight my outboard motor fouled on a net that was stretched from bank to bank in a remote creek in the Santee Delta. As I cleared my propeller and pulled the net into my boat I found that it was loaded with garfish and a couple of shortnose sturgeon, a much smaller fish than the Atlantic sturgeon.

I had heard about the local affinity for garfish so, when I finished the patrol, I stopped by the guide house at the Santee Gun Club and asked the men who were sitting around a fire picking ducks if they would like any of the fish. They jumped up and eagerly hauled the net out of the boat on to the ground and soon extracted a wheelbarrow full of garfish. They also neatly folded up the net and tucked it into a burlap bag for me. I took the sturgeon to the marine lab in Charleston for scientific study, because they were an endangered species and illegal to keep.

Knowing the meat in a gar was very boney and stringy, I asked one of the guides how they cooked them. He said that he cut the gar down the backbone with a hatchet and used a sharpened spoon to scrape the meat away from the sinewy tissue. The meat was then cooked into a stew with vegetables and served over rice. Several days later one of the guides surprised me with a jar of gar stew his wife had made. I found it quite tasty.

Over the years I encountered increasing numbers of Vietnamese fishermen. They seemed to concentrate around the easily accessible waters near Mount Pleasant. They were expert cast netters and could fan out a twelve-foot cast net while standing chest deep in the water. They also used gill nets before they were made illegal in inshore waters.

Pulling alongside one of their boats anchored at one end of a gill net set off the Shem Creek channel one day, I checked their licenses and examined what they were catching. When I asked to see their fish, they reached under the console and produced a huge bowl of menhaden fillets immersed in a pickling liquid mixed with sliced peppers and onions. They also had a few trout and flounder on ice in a cooler. When I asked what they were going to do with the menhaden, they looked at me with a surprised expression and replied that they were going to eat them.

I found out later that menhaden, a very oily fish, is full of healthy nutrients, especially if eaten raw. Frankly I think they would melt if you tried to cook them. I think I will stick with a vitamin pill.

Most of the Vietnamese were good hardworking sorts. A small number of them were involved in the crabbing business; several either owned or operated shrimp trawlers. I had problems with a couple of them turning in the required landing reports. I had to explain through a translator, usually a younger family member, that the reports of their catch were required as a condition of the license, and that if they failed to turn them in, they would lose their livelihood. One or two did rack up enough offenses to lose their commercial-fishing licenses, and one left town when the word got out that I was looking for him to lock him up for several unpaid tickets.

We had problems with some of the Vietnamese who operated fish markets around Rock Hill. They sent contingents down to go fishing on the several head boats, recreational boats that carried large numbers of people at a time to offshore fishing grounds. These boats operated out of Shem Creek.

The group from Rock Hill brought back their catch to be sold with no regard for size or catch limits.

One afternoon I was checking the contents of the fishermen's coolers on the afterdeck of one of the head boats just after it returned to the dock. Each large cooler I examined was loaded to the top with grouper, snapper, and porgy. There were federal restrictions that applied to the snapper-grouper fishery, and I didn't even get beyond the top layer of fish before I began to discover multiple violations. I knew that I couldn't check all the coolers on the boat so I chose a random sample and had their owners carry them down the ramp over to a corner of the dock.

Just about all the vermilion snapper, called "Beeliners," were of an illegal size, and they had vastly exceeded their catch limit. Their excesses also applied to the grouper and porgies. There were huge piles of illegal fish sitting on the dock by the time I had graded three 160-quart coolers.

I wrote each of the Vietnamese fishermen two or three tickets and told them that I was seizing their catch as well as their coolers. Since they could not be sold, I carried the whole lot to a downtown homeless shelter, and they seemed glad to have them. I learned later that every time I brought a load of contraband fish, a thriving seafood market materialized at the back of the shelter.

The head-boat intercepts were conducted at varying intervals, always with pretty much the same result. The second time I boarded one of the boats in Shem Creek, many of the fishermen simply walked down the ramp and abandoned their coolers full of fish. With no markings there was no way to tie the fisherman to his cooler. Losing the cooler and the fish was cheaper than paying the fine, so I began to put pressure on the head-boat operators.

They knew a few tickets for violations of the federal snapper-grouper regulations could entirely close down their operations. I had tried to keep the boarding somewhat low-key, just concentrating on the individual fishermen, but the trend in abandoning coolers escalated matters to an entirely unexpected level. The boat operators were already in a stir because they said my frequent visits were affecting their business.

We informed them that we were looking at a serious resource problem with thousands of illegal fish being brought to the dock to supply markets as far inland as Atlanta. I told them it was not my mission to put them out of business but that the illegal fishing had to stop. They explained that they made announcements on the public-address system on the way out and that they had size and catch limits posted all around the boat. One owner further explained that the crew depended on tips from the fishermen and that there was just so much policing that they could do.

I offered the proposition that, if they worked with me, I would try to keep them out of the process, but in return I was going to have to see some progress in ending the problem. We conceived a plan by which the boat captain would call me on a cell phone when they were about an hour away from the dock. When I got the call, I would gather together every officer I could find. As they arrived, they hid their vehicles across the street behind an office building and waited at some distance from the dock for the arrival of the boat.

An elevated latticework-enclosed platform behind the kitchen of a nearby restaurant provided an ideal place to see the boat and the apron where the fishermen's coolers were unloaded. On arrival, after determining the coast was clear, the fishermen would bring their vehicles over near the dock to load their coolers. I would radio the group of officers and give them a description of the vehicles as they left.

We were looking only for fishermen who came off the boat carrying multiple or really large coolers. I could tell if a cooler was topped off by the effort required to lift it. The officers stopped these fishermen a good distance away, just before they exited the parking lot. The fishermen's vehicles were directed to an area behind an automotive shop, where their coolers were checked. Huge numbers of tickets were issued the several times we conducted such an operation. All the activity eventually attracted the attention of federal fisheries enforcement officers. They made some serious federal cases against the boat operators and put an end to the excesses.

There was another kind of net rarely seen in local coastal waters. I discovered it in the darkness of night when I imbedded my boat right in the middle of it. I was familiar with the shoreline of the Cooper River across from the U.S. Navy Base, and I knew where every dock and piling along that stretch was located. I was running up the river close to the Clouter Island shore just north of the mouth of Clouter Creek when I ran right into a large pound net that had apparently been established there earlier in the week for the purpose of catching herring. I felt like a fly caught in a spider web.

Pound nets have a long wing of netting set on poles around six feet apart. A net extends from the shoreline out around seventy-five feet and terminates in a large boxlike trap. The wing of the net blocks any fish swimming up the river. As they swim out toward deeper water they are diverted into the trap through a series of funnels.

Standing by the gate to a rice-field trunk, a structure used to control water levels within impoundments managed for waterfowl hunting

Afterward I felt lucky that I hadn't collided with one of the long poles firmly set in the river bottom. I had run between two of the poles, ripping loose the netting, which fell back over me completely covering my boat like a huge cast net. It happened so suddenly that I didn't have a clue what was happening or what direction to go in to extricate myself. I groped around beneath the heavy, wet netting, found my flashlight, assessed the situation, and started clawing my way from under the entangling webbing of the net.

I was really surprised when I backed out and put the spotlight on it, to see such an elaborate contrivance. Until that moment, I had never seen one. I failed in further examination to find any tag or sign that would indicate the name of its owner or the license number of the net, so I continued my patrol that night with extra vigilance in the event there might be more of those things set further up the river. The next day, I found out from some crabbers that it belonged to a man from Moncks Corner, who was later ticketed for failing to mark his net.

Shrimpers

Shrimp trawlers come in every shape and size from super trawlers sixty feet and over, to the more common thirty- and forty-something-foot models, on down to modified outboards twenty feet and under. Keeping track of them was an important component of my marine-enforcement responsibilities.

Trawling for shrimp is a heavily regulated fishery: there is a legal season; there are areas always closed to trawling; there are areas open to trawling at certain times; and there are times of day when trawling can begin and when it must end. Bycatch-reduction devices and turtle excluders that meet rigid specifications must be installed in trawl nets.

Trawlers must have South Carolina trawling permits visibly displayed. Their captains must have licenses. Trawlers are required to keep records on their catch activity and send reports regularly to the Marine Division.

They must also conform to a host of state and federal laws that regulate boating safety—such as the laws requiring automatic man-overboard signaling devices, radios, navigation lights, life jackets, and life rings—and they must have state registration or federal documentation onboard. Operating a shrimp trawler is not an easy way to make a living, and the vast majority of shrimpers are good, hardworking people.

As environmental awareness began to emerge, the methods and activities of the trawler fleet were subjected to increasing scrutiny and regulation. The huge loggerhead turtles have an annual nesting cycle that brings them close to shore. Increasing alarm over the large numbers of dead turtles found up and down the resort beaches along the coast gave rise to ugly public

On offshore patrol during the shrimp season in a nineteen-foot radar-equipped Action Craft flats boat, the first of its design used in coastal law enforcement

hearings with both sides making unfounded accusations. The trawler captains thought that they were being unfairly singled out and attributed the turtle mortality to all manner of circumstances, none of them very convincing.

In the late 1980s Congressman Arthur Ravenel—regarded by many of the shrimpers as having poor judgment and being in the thrall of about every known environmental group—even called the shrimpers "turtle killers," a statement that didn't do much to calm things down.

As the regulatory process picked up steam, the trawlers were made to limit the length of time per trawl. They had to install an ever-changing array of turtle-excluder devices (TEDs) in the throats of their nets. Shrimpers also faced the threat of federal action to shut down the shrimping season if unacceptable turtle-mortality rates continued.

Law-enforcement agents from the National Marine Fisheries Service came to South Carolina and, along with state officers, boarded trawlers all up and down the coast for almost a week to ensure that regulations were being followed. The shrimpers were outraged at the boardings and the burgeoning restrictions, which they felt would keep them from making a decent living.

Some of them threatened to blockade the shipping channel, but cooler heads prevailed, and none of the threats was ever carried out. Transmissions over the marine VHF radios on the trawlers sounded like a Howard Stern broadcast as the shrimpers described their visceral estimations of the environmentalists, the government, the Wildlife Department, and those blankety-blank game wardens.

To add more aggravation, a new federal regulation was implemented requiring the installation of bycatch-reduction devices (BRDs) in the tail bag of their nets. That device was designed to allow the escape of the small, unmarketable fish, bycatch that would otherwise be thrown away. After an interval of time the shrimpers gradually came around. One of the McClellanville shrimpers even designed a more-efficient and trawler-friendly turtle-excluder device, called the soft TED or Morrison TED, and worked with local marine scientists in demonstrating its value.

During random boardings we occasionally caught shrimpers who had sewed the openings of their TEDs shut. The penalty for doing that was severe, and it didn't take long for the word to get out around the docks and

Checking a loggerhead turtle removed from the net of a shrimp trawler. Crews were required to use resuscitation measures on turtles before returning them to the water.

over the radio that being caught violating the TED regulations was a costly experience.

Perhaps the most serious of the trawling violations—the ones that result in heavy fines, seizure of boats, and suspension of licenses—were the offenses of trawling out of season and trawling in prohibited waters. Another restriction that the trawlers had to observe was the official trawling time, which for the better part of the season was sunrise until sunset. The most common of the trawling violations was trawling before or after legal hours.

Problems within the fleet usually started as the trawlers jockeyed for position just before sunrise on the most productive shrimping grounds, just offshore of the barrier islands. They were motivated by the firm belief that the boat out front on the first run of the morning got the most shrimp. The after-hours trawlers were usually trying to get just a few more shrimp—or "bugs" as they called them—before calling it quits, or they were trying to take advantage of a late ebb tide that would wash the shrimp out from the inlets to awaiting nets offshore.

Early in the morning I scanned the VHF channels most often used by the trawlers to find out if anybody was getting out of hand. The trawler captains could be critical of each other for not abiding by the rules, but they rarely called in the law because the consequences could put the offender out of the trawling business for a while.

The success of the shrimp season was governed by the weather and prevailing market prices. If it had been a hard winter, the water temperature would lower to the point of killing a great many overwintering shrimp, which would have been the producers of the forthcoming season's crop. If there was prolonged drought during the season, the size and mobility of the shrimp was affected. Obviously long periods of stormy weather affected the shrimpers' ability to go offshore, although some of the larger trawlers ventured out in heavy seas that were too much for the smaller ones to manage.

Market prices could be all over the landscape and were affected by availability over a wide area of the shrimping centers along the East Coast and in the Gulf. Shrimp prices have been increasingly affected by emerging competition from domestic and foreign mariculture operations. Only recently have protective tariffs been imposed to restrict the importation of mariculture shrimp. Other problems include escalating fuel prices and the loss of commercial-fishing infrastructure such as wharf-side packing sheds, ice houses, and docks as waterfront property becomes more valuable. Both the shrimpers' supply and markets were drastically affected by the advent of shrimp baiting. Ostensibly a recreational activity, shrimp baiting enables thousands of people who have a taste for shrimp to catch their own easily. These various market or regulatory factors, alone or in combination, caused some shrimpers to pursue desperate measures in order to obtain more shrimp to sell.

The number of hours I spent patrolling the inshore and offshore waters to enforce the shrimping regulations, usually in the dark, is almost uncountable. Some of this time fell in the category of what game wardens called —for purposes of their daily report—"routine patrol," which was simply covering the territory to find out what was going on. I discovered early that, if the trawler captains thought you were serious about what you were supposed to do and would actually respond to their complaints, no end of helpful information would come your way. One incident involved a North Carolina trawler that other shrimpers saw repeatedly trawling after legal hours off Bull and Capers islands. I received numerous calls from the McClellanville fleet saying that I should do something about it.

I convinced several of the trawler captains to become more active in solving the problem, to undertake a collaborative effort to document the offenses by taking readings off their radars when they saw the offender and accurately recording the time. I told them that the word of just one trawler captain might not stand up in court and that I needed as many witnesses to the offending activity as possible. Based on their information, a warrant could be issued, and I told them I would personally serve it on the offender.

The captains of three McClellanville trawlers observed and documented several nights of after-hours trawling by the North Carolinian. I met the captains at the magistrate's office in McClellanville, where I helped them prepare the affidavit and obtain the warrant, which I took in hand. As luck would have it, the offending trawler had left that day for North Carolina to offload his week's catch and was not seen in South Carolina waters until several weeks later.

Belle and I were patrolling in my johnboat in one of the inlets around Capers Island when a call came over the marine VHF radio from one of the McClellanville trawler captains. He told me that the boat I was looking for was shrimping around two miles off the east end of Bull Island and that he was in full tow heading west. He also asked me if I still had the warrant with me, which I did.

Fortunately the ocean was fairly calm, and I made a run through Price Inlet between Bull and Capers islands and headed offshore to the location I had been given. When I was well underway, I received another call from the McClellanville trawler captain saying that the boat I was looking for had just picked up its net doors and was heading straight out to sea. Its captain had apparently overheard the VHF traffic regarding his whereabouts and was trying to flee.

The distance from me to the outbound trawler was around seven miles. The chase was on to apprehend a sixty-foot trawler bent on escape. By the time I got to him, he was about five miles offshore. As I was closing the distance, I noticed the trawler had slowed to an idle to allow the crew to bring in the nets and rigging. I came up behind her, threw my bow line around one of the mast stays on the transom and climbed up over the stern.

The crew was busy securing the nets and did not appear to notice me coming aboard. I walked right past them to the wheelhouse, introduced myself to the much-surprised man behind the wheel, and asked him if he were Captain So-and-So. He responded "yes," and I told him that I had a warrant for his arrest and that he was going to have to turn around, go to McClellanville, and appear before the magistrate. After an initial debate as to whether I had any jurisdiction on the high seas, I convinced him that I did by producing my National Marine Fisheries Service commission, which gave me enforcement authority in federal waters.

I read him the charges on the warrant, gave him his copy, and instructed him to head for McClellanville after I had reboarded my boat. At magistrate's court he had to come up with several hundred dollars for a cash bond. There was some initial talk of a jury trial, but his North Carolina lawyer consulted a local attorney, who advised him that his client probably would not stand a chance in a trial with a local jury. The captain forfeited his bond and was suspended from trawling in South Carolina waters for the rest of the season. I don't believe he ever came back.

Sometimes if the weather was right, I headed across the harbor an hour or so before legal trawling time, ran out behind the jetties, pulled my boat up to the rocks, and waited for the trawler fleet to come out. My presence there was generally prompted by reports that some of the trawler captains were getting out of hand, either cutting in front of other trawlers or dropping their nets and beginning their tows before legal hours.

One morning Belle and I were in the rocks off the North Jetty. It had been a black-dark night but the ocean was calm. I was already sitting on the bow of my boat holding onto the jetty rocks with the heels of my boots as the fleet came steaming out of Shem Creek. They arrived at the jetties around four thirty or five A.M. with their green and white mast lights burning. Some turned to go through Dynamite Hole to trawl off Morris Island

and Folly Beach, and the others turned eastward around the end of the jetties to set up offshore of Sullivan's Island, the Isle of Palms or Capers Island. About six trawlers came around to my side.

I could clearly hear the sounds of activity on the trawler decks. Net chains and doors rattled and creaked; cable winches whined; and the trawler engines idled. After working among the trawler fleet for a while, I had learned that each of the separate little noises indicated a particular activity, and I could tell pretty much everything going on in the distance and the darkness of night.

The sounds of distant deck activity quieted down. What I usually expected to hear were the idling engines of the trawlers and the lap of the net doors just above the water surface. At the moment of legal trawling time the boats begin running as the nets are let out on cables. The throats of the nets are held open by the doors as long as there is forward motion of the trawler. The engines of a trawler towing a net have a very distinctive throb. When the nets are set, the afterdeck light typically goes out, and the deck crew, known as "strikers," go inside to take a break or fix breakfast. The average length of time for a tow is generally around an hour to an hour and a half.

Two of the six trawlers within three hundred yards of me extinguished their afterdeck lights, and I began to hear that distinctive engine throb of nets under tow. Pushing my boat away from the rocks, I started my engine but kept my running lights turned off. I rooted around in my boat bag and found my gum-ball-machine-looking rotating blue light and got it positioned to plug into my cigarette lighter.

The trawlers were several hundred yards apart and still in the vicinity of the other boats. It required all my concentration to keep track of which boat was which because at night distances can be deceiving. As I closed in on one of the offending trawlers, I had to avoid the net cables extending out along each side, plug in my blue light, aim the spotlight so I could read the name of the trawler, and holler for them to switch to VHF radio channel 67, where I could talk to them and tell them to stop and take up their nets. Then I immediately had to run to next trawler to play out the same scenario. I accomplished all these acts in short, intense moments of time. I really never thought much about it then, I just reacted and thought about it later.

I boarded each trawler to take the necessary information for issuing the appropriate citation. Coming over the rail, I heard the same old refrain, "Where were you yesterday when everybody else out here was draggin' early?"

Disembarking over the stern of a trawler with a National Marine Fisheries Service agent (left) after we checked it for gear compliance

I practiced a lot of preventative law enforcement by getting out among the shrimpers just before legal trawling time and running around and through the assembled fleet. Sometimes there would be so many trawlers jockeying for position that I really had to keep a sharp eye on where I was going and what might be coming up behind me. While dashing around the trawler fleet, I could hear the marine VHF radio transmissions crackle to a crescendo. A few would ask was the official time was; others would issue warnings that "the man" was out running around and taking names.

The river draggers, those who trawled for shrimp at night way up in the harbor, rivers, or creeks—well within the restricted—area were much different and a lot harder to catch. The problem was compounded by the fact that most of them had boats that were much faster than mine, so I had to use stealth instead of speed. I found out that some were casing my house to see if my car and boat were there before they hit the river. A crabber divulged that information as I was checking him in the Ashley River. He told me I wasn't so smart because those draggers knew my every move. I quickly got the drift of his conversation and set about implementing "Plan B."

I had two boats then, a fifteen-foot Boston Whaler and a fourteen-foot Duracraft johnboat. I used the johnboat chiefly on marsh-hen and duck patrols and kept it at Fort Johnson most of the time. The Boston Whaler stayed attached to my patrol car, and when I was at home, they were parked on the street.

I figured that if they were casing my house, the presence of my car and boat on the street would give them reason to believe that I was enjoying a good night's sleep and cause them, with that assumption in mind, to be less vigilant as they pursued their illegal activities. What they didn't know was that earlier that day I launched the johnboat at the City Marina and tied it up on one of the far docks away from the boat ramp.

Later that night when the tide was right, Belle and I walked the few blocks from my house to the marina. We entered my boat, came around the seawall of the marina, and headed slowly upstream. I hugged the west bank of the Ashley River, keeping a sharp eye on the darkened river scene unfolding before me. Rounding the long, sweeping curve of the river beyond the Citadel, I could just barely make out, in the lights reflected from the power plant on the far side of the river, the low, dark outline of a boat moving upstream on the east side of the channel.

An outboard motorboat seized for trawling at night in the Ashley River

I kept close to the marsh grass on the west side of the river in order to hide my profile and to absorb as much engine noise and wake ripples as possible. I knew I had to calculate my move carefully because, if the river dragger was who I thought it was, he had a 140-horsepower engine, exactly 110 horses more than I had.

I was moving at a fairly steady clip, getting closer and closer. I could see the boat silhouetted in the light across the river and the prop wash and the towline in the water. I was about fifty yards behind him, and he was some seventy-five yards out in the river from the bank. At that point I cut the long diagonal, shoved down on my throttle, and was instantly alongside him with my hand on the rail of his boat and a spot beam shining in his face.

Before he could come his senses and react, I demanded he turn off his boat and give me his key. To my relief he did. He probably realized that I recognized who he was and remembered he could not outrun Motorola. The evening was clearly not going as he had envisioned it; he appeared disoriented and confused as he stared at me in disbelief.

I informed him that I was going to write him a couple of tickets for trawling in a restricted area and for operating a boat without running lights and that I was going to seize his boat, motor, net, and shrimp. I knew he had launched out of Wappoo Cut landing, some miles down the river, and I instructed him to follow me there, at which point he would be free to leave. On the way there, I got on the portable radio and asked the Columbia dispatcher to wake up a couple of local officers and get them to come on the radio.

A sleepy voice responded a short time later, and I asked him to meet me at Wappoo Landing with a boat trailer to haul the seized boat over to Fort Johnson. At the landing the frustrated shrimper sullenly entered his truck and drove off, tickets in hand. My colleague arrived shortly afterward. We loaded the boat onto the trailer and carried it to our compound at Fort Johnson, where we inventoried the contents of the boat and put all the shrimp in a cooler with ice. The shrimp would be sold to a wholesaler in the morning and the check held pending the outcome of the court case.

The word was out that someone was dragging the flats at night between Fort Sumter and the James Island Yacht Club. Officer Wiley Knight and I launched just before the ebb from the Charleston City Marina and drove over to a small marsh island near Fort Sumter, where we beached the boat, walked over to the dunes, and found a place to sit where we could watch the sunset and observe that portion of the harbor.

We had been telling "war stories" for hours when we began to hear what sounded like voices coming from the direction of an area out in the harbor called Middle Anchorage. We listened intently for some time and heard several shouts. We could not see or hear anything that looked like a boat in that direction and decided we had better go and have a look.

We pushed the Boston Whaler off the beach and headed toward where we had heard the voices. I cut off the engine every few minutes to get a new bearing on the voices. We still could detect no sign of a boat in the area. When Officer Knight turned on the spotlight, we heard loud shouts not too far away. He swung the beam back and forth across the water and saw a reflection off a dark object about one hundred feet away.

As we got nearer we saw in the beam two black men holding on to a black garbage bag that barely had enough buoyancy to keep both of them afloat. We went right up to them and tossed one of the boat cushions, which they immediately grabbed. They were talking rapidly in a language that we could not understand and were clad only in undershorts. One of them kept trying to shove the bag over the side of the boat, and I told Wiley we had better know what was in that bag before we got them aboard. As we pulled the men into the boat, we could not understand what they were saying, and they did not appear to understand us. Officer Knight and I were both in plain clothes, so I told him that this might be a good time to identify ourselves as having some official capacity. He pulled out his badge, a universally recognized symbol of authority, and shined the light on it where they could clearly see it.

Their exuberance became immediately subdued. Officer Knight pulled over the bag, untied it, and began pulling things out. The only things in the bag were their shoes and their clothes, which he handed over as he motioned for them to put them on.

We carried them to the Coast Guard base, walked them up to the radio room, and left them in the custody of a couple of the radio operators. I found out later they were Haitians who had stowed away on a small break-bulk freighter moored at Union Pier and had jumped overboard when they were discovered by the ship's crew. I felt a little ambivalent about their fate because some of my own ancestors had also arrived at this very same port as émigrés from Haiti back in 1791.

Through the grapevine I had gotten word that a Mount Pleasant crabber, Rocky Borowski, had been dragging the flats at night between Patriots Point and Crab Bank. He operated out of a dark-painted seventeen-foot boat with a big engine and had a lot of experience crabbing around the harbor. I had been told he would be hard to catch. He always scouted the area well before he put his net over and kept a sharp lookout while the net was under tow.

One night I was walking around perusing the docks over at Shem Creek. As I was standing in the shadow of a dockside building, I noticed an outboard coming from up the creek and running without any lights. As it passed by, I was high enough to see that the boat contained a trawl net and doors. It didn't take a genius to figure out what was about to happen.

I drove over to the Simmons Street landing on Shem Creek and checked out the licenses of the two vehicles there. One vehicle, a pickup, was registered to Mr. Borowski. Now I knew something about the time, the tide, and the landing that he used. I knew that I didn't have anything fast enough to catch him and that the area where he was trawling was wide open with no place to hide, so I started cooking up the proverbial "Plan B."

The next morning I called my fellow warden Corporal Jimmy Warko from Green Pond, who had a sixteen-foot Glassmaster bass boat and a 235-horsepower engine with a four-bladed racing prop. Officer Warko loved to go fast, and his boat could easily reach speeds of 65 to 70 mph. Riding at night with Officer Warko was a white-knuckle experience that I had first endured in St. Helena Sound, near Beaufort, South Carolina.

He agreed to join me for some night patrols around Charleston Harbor beginning that night. Late that afternoon we launched at the City Marina, slowly came around the city peninsula, and headed up the Cooper River. We fed mosquitoes on the shell bank at the tip of Drum Island for several hours and then slowly began to move back out into the harbor, staying close to the Ports Authority docks. We went all the way over to the flats on the James Island side of the Ashley River and then headed back toward Castle Pinckney.

Just as we passed the upriver end of Castle Pinckney I looked over toward Crab Bank and saw, back lighted from the houses on the waterfront of Mount Pleasant, the barely discernable, low profile of a dark-running boat just off the ship channel, probably about three quarters of a mile away.

I pointed out the target to Officer Warko, who studied it for a moment and said, "It looks like he could be dragging to me." I said, "Let's get 'em." At that he shoved the throttle full forward, and the boat lurched out of the water with a roar. Within less than a minute we were closing in on the target boat. We saw the figure in the boat run to the back, bend over, turn, and start back to his console. Before he could cover the distance, we were alongside him and had him lighted up like a football stadium. There stood Mr. Borowski with an expression of dazed consternation.

We pointed the beam in the water around our boats and saw a six-inch Styrofoam ball bobbing on the surface not fifty feet away. We took temporary possession of his boat key, idled around, and picked up the float and line, which we found attached to the tail bag of a full-size trawl net with doors.

We returned his key and got him to bring his boat over and pull the net aboard. He kept saying " I can't believe that you got over here that fast." He said that he had seen us come from behind Castle Pinckney and was keeping an eye on us. He just couldn't believe we covered that distance so quickly. We put him off at the Shem Creek Landing, towed his boat across the harbor to a boat landing, and hauled it over to the Fort Johnson compound, where it and the net were held until after the trial.

My first ride in Officer Warko's fast boat had been about a year earlier. He had gotten word that some small drag boats were coming across St. Helena Sound into the estuary behind Pine and Otter islands, and he wanted me to join him in a stakeout. I met him at Bennetts Point Landing just at sunset and we ran over to the South Edisto and found a narrow creek that threaded through the marsh behind Fenwick Island and led into the deeper creeks behind the islands.

He steered the boat around a sharp turn into a little basin that was completely hidden behind the marsh grass. After sitting there in the dark for several hours, we heard what sounded like several boats entering the estuary from the mouth of the Ashepoo River. We listened to the engine noises for some time, and then they were suddenly silent. As we waited in our dark little pool for about another hour, Warko began to speculate that the boats were probably just sitting out there waiting to see if they could hear anything, just as we were doing.

The tide had been in ebb for just over two hours, a situation that could become a problem as the water depth under our boat continued to diminish. At last we heard the sound of an outboard motor cranking up in the distance. It idled for a long time, and then we could make out the rattle of chains. All we heard for the longest time was the faint throb of an engine, not the steady drone of an engine towing a net.

We knew from the reading on the depth finder that we had to exit our hiding place quickly. We also knew that, once Warko cranked up that souped-up engine of his, our presence would be announced far and wide. He decided to make a full-bore run to where he thought the drag boats would be. Even the whine of the trim and tilt as the propeller descended into the water, sounded deafening following the hours of quiet. That 235-horsepower engine came to life, and Warko shoved the throttle into the corner. The bow of the boat shot into the air, and a giant plume of spray and mud exploded from the stern. It probably took ten to fifteen seconds to bring the boat up on a plane and the roar was mind numbing.

As I held on for dear life, Warko maneuvered the careening boat around curve after curve in the darkness. My eyes were watering from the blast of cold air across my face. As we rounded one wide turn, I heard Officer Warko say, "They are over there!" In an instant we were beside them. I shined the spotlight first behind their boat. There was no towline in the water. Then, as I illuminated the occupants, we could see them sitting there smirking. I reached over and pulled our boat over to theirs and one of them said, "We wondered when you would come out."

We later found out through the ever-active grapevine that our departure from the Bennetts Point Landing had been noticed, and several quick phone calls had been made. They had decided that, since they were already there, they were going to stick around and have some fun needling the game wardens.

One of the tricks the night draggers used was hauling a couple of cinder blocks at the end of a tow line up and down the creek for an hour or so to see if they could draw out any prowling or hidden game-warden boats. If they were not approached during that time, they put their nets overboard and went to catching shrimp.

One night we were outfoxed by that ruse while on a surveillance from Morgan Island in Beaufort County. We knew that there was quite a shrimp run in Morgan River and that the draggers were taking advantage of it. The shrimp were in such abundance that a drag of only twenty or thirty minutes could yield a catch up to a hundred pounds. Another officer and I had been dropped off at the dock on Morgan Island in the late evening. Morgan Island is home to hundreds of rhesus monkeys bred for medical research. We had walked through swarms of chattering monkeys swinging from the live oak trees to reach the edge of Morgan River, where we found positions from which we could see or hear any activity.

Other officers occupied boats up and down the river at some remove and stood by to come running if we reported by radio anything that sounded like someone dragging. We sat on the branches of a live oak tree whose large limbs extended out over the water, and we variously occupied ourselves by taking short snoozes or slapping at the pesky mosquitoes.

Around one in the morning we came to full alert at hearing the approach of a fast-moving, dark-running boat. We were to keep radio silence until we were convinced that someone was fully under tow because we knew that the draggers often monitored our frequencies. We soon heard the telltale sound of an engine under tow. We listened for around ten minutes before we were convinced and sent out the signal. In a moment we heard the roar of motors coming from opposite directions rapidly closing in on the position we had reported.

We listened to exchanges of loud voices for a while, and then one of the officers hailed us on the radio and said that the boat had been dragging cinder blocks, which was not an offense in South Carolina. The boat operator did receive a ticket for running without lights, so the operation was not a complete skunk.

In most of the illegal-trawling cases made against the St. Helena Sound crowd, the defendants would invariably ask for a jury trial. Part of their decision stemmed from its value as a delaying tactic. Any suspensions could not begin until after a conviction, and meanwhile they could post a bond for their boat and equipment and continue shrimping until the end of the season. Another reason for asking for a jury trial was that the juries in that area almost always decided for acquittal.

One of the Beaufort officers had made a night-trawling case on a particularly intractable violator, who subsequently made the predictable request for a jury trial. A climate unfavorable to that officer's cases had long existed in a particular magistrate's court. Our district captain, Ed McTeer, the son of the legendary "High Sheriff of the Lowcountry," had picked up a few tricks from his father over the years in the arcana of voodoo, which still had a congregation of practitioners and believers in the hinterlands of Beaufort and Jasper counties. In an attempt to counter the annoying trend of not-guilty verdicts, Captain McTeer hatched an unusual plan.

On the day of the trial he and the arresting officer arrived early at the magistrate's office. Presently the magistrate drove up and nodded politely to some of the jurors, who were standing in the shade along the edge of the parking area. Captain McTeer, just a little ahead of the judge, walked up the front stairs and "accidentally" dropped a handkerchief containing a quantity of white powder, which spilled out over the steps, an act clearly visible to all present.

The judge and several of the group following him jumped back, and there was an audible murmur among the crowd. A lot of hushed talk went on outside before the trial started; while McTeer and the officer sat quietly on a bench inside the courtroom. That trial and a good number of trials that followed produced dramatic reversals of fortune for defendants who had long depended on the tender mercies of local juries.

In addition to voodoo sometimes a combination of luck and bluff comes into play when making a case. I got a call late one afternoon from a commercial fisherman who reported that he had just seen a trawler dragging in Green Creek behind Folly Beach.

I asked a few questions—such as "Are you sure?" "Did you see the tow cables down?" "Was it definitely moving through the water?" My final question was, "Would you be willing to testify to what you saw?" When he said yes to all queries, I dashed out of the house, jumped into the car, which had the boat and trailer attached, and drove as fast as possible to the Folly River Landing. I think I was in the water fewer than twenty-five minutes from getting the phone call.

As I entered the mouth of Green Creek at Folly River, I saw the reported trawler with the doors up out of the water and hanging on the outriggers. The nets were on the deck, and it was under way. I circled the trawler, came alongside just forward of the outriggers, and hailed for the captain to stop. I came around to the stern and climbed over the transom, handed my bow line to a striker, immediately stepped over to the heap of netting, and pulled the tail bag out. It was still tied and full of live shrimp.

I went forward to the wheelhouse and informed the captain that he was going to be given a ticket for trawling in an area never open to trawling and that I was going to seize his trawler and his catch. The captain launched into the usual round of vehement denials and stout protests.

I asked him where he kept his boat moored and he replied "Bowen's Island. This is Mrs. Bowen's boat." "Good Grief!" The much-revered May Bowen operated the well-known Bowen's Island seafood restaurant near Folly Beach. I radioed for a couple of officers to come and meet the trawler at the dock and take possession of the shrimp, which were to be taken to a wholesaler and sold. The check, as usual, would be held until the final disposition of the case.

The captain was informed that the trawler was under seizure and that he and the crew had to vacate it until a bond was posted to secure its release. One of our officers stayed to guard the boat until Mrs. Bowen posted the bond the next day so that it could resume fishing.

Mrs. Bowen's lawyer, her grandson Robert Barber, called me and said that they wanted a jury trial. A tenant in one of my downtown apartments, attorney Jack Ungaro, agreed to represent the state's case without fee. I always found it somewhat complicated to act as both witness and prosecutor in jury trials, and it was helpful to have a lawyer to help organize things, especially a pro bono lawyer.

At the time of our initial discovery meeting, a kind of a legal "show-and-tell" time, I had only one eyewitness to the act of trawling in Green Creek, the fellow who made the phone call. He was intermittently employed as a striker on crab boats or shrimp trawlers. His reputation for reliability was not the greatest, and he had a lengthy criminal record for various misdemeanors. He was also known to be fond of the grape.

The only testimony I could offer was that, when I boarded the trawler in Green Creek, the nets were still dripping wet and there were live shrimp in the untied tail bag. Mrs. Bowen's boat captain steadfastly denied that he was trawling in Green Creek that evening. Just a week before the trial date, I learned that one of the deck hands on the offending trawler, a female, was the wife of one of the biologist technicians at the Fort Johnson Marine Center, a Wildlife Department employee. After finding him in one of the laboratories, I impressed on him the gravity of the charges and solicited his help in getting his wife to come forward as a witness.

She called me at home that night, and said she was afraid to get involved. I told her that she was not "getting" involved, for she was already involved as a participant in an illegal act. I told her I could remove the burden of her voluntarily appearing to testify by serving her with a subpoena, by which she would be compelled to appear.

The idea of a subpoena seemed to scare her. She said that she would have to think about it and would call me back. I was going to let her stew for a day or two when she called and asked to have a meeting. I reiterated the serious nature of the charges and said I would very much appreciate her cooperation. She relented, agreeing to write out an affidavit as to what had transpired in Green Creek that day and to testify in court. The case was to be heard before a jury that Mr. Barber and I had selected some weeks before. The magistrate was Harry "Skeeter" Shaw in Mount Pleasant.

Our first witness, the one who made the initial phone call, arrived drunk, and Mr. Ungaro thought that it would be a bad idea even to let him in the courtroom. I told him to stay outside by his truck in the parking lot in case we needed him.

Mr. Ungaro and I, along with our new female deckhand eyewitness, entered the court. As we passed Mr. Barber and his client, already seated at their table, we nodded in acknowledgment, then walked over to our table and sat down. I noticed the captain leaning over, whispering in Mr. Barber's ear, and looking agitated. Both were periodically turning and staring in our direction.

Mr. Barber came over and asked if Mr. Ungaro and I would come outside for a moment. Out in the parking lot he asked us what the girl was doing there. Mr. Ungaro informed him that she was on the trawler in Green Creek on the date and time of the violation and that she was prepared to testify that they had put the nets over and trawled for shrimp in Green Creek. He asked why we had not brought this forward during the discovery hearing. We explained to him that she had only recently come forth.

We went back into the courtroom, where Mr. Barber asked the captain to go back outside with him. When they returned a few minutes later, Mr. Barber approached the judge's bench and said that, because of the disclosure of new information, his client was going to forgo the jury trial and plead guilty to the charge.

It took a long time for me to get the courage to eat again at the Bowen's Island Restaurant, which was one of my favorite places. I did eventually go out and have a long talk with Mrs. Bowen. While I could not say that, when the conversation was over, she was any happier, at least she understood my side of the story.

The only time I was ever sued in an official capacity proceeded from a shrimping incident, which occurred in the restricted area of Bull Bay.

As the sun rose on a mid-November morning in 1995, a Georgetown officer, Sergeant Scott Powell, and I met at a landing on the South Santee River to run a patrol of Bull Bay between Sandy Point and the eastern end of Bull Island. Officer Powell had a fast boat that could cover a lot of territory in a short time, and in the coolness of the morning we rapidly traversed the small creeks and waterways out to where Five Fathom Creek enters Bull Bay at Sandy Point. Five Fathom Creek runs straight out from McClellanville to the ocean.

From Sandy Point we made a short run out toward the first in a line of large poles stretching across the bay to delineate the boundary between the seaward waters that were open for trawling and those inside that were closed. The bay was calm, and visibility was exceptionally clear in the crisp morning air. In the immediate area we observed about twenty-five trawlers working outboard of the line, and one that was clearly around three hundred yards inside the restricted area.

Officer Powell shoved the throttle in the corner, and—in one of those face-flapping-in-the-wind speed runs—we quickly intercepted the boat, a small stern trawler. As we were taking information from the boat operator, I spotted another boat over toward Bull Island, about a mile and a half away, which appeared to be well inside the line of poles.

We kept the first boat captain's license and instructed him to take up his net, proceed to the landing at McClellanville, and wait for us. We initiated another white-knuckle, high-speed run across the bay in the direction of the second boat. As we closed the distance to him, we could see that he was turning and heading back out to sea. When we arrived alongside him, he appeared to be still well behind the line. After enduring the usual amount of dispute, we secured his license and instructed him to meet us at the McClellanville landing.

Officer Powell radioed district headquarters to find several officers to meet us there and help with the inventory and transportation of the boats, equipment, and catch—all of which we were going to seize. At the landing I issued tickets for "trawling for shrimp in an area not open for trawling." The boats and equipment were transported to the Fort Johnson compound on James Island, and the shrimp was sold to a seafood dealer in McClellanville with the checks held pending resolution of the case.

Before the scheduled appearance at magistrate's court, Gedney Howe, a well-known Charleston lawyer who represented the first shrimper, got the court date continued to the spring of 1996. His client posted a bond on his boat and equipment, put them back in the water, and went back to work. The second shrimper appeared before the judge and indicated that he wanted a jury trial. Because he had posted no bond, his boat and gear remained in custody.

When the first shrimper's case finally came to trial, Mr. Howe raised the issue that several of the laws regulating the closure of certain areas to trawling—including the one his client was charged with violating—were confusing, contradictory, and in direct conflict with other laws. The Wildlife

Department's lawyer, Jim Quinn, retorted that the passage of the more recent law, under which the defendants were charged, implied the repeal of the older law, which the defendant's lawyer claimed was in conflict.

Further complicating the issue was the fact that the old law was still included in the South Carolina legal code. It had never been legislatively repealed. I might add that at no time on that November morning when we apprehended the first shrimper in the restricted area did he appear to be in any confusion regarding the ambiguities of the law. The magistrate agreed with the defense counsel's assertion and found the shrimper not guilty of the charges. The department's attorney immediately announced that the state would appeal the ruling.

Some time later I received a phone call from Bob Lumpkin, a lawyer from Georgetown, who informed me that he was going to be representing the second shrimper at his jury trial. I related to him the status of the first case, and I asked if he was agreeable to continuing his case until the outcome of the appeal was determined. I told him that, if the magistrate's judgment that the law itself was questionable was sustained by the Court of Appeals, then I would ask the judge to find his client not guilty. However, if the verdict was overturned, then we could proceed with his client's trial. He agreed to put his client's case on hold.

After the appeals court finally affirmed the verdict of the magistrate in January of 1997, I called the Georgetown lawyer. I told him that I had already asked the magistrate to find his client not guilty and that his client could pick up his boat and equipment and the check for the seized shrimp at the Fort Johnson compound at any time convenient to him.

Six months later the District Nine captain, Henry Garbade, who had been promoted to the position following the retirement of Captain Ed McTeer, sent me a copy of a letter from the Anastopoulo law firm in Charleston to a claims representative on the State Budget and Control Board. The letter related that their firm was representing the shrimper formerly represented by Mr. Lumpkin, whose case I had earlier asked the magistrate to dismiss.

The plaintiff's lawyer, Constance Anastopoulo, stated that, after her client's boat had been sitting out in the elements for more than a year and a half, it was unusable in its current condition and that her client had been wrongfully deprived of his livelihood as a result of its seizure. She demanded that the state pay her client for the cost of the boat and lost income or she would file suit, alleging that the Department of Natural Resources and I were liable for false arrest, wrongful imprisonment, assault and battery, wrongful deprivation of property without due process, disparagement of property, defamation through slander and liable, and intentional infliction of emotional distress.

The state failed to cough up as requested, so she made good on her threat and brought a suit on everything but the allegations of assault and battery. It is truly amazing how a lawsuit can take on a life and a momentum of its own regardless of the fact that a complaint may be completely devoid of legal substance. In his affidavit the plaintiff, of course, denied that he was ever near the restricted area and stated that it was common knowledge that I was out to write a ticket on any small-boat owner regardless of whether he was in violation or not because of "pressure" from the large trawler owners. In a conversation outside the conference room, during a break in one of the depositions, Ms. Anastopoulo, told my attorney, Alexia Pittas-Giroux, that I was a "rogue game warden" who handed out tickets right and left to perfectly innocent fishermen. Ms. Anastopoulo also intimated that I should be made to suffer (pay) for my unscrupulous behavior.

Ms. Anastopoulo rounded up a commercial crabber with a reputation for multiple resource violations, who gave a totally pointless statement to the effect that years before I had graded all his crabs in the back of my pickup truck at night and had given him a ticket for possession of undersize crabs. He added that I had once hollered at him from a dock in Shem Creek to go back and pick up some paper he had tossed out of his boat. I found out that the Anastopoulo law office was making a lot of calls to area crabbers, trying to find someone to substantiate their colorful image of my "rogue" status.

My attorney succeeded in getting the Wildlife Department removed from the suit and the jurisdiction moved from state court to federal court. She felt that the federal courts were more receptive to motions for summary judgment. Then the paper chase heated up. The attorneys began making motions and countermotions, and the case file was getting thicker by the day.

Perhaps the strangest spectacle during the whole process was the deposition taken from the plaintiff, who contradicted practically every allegation he had made in his complaint. His claims about his loss of the use of his boat and its current mechanical state became a little flabby when it was revealed that he took almost a year to come and pick up the boat after he was notified that he could do so.

In one line of questioning during the deposition, despite his lawyer's scowling expression, he almost gave me a testimonial. My attorney asked the plaintiff, "Do shrimpers and other fishermen fear Officer Moïse?" He replied, "There's talk in McClellanville, yes, they do fear him." My attorney asked, "Why do they fear him?" He said, "Because of his reputation of being 'The Man That Will Get You.'" My attorney asked, "What does 'The Man That Will Get You' mean?" He responded, "In my opinion, if you get on his list or get on the bad side of him or he's told from his boss to go get somebody, he's going to get somebody. He does a good job." My attorney, somewhat surprised at this disclosure, responded, "You say that he does a good job. When he wants to get somebody, he gets them." He replied, "He does a good job, he gets them."

The only time I ever attended court on this matter was for the hearing when my attorney entered a motion for a summary judgment to dismiss the suit. The federal judge deliberated over the motions and decided in my favor in October 1998. In April 1999 the plaintiff's lawyer filed a motion to add or amend findings of fact and to alter or amend the judgment of dismissal. One of the reasons given in the lawyer's motion was that the judge had used "pejorative terms" when describing the nature of the lawsuit in his order of dismissal.

Other reasons stemmed from the persistent notion of the plaintiff's lawyer that I "was determined to arrest someone," that I exhibited "ill will and wanton indifference to her client's rights," and that I had "a propensity to target individuals in the application of the law." The judge responded to that motion with a speedy denial. The whole episode had taken forty-two months to die the death it deserved.

Crab Pots and Poachers

When I first started patrolling the rivers around Charleston, there was a large concentration of crabbers in the Wando River. I remember local names such as Manigault, Coakley, Gaskins, Aytes, White, Crane, and Smith as well as a good number of Hispanic and Asian names over the years.

Most of the crabbers worked their pots from small boats. Each one typically maintained forty or fifty pots, which were pulled in by hand. Many carried an assistant, called a "striker," who graded the crabs after they were emptied out of the crab pot into the grading box.

The crabs smaller than five inches were tossed back, and the remainder were sorted into baskets of "number ones" or "twos and threes." Number ones were the larger blue-clawed males, or "jimmy crabs." The twos and threes basket held a mixture of the smaller "jimmies" and the red-clawed females, or "sooks." The number ones brought the highest price.

When I was grading crabs, I went first for the baskets of twos and threes. Some crabbers were known to put undersize crabs that were illegal to sell in the bottom part of the basket and cover them with legal crabs. Occasionally they would even slip a few sooks in the bottom of a basket of number ones. If you looked closely through the cracks around the bottom of the basket, you could spot the red-clawed females without having to empty it. Occasionally I found baskets where—buried beneath a deep layer of legal "twos and threes"—were concealed egg-bearing "sponge" crabs with their sponge-bearing aprons torn off. It was illegal to sell crabs with their aprons removed or to possess sponge-bearing crabs.

In a fifteen-foot Boston Whaler rigged out for an extended patrol. In addition to the twenty-gallon tank forward, there were two six-gallon tanks aft.

Some crabbers were extremely territorial and claimed whole creeks and stretches of the river for themselves. Often they became aggressive when another crabber encroached on what they fancied as their territory. Turf battles were one of the chief law-enforcement problems in the regulation of that business and required a large number of officer man-hours to investigate and resolve.

The crabbers' main means of retaliation against perceived interlopers was cutting off their pot floats. This act of vandalism not only deprives the owner of the use of his pots but also wastes the resource; the lost pots continue to attract crabs, which die and in turn attract other crabs until the pot becomes overgrown with seaweed or deteriorates.

During my early years in the river, there was at least one broad-daylight killing resulting from one crabber stealing another's crabs. Several other crabbers drowned under mysterious circumstances while out working their pot lines. I will never forget the pitiful gatherings at Remleys Point Landing on the Wando River, where friends and relatives of a missing crabber maintained vigils for days as searches were conducted, and the awful commotion that ensued when the body was at last recovered and brought back to the landing.

There were frequent clashes that involved fisticuffs and ramming boats. At one time there was a full-fledged crab war among crabbers in the Charleston and Mount Pleasant area, where pots were cut and weapons brandished. The war started from differences between local crabbers and several Virginian crabbers who had moved into the area. The Virginians fished a lot more pots and spent more time on the water. Some of the locals regarded them as "foreigners" invading "their" territory and catching all of "their" crabs. It turned into a volatile situation, and several of the meetings held in an attempt to moderate some of the issues and misperceptions turned into ugly shouting matches. The meetings grew so rancorous that game wardens were assigned to be present to prevent violence.

My personal contribution toward ending the war was to step up my crab grading. Ordinarily I randomly selected a basket of crabs and graded all the crabs in that basket. On a good day most crabbers will have anywhere from ten to twenty baskets of crabs on board. To facilitate the grading process, I designed and had made a special stainless-steel crab grader. It had a long bar to use as the handle and two circles mounted exactly five inches apart, the legal width across the back for a keeper. The instrument greatly facilitated the grading process.

A stainless-steel measuring device I invented for quick grading of blue crabs, conchs (whelks), and stone-crab claws

Using my grading device to measure conchs on the deck of a trawler in Shem Creek

For the duration of the war, when I checked a crab boat, I gave it a thorough inspection, and if I found any sort of weapon, I graded every crab in every basket in the boat, a time-consuming process that could take hours. Hey, what else did I have to do?

This unorthodox practice served to focus the crabbers' anger on me and not on each other. Some were even getting larger engines so they could outrun me. After a while they were actually banding together to bring official pressure on me to stop "harassing" them in the river.

Soon the war was over. While it didn't exactly end in a lovefest among the crabbers, most of them tried to avoid difficulties. Laws have since been enacted that can ban from the business for a substantial time anyone caught cutting floats or stealing crabs. The implementation of those regulations sent a strong message to those prone to such activities. The practical effects of their enforcement had a long-term calming effect in lowcountry waters.

Once Eddie Gordon, the owner of the crab plant in McClellanville, contacted me and related a woeful story of some of the Cape Romain crabbers being put out of business by a few Georgetown crabbers who were cutting their floats. The next morning I went to McClellanville, where I interviewed several affected crabbers to try and determine where most of the cutting activity was going on, what time of day it was likely to occur again, and whether they had any particular suspects in mind. After finding out what I needed to know, I asked Mr. Gordon if he would loan me five new crab pots with the floats marked clearly with a number that would be new to the area.

I picked up the pots and a bucket of bait around midmorning the next day and stacked them in the front of my johnboat. I scouted several of the large creeks in the Cape Romain area to find a hiding place that overlooked the suspect's pot line. In those broad, flat expanses of marsh there are not a lot of opportunities for concealment. I found a particularly thick skirt of marsh grass bordering Casino Creek and gathered several boatloads of dead marsh grass from both sides of the creek in order to build a thick platform on top of the marsh just behind the fringe of grass. I piled up enough of a layer to keep me well out of the mud. Then I placed my five decoy pots in a line parallel to the suspect's, which were on the other side of the creek.

The suspect launched his boat at Pole Yard Landing on the North Santee River, and he had pots set from there to Cape Romain. I figured it would be somewhere around midafternoon before he arrived in the area I had "prepared." I concealed my johnboat some distance away in a narrow creek barely the width of my boat and slogged across seventy yards of marsh to reach my grass nest. I had brought along binoculars, notepad and pen, and a pack of Nabs.

In the five hours I waited, the heat and humidity became increasingly uncomfortable. Finally I heard the distant sound of an approaching outboard engine. The boat came into view on my left and stopped. As the two people in the boat worked one of their own pots, I could hear conversation, but they were still too far away for me to understand what they were saying.

They rebaited their pot, pitched it overboard, and turned to run over to the side of the creek where I had set the decoy line. They approached the first float, grabbed it, and towed it behind the boat until they came to the next decoy float in the line. They pulled it on board and tied it to the first one and dragged them both close to the bank and let them go, a gesture usually meant to serve as a warning.

I stared intently through the binoculars, putting them down only to take notes on the time that each float was handled and what was done to it. They got close enough so I could begin to understand what they were saying. I began writing all that down too, along with their boat's registration number and commercial-tag number. As they passed each of the remaining three decoy buoys, they pulled up the trap, stuffed the buoy in it, and threw it back overboard, where it sank completely out of sight. As they passed right in front of me, they were fewer than seventy feet away.

They went back across the creek, continued working their line, and finally disappeared from view. When I could no longer hear the sound of their engine, I stiffly arose from my little pile and began to retrace my steps back to the johnboat.

Returning to Casino Creek, I retrieved the two pots that were tied together and marked the marsh grass near the area where the three traps had been "deep-sixed," so I could come back and retrieve them by towing a grapnel along the bottom. Speeding back to McClellanville, I loaded the boat onto the trailer and drove over to a seafood buyer on the other side of the village where the crabber usually sold his crabs. He came driving up a short time later and parked just behind my truck.

I walked up as he and his striker exited their truck and told them I had a story they might find interesting. "Here," I said, "Let me read from my notes." I proceeded to tell them the precise time they interfered with each crab pot, including a good bit of their conversation while they were doing it, including one rude comment they had made about game wardens.

I told them that each pot they interfered with was a separate violation and involved serious money. I also told them that I was contemplating charging them with conspiracy to deprive another wrongfully of his catch. I pulled out my ticket book and issued them five tickets each for the maximum fine, which was then four hundred and fifty dollars for each violation. I decided to let them stew a bit over the possible conspiracy charge.

Another little demon they had to contend with was the newly implemented point system, where conviction on just one charge of "interfering with crab pots" carried a sufficient assessment of points to take away all their commercial-fishing privileges for a year. At first they talked about asking for a jury trial. Their Georgetown lawyer called me a day later wanting to know about the circumstances of the case and if anything could be done to keep them from losing their livelihood.

I explained to him the entire situation and that I had been an eyewitness to the incident and had extensive descriptive notes on what I had seen— information I would gladly share with him. He called about a week later and said that his clients would not contest the charges. The troublesome crabbers were off the water and out of everyone's hair for the next twelve months.

Over the years my fellow wardens and I spent countless hours hunkered down around the lowcountry marshes doing surveillance on crab-pot lines. Every now and then a recreational boater strayed into an area we were watching and pulled up a crab trap. Sometimes they just emptied the pot of its crabs and threw it back, but other times they attempted to make off with the entire rig. In either case they were soon intercepted by one or more game-warden boats.

We usually told them that as stiff as the penalty was, it was better to be caught by us than by the owner of the pot. There were numerous reports of crabbers running down boats that had been spotted pulling their pots and either ramming them or jumping aboard and subjecting the offending party to a thorough bruising.

I remember one shirtless crabber rushing up to my boat in the middle of Charleston Harbor, his back and chest covered with ugly red welts. He breathlessly told me that he had just been attacked with a paddle by another crabber, pointing out his assailant in the distance. I saw the broken blade of the paddle lying in the bottom of his boat.

On asking him what he thought had precipitated the altercation, he responded he had gotten the other crabber's pot line entangled in his propeller. I asked him how he could have done that when his own pot line was way over on the other side of the harbor. He claimed that he was just riding around.

I instructed him to wait where he was while I went over to interview the other crabber, who told me that he had seen the victim of his assault stealing his crabs, an activity not inconsistent with the victim's reputation. The assailant related to me that after he had seen his pot being worked, he started a full-speed pursuit from behind Crab Bank. When the victim saw him coming, he turned his boat and started running away. The assailant said that when he caught up with the victim, one of the assailant's lines was still hung up on one of the cleats on the gunnels of the victim's boat, with the float and trap bouncing on top of the water behind the boat. The assailant admitted that he lost his temper, grabbed his boat paddle, and began swinging it at the victim. I saw the top half of the broken paddle leaning against his transom.

I returned to the victim, who by then had formed the strategy of taking out a warrant for assault on his tormentor. I advised him that it was likely the other crabber was going to take out a warrant for him for theft of fishing gear, and probably a better decision was to be thankful he didn't take a

In disguise while working as an undercover investigator

head shot with the paddle and get knocked overboard, as it was certain that his assailant would not have fished him out of the water. He departed grumbling, knowing full well that he had received his just deserts, and as far as I know nothing further came from the altercation.

One old crabber from Mount Pleasant, no stranger to the legal process, ran a seafood company on Coleman Boulevard. He was a hardworking, generally good-natured man. He operated an enormous old wooden boat called the *Behemoth,* which seemed to stay broken down most of the time before it eventually sank at a dock in Morgan Creek, where the Isle of Palms Marina is now located. During one of his mechanical hiatuses, a rival crabber began working his pot line and even brought the crabs stolen from his pots to his seafood store to sell.

It didn't take long for word of that scam to get back to the captain of the *Behemoth.* It seems the offending crabber was joking and bragging at several local juke joints about selling the man his own crabs. There had been a history of bad blood between them, acrimonious territorial disputes and accusations of one robbing the other's pots. Both parties were known for their propensity for strong drink and were rarely seen without a can of beer in hand, a situation that led to a lack of restraint and overcame reason.

One afternoon the offending crabber and his girlfriend drove up behind the Coleman Boulevard seafood store with a load of crabs. The old captain confronted the driver. Both had been drinking and the exchange rapidly escalated into a shouting match filled with threats and invective. The old captain ran behind a large outdoor cooler and grabbed a .30-30 rifle. Running back to the truck, he pointed the rifle through the window behind the girlfriend and shot the offending crabber stone dead.

I had written the deceased a ticket for undersized crabs the week before, which later had to be cleared off the books as a nolle prosequi. Then I was subpoenaed by the old crabber's attorney to testify as a character witness at the sentencing phase of his trial. I told the judge that the defendant was a good person who had obviously done a bad thing and went on to enumerate his better qualities. He was a "character" all right. He was sentenced to a short term of imprisonment in the Charleston County Jail.

I remember sitting on top of an impoundment bordering the South Santee River one afternoon on one of the most oppressively humid days I had ever endured. I was there to conduct surveillance on a line of crab pots whose owner claimed he had been regularly robbed. I had driven my nineteen-foot Action Craft up a deep canal out of sight from the river and tied it to a small tree growing on the bank. I walked about three quarters of a mile down the dike paralleling the river and got in position to observe a fairly long string of crab pots strung out along the channel.

Hours passed with nothing but the constant buzzing of the bugs and the occasional screech or yawp of a heron or egret in the nearby impoundment. The heat and humidity were oppressive. I could not have jumped into the river and been any more soaked than I was. After a while I noticed the breeze beginning to pick up, providing welcome relief from the searing heat. I had been hearing for some time the distant rumblings of thunder and saw that the sky south of me was becoming increasingly dark. Suddenly I felt a telltale blast of really chilly air, a clear sign that a storm front was arriving like a freight train.

The distant rumbles gave way to loud thunderclaps. In an instant the sky turned inky black, and a torrential deluge soon followed. I barely had time to root out a poncho from the depths of my carry-around bag and pull it over me. The wind was howling, and the lightning bursts were so close that they sounded like shattering panes of glass. I could feel the electricity in the air as I sank as low as I could down the face of the dike without sinking into the waters of the impoundment.

The rain was coming in sheets. The thunder was so loud from the close and constant lightning strikes that it sounded like one continuous rumble. I knew that if I got hit, I would never know it, so I just continued to hug the earth and pray that it didn't happen. Thirty minutes later there was not a cloud in the sky. Over the course of my career, I experienced many storms, but that one was about the most intense I have ever endured out in the open.

When patrolling the rivers and waterways, I frequently checked crab pots to make sure that they were being worked. The law required that they be fished at least every five days. The presences of algae growth on the floats or cannibalized crabs in the pots were sure indications that the line was not being worked or had been abandoned.

Early one morning, as I was checking crab pots behind Dewees and Capers, I was finding an unusual number of stone crabs that had both claws missing. The regulations on taking stone crabs required that only one legal-size claw could be removed. The claw had to be at least two and three-quarters of an inch long in a line extending from the tip of the immovable claw to the elbow. If the crab only had one claw, the crab had to be returned to the water intact.

The law also prohibited the removal of any claw from a female bearing a visible egg mass. I was convinced by what I had seen that just about every crabber working that part of the waterway was violating the law and launched a plan to prove my theory. Returning to the landing, I drove to a Mount Pleasant hardware store, where I purchased a hard steel scribe. Then I went to a nearby shopping center and bought a large bath towel.

I returned to the landing later that evening, well after the crabbers had worked their lines and left the water. I went out and pulled enough pots to obtain a sample of stone crabs that could represent the full potential of violations: taking the only claw, taking both claws, and taking from a sponge-bearing female.

There were five crabbers working that particular area, and I had to pull a lot of pots to find the requisite fifteen stone crabs I needed for my plan to work. When I had gathered the crabs with the twenty-five representative claws I needed, I wrapped each crab in the towel to keep it immobile and then began to mark the flat surface of the shoulder of each claw with the steel scribe. The crabs with only one claw were marked with an *X.* The crabs with two legal claws were marked *XI,* and the sponge bearing females were marked with an *XII*. In addition I marked the claws with an *L* or a *R* to indicate whether it was a left or right claw.

Going back through the area, I pulled up one pot from each crabber's line, placed three individually marked crabs in the top part of each pot, relatched it, and replaced it in the line. The next morning I waited, tied up to an Intracoastal Waterway marker behind the Isle of Palms, for the crabbers to return from working their lines. As each crab boat approached I motioned them over and asked to see their stone-crab claws. The first four crabbers I checked had taken all the claws off the marked crabs.

They were very curious as I picked each claw out of the bucket and closely examined it. When I found a marked one, I checked it off on my list and placed it in a widening row of claws on top of my console. They were outraged at getting three different tickets and claimed that it was entrapment. I explained to them that entrapment was encouraging them to do something they would not normally do, and in this instance that certainly could not be the case.

I was looking for the fifth crabber, Floyd "Dunie" Bonney, to come by and asked one of the departing crabbers I had checked if he had seen him. He told me that Mr. Bonney had come out earlier and had long been back at the landing.

I knew that Mr. Bonney operated a seafood restaurant on the Isle of Palms, so I went back to the landing and drove over to his establishment. Entering the front door, I asked one of the waitresses if the crabber was in. She escorted me to the kitchen, where we found Mr. Bonney washing pots and pans. When I asked him if he had caught any stone crabs that morning, he replied that he had and that they were on the stove cooking. I waited until they were done, and after he drained them in a large colander, I began checking them. I found five marked stone-crab claws, in addition to several undersized ones. He got four tickets.

I let on to several crabbers that I had other secret markings to supplement the more obvious ones I had used. Once the crabbers found that they could be caught, the numbers of no-clawed stone claws showing up in crab pots considerably diminished.

One day in the summer of 1979, I got a phone call from a crabber on Edisto Island who had a reputation for being a little on the eccentric side. He told me that he thought a crabber from a neighboring county had come into "his" territory and had been stealing "his" crabs as well as a number of his pots.

I went down the next afternoon to talk to him about his difficulties, and he said he knew that the other crabber had to be doing it because there had been no trouble in the area until he showed up. The Edisto crabber told me that the other crabber usually put in the water fairly early at Dahoo Landing, right by the Edisto Bridge. We rode around in his boat, and he showed me the area where he set his pot line and where he had been having the most trouble with missing pots, which turned out to be along the Intracoastal Waterway about half a mile north of the bridge.

A small island along the waterway ringed with washed oyster shells offered a place to hide the boat out of sight of the main channel, and for us to be concealed while watching a string of four or five of his crab pots. I made arrangements to meet him before daylight the next morning.

We pulled his boat into the marsh grass on the back of the island, walked across it, and lay across some boat cushions placed behind an oyster-shell embankment. We were both peering over the top of the shell bank watching the sunrise when we spotted an enormous alligator lazily swimming back and forth across the waterway. It approached one of his crab-pot floats, took it in its mouth, and bit off a fair size chunk of Styrofoam.

This was something that neither of us had seen before, and I speculated that the gator, not the suspected crabber, might be the source of his problem. He replied that the gator might explain some of the missing pots, but he said that it did not account for the crabs that were missing from the pots he could find.

About that time we heard the sound of a boat coming from the direction of Dahoo Landing. Scrunching a little lower behind the bank, we saw the crabber we were looking for and his striker pass by and continue on until they were out of sight, never even hesitating as they passed by my crabber's pot line. I told him that they had to return, so we would wait and see if he would do anything on his way back.

Apparently they had only a few pots north of the bridge because we soon saw them returning and passing by the two most distant of my crabber's pots. Suddenly his boat came to a stop, and I distinctly heard one of them say, "Great Gawd, look at that big gator. Quick, give me the gun." He had just discovered the gator we had been observing all morning, which was then directly between them and where we were hiding.

The crabber aimed the rifle over the windshield of his boat and fired eight or nine times, the bullets ricocheting across the water, some slamming into the shell bank in front of us. A few of the bullets frayed the stems of marsh grass right in front of us. I had to hold my crabber down. He was desperate to cut and run.

When there was a lull in the shooting, I told my crabber to stay low until I came back. I jumped up and ran down the shell bank, holding out my badge and shouting for them to stop shooting and come over to me. I was a little surprised when the boat came right over, and I was even more surprised to find the man doing the shooting was Johnny Seigler, an old classmate of mine from my military-high-school days.

I explained to him that shooting an alligator was illegal and that he was going to get a ticket for it. I asked to see his hunting license, and he said that he didn't have one. I said that, since he had a gun and was shooting at a wild animal, he was required to have a hunting license, so I issued him an additional ticket for not having a hunting license in his possession. They went on their way not even knowing that my crabber friend was still hunkered down behind the shell pile and shaking in his boots fewer than seventy-five feet away.

A few days later, I was informed that Mr. Seigler had requested a jury trial and retained a defense lawyer. The trial was to be held at magistrate's court in Ravenel, south of Charleston. I rounded up some legal help from the solicitor's office and wound up with not just one, but two, assistant solicitors, Richard Stoney and Charles Condon, who was later elected Ninth Circuit solicitor and then attorney general of South Carolina.

We got busy with assembling our case, which was mostly based on my testimony since we could not convince the crabber I was trying to help to come to court to testify. He said that he was too scared, and we figured that he would be of little use even if we subpoenaed him. We amended the original charge of "shooting an alligator" to "attempting to shoot an alligator," which was covered in the same code section but was a more generally worded charge. I could not testify that I had seen any bullets hit the alligator because I was too busy dodging bullets myself.

Arriving at court on the trial date in January 1980, we were treated to the sight of W. McAlister Hill, Mr. Seigler's defense lawyer, standing on the front steps with the defendant's father, who was impressively attired in the uniform he wore as the sheriff of Colleton County. His sheriff's patrol car was conspicuously parked right in front of the court. The jury had been selected about a week earlier, and apparently the defense lawyer had been caught off guard because we wound up with an all-female jury, not a bad situation in a case involving shooting at an animal.

The magistrate stated that the charges of attempting to shoot an alligator and hunting without a license would both be tried at the same time, and we commenced the trial with me in the witness box being questioned by Assistant Solicitor Condon. I stated what I had seen and heard, and noted that at the time of the incident the defendant never denied that he was shooting at the alligator.

Mr. Condon's direct examination was brief and to the point, which was not the case when I was cross-examined by the defense lawyer, who asked leading questions in an attempt to get me to admit how dangerous alligators were. We danced with that issue for around thirty minutes before he gave up and went into questions of how I could have seen what his client was shooting at if I was hiding behind the shell pile. I reminded him of the statement his client had made just before the firing began: "Great Gawd, look at that big gator. Quick, give me the gun." I told him that I had seen his client take aim and begin firing just before I ducked down to keep from being hit myself.

Threaded in among the many questions Mr. Hill directed at me were lengthy statements of the dangerous nature of alligators. From time to time he reminded the jury that the defendant was not to be confused with his father, who had the same name, the respected, long-serving sheriff of Colleton County.

At length I was dismissed as a witness, and Mr. Seigler took the stand. He was sworn in and launched into a story claiming that when he brought out the rifle and began shooting it, he thought that he was shooting at a garfish. "An alligator gar," he said. He stated that he had never seen an alligator, so I must have misheard him that morning.

When Assistant Solicitor Condon began cross-examining the defendant, he walked him back through his story about shooting at a garfish. Then he asked him if garfish were good to eat. Mr. Seigler stated that as far as he knew, they were not good to eat. Mr. Condon inquired if garfish posed any kind of threat, if they could be considered dangerous. The defendant stated that he didn't think they were dangerous at all.

The brisk interrogatory continued with the question of whether the defendant took shots at all the garfish he saw in the water. He responded, obviously annoyed, with an abrupt "No!" Pursuing that theme, Mr. Condon asked him why he had chosen to shoot at that particular garfish. He said that he couldn't remember. Mr. Condon's last question to him was, "Is killing garfish a fun thing to do?" The defense lawyer objected. The women of the jury, who had no doubts about the identity of the defendant, were not impressed with the revelations of his gratuitous shooting, regardless of what his target may have been.

Mr. Hill, sensing that he might be losing his grip over what he had considered a certain outcome, launched into his closing statement with a long harangue over the dangers to children from the numerous alligators that lurked in the coastal waters. No more mention was made of garfish. He appealed to the protective instincts of the female jury and concluded with the astounding assertion that his client should be given a medal for shooting an alligator instead of being prosecuted for it. His statement caused an audible murmur in the jury box.

They were out only around thirty minutes and returned to the courtroom with the verdict written on the back of the Wildlife Department ticket that the magistrate had sent in with them. The foreman handed the folded ticket to the magistrate. As he opened it up and read their verdict. I could see his hands slightly tremble as he stated that the jury had found the defendant guilty of the charges. At that Sheriff Seigler got up and stormed out of the courtroom.

The magistrate stated that he was going to impose a fine of twenty-five dollars. He then said he was changing his mind on the hunting without a license charge. Shooting at an alligator was not hunting, he said, and he found the defendant not guilty of that charge.

The assistant solicitors had headed back to town when the jury had adjourned to deliberate. I stated to the magistrate that his dismissal of the hunting charge was not the understanding we had at the beginning of the trial. He curtly said that was then, and this was now, and that was that. I never took another case to his court.

Cast Nets and Bait Balls

efore 1988 the practice of casting for shrimp over bait was totally unregulated. Years before that method became popular, an old African American waterman, Lester Nelson, used to cast over bait for shrimp up the Ashley River behind the Citadel. He sold his catch from the back of his truck at various locations around Charleston.

I first encountered Mr. Nelson in the early 1980s way up the Cooper River in Yellow House Creek when Belle, my Boykin spaniel "partner," and I were on a night patrol. We had come to the northern terminus of Clouter Creek, where it enters Cooper River. I was running slowly, occasionally cutting the engine and drifting to listen for any activity. I was running a little faster than idle when I turned into Yellow House Creek. It was pitch-black dark, but I was familiar with most of the turns and could barely make out the outline of the marsh grass on the bank on either side of the creek.

As I came around a bend in the creek, I saw some seventy-five yards ahead of me an eerie light glowing right in the middle of the channel. I quickly steered the boat into the marsh grass on the bank and cut the engine. I studied that light for around thirty minutes, occasionally detecting some motion around it and hearing some indistinct, muffled sounds. For the life of me I could not figure out what was going on.

"Well," I thought, "there is only one way to tell." I cranked up the engine and headed directly for the source of the mystery. As I approached, I could begin to make out the form of a boat, and I pulled alongside. I saw a smoky pine-knot fire burning in a galvanized washtub in the middle of the boat and a man who was in the act of working a trotline.

I introduced myself, and as I was checking his licenses, I found out he had a gill net set a short distance up the creek. He used the gill net to catch bait for his trotlines. He said that he also set trotlines for catfish up in the lake when the season was right.

I found out that he didn't throw anything away. He took all the trash fish, fish heads, innards, etc., threw them in a large barrel in his yard, built a fire under it, and set it to a boil. All the fresh stuff he threw in the barrel joined an already fermenting gruel from his other forays. He said that a thick layer of fish oil would form on the top of the contents of the barrel and that he would mix that with mud and use it to bait shrimp during the summer and fall months.

If the wind was right, I could tell when Mr. Nelson was shrimping up the Ashley River because I could smell his boat long before I could see it. He could catch the shrimp too. He sold his catch out of the back of his old truck in areas around Cainhoy and Huger and over at the Longshoremen's Hall. His weathered bateau was older than I was, and I was impressed with the long hours he worked in the water.

I found out later that he had supported his family and put several children through college by dint of his hard work. Sadly, nearly everything he did was becoming a violation of the law. Setting gill nets inshore of the coastline and selling shrimp caught over bait were made illegal, and Mr. Nelson was put out of business.

Shrimp baiting caught on like wildfire following a series of public hearings held throughout the state to get public input on whether the state should regulate or prohibit the practice. The gruesome tales of the vast amounts of shrimp caught over bait by out-of-state commercial cast netters, especially down around the Beaufort area, fired the public's imagination. It was not long before the media got hold of the baiting issue and spread the word even further.

The state implemented many regulations governing this fishery, including licensing and setting a season for it, but the public had discovered shrimp baiting, and the onslaught began. What was once practiced by relatively few commercial operators and a small number of recreational cast netters now draws the attention of almost fifteen thousand annual license holders from every corner of the state. The profusion of boat lights on the waters at night in the most popular areas near boat landings look like a waterborne carnival.

This practice instantly gave rise to another front in the perennial enmity between recreational fishermen and commercial fishermen. The trawler owners, already smarting from heavy regulation designed to reduce sea-turtle mortality and finfish bycatch, clamored for tighter restrictions on shrimp baiting, which they viewed as clandestine commercial encroachments under the guise of recreational shrimping.

As an example, in 1989 Captain Junior Magwood wrote a letter to the Wildlife Department commissioners over the heading of "Raping of Our Estuaries."

Dear Sirs:

The South Carolina shrimpers are deeply concerned with the esca-lation of commercial taking of shrimp in our estuaries by means of cast netting and pocket seines.

For years we have been trying to close our bays and sounds to com-mercial trawling, and we finally succeeded this year. Now a new type of commercial harvesting has arisen, BAITING! If the conservation of shrimp and sport fish is to be considered in the estuaries, the taking of shrimp commercially should be halted.

The public should be able to exercise their God Given Rights in a reasonable manner without harassment. In our view, the only way to

Junior Magwood, captain of the trawler Tressy Marie, *showing Ben Albrecht and Freeman Taylor the entire catch from his first trawl of the morning on opening day in Bull Bay*

avoid an accident or be able to control the commercial aspect of this new development is to close shrimping from sundown to sunup, as it is now imposed on commercial shrimpers in the oceans.

We respectfully request your help in resolving this environmental disaster.

Captain Junior Magwood was not the only trawler captain to express strong reservations about the outcome of the burgeoning interest in shrimp baiting, but he was certainly the most vocal.

Some shrimp baiters erected lines of two-by-two-inch permanently set stakes along as much as three quarters of a mile of shoreline, claiming the length of it as their own territory. The stakes marked the spots where the bait was deposited in the water. Approaching anyone who cast near or between their poles, they heaped verbal abuse and threats upon them.

There were reports of weapons being brandished. On several occasions even property owners whose docks protruded into marked territory were threatened if they attempted to cast a net off their own docks. On some nights the bait poles would be so thick and numerous in a few areas you had to run slowly with your spot beam on to avoid running into them.

Some years before the practice of shrimp baiting became such a hot-button issue, the General Assembly passed a law making it a seriously punishable offense for anyone willfully to impede another in the act of hunting or fishing. This law was invoked several times early in the controversy, especially against those who threatened and intimidated others.

In several instances plainclothes officers were sent into an area where problems had been reported. The complaints were immediately confirmed when the officers were almost rammed by a boatload of thugs demanding they leave and making threats about what they'd do if the officers didn't. Some of the lawbreakers involved in those early encounters met the full force of the law and were carried off in handcuffs to the county jail. In addition to having to pay a large fine, they had their statewide hunting and fishing privileges suspended for one year. It didn't take too long for the word to get out and have a calming effect on some of the territorial claims.

The real culprits were the few who entered the recreational shrimping areas, which was anything inland of a line running along the shoreline of the barrier islands, for the purpose of catching shrimp to sell. They were hard to apprehend and even more difficult to prosecute successfully.

Shrimp baiting was primarily a night fishery. Little was done during the day except in some of the larger bays. In order to make a case, you had to prove that the culprit caught the shrimp over bait. You had to track the

On the beach at the Isle of Palms during Hurricane David, September 1979

shrimp from the water to the landing and from there to the culprit's house or some other location, where you might manage to observe a transaction taking place—all of which usually happened in the darkness of night.

The official answer to these and other problems was numerous regulations and stiff penalties. Participants in this fishery were limited to ten poles per boat. Each pole had to be marked with reflector tape to make it visible at night and with a sticker bearing a number corresponding to the license number. Other regulations included the imposition of a sixty-day shrimp-baiting season, limits on the amount of shrimp one could catch in a day, and maximum distances in the lengths of the bait-pole sets as well as distances the shrimp baiters had to stay away from each other.

Despite the outcry from the trawler fleet and from those who had grown up free casting without the aid of bait, there was no evidence that the use of bait had any measurable impact on the sustainability of shrimp populations. Those who wished to cast the old fashioned way could still do so year round as long as they observed the recreational limits and did not use bait or sell their shrimp.

Most of the regulations resulted from the failure of shrimp baiters to control their own behavior. Just about all of the shrimp-baiting regulations were designed more to equalize opportunity than to protect the resource. Efforts to impose additional controls met stalwart resistance until the late 1990s.

So many people take advantage of shrimp baiting that it taxes the man power of the Wildlife Department to regulate it. Recent restrictions have increased the mesh size of cast nets so that smaller shrimp may escape. Also dock owners are permitted to cast over bait off their own docks.

The opening moments of the sixty-day shrimp-baiting season, which runs from the middle of September to the middle of November, resemble the headlong rush of people onto the old western land grants you used to see in the movies, where participants stormed forward en masse to stake their claims to what they fancied was the choicest territory. No one can leave the dock or landing with shrimp-bait paraphernalia aboard his boat until the very moment the legal season opens, which is at high noon.

There were always those who tried to jump the gun or didn't read the law and were caught in the waterways while in headlong flight to the shrimping grounds or, even worse, out with all the bait poles set before the legal beginning of the season. They were subject to the charge of having shrimp-baiting paraphernalia in the boat out of season. Sometimes they were made to pull up their poles and go all the way back to the landing. If they had actually put their baits out and were casting, it was the proverbial "Katy, bar the door," and the tickets would flow.

Recreational shrimp baiting is a well-established practice now and properly enjoyed by many as a way to fill the family freezer with tasty shrimp. I still think sadly on the demise of Lester Nelson's career.

Dove Fields and Cracked Corn

 dove shoot in South Carolina is as much a social event as it is a hunt. It usually involves a good number of people—usually men but sometimes women and children—and a wide variety of retrieving dogs.

Dove-hunting clubs are common throughout the state. Some of the dove shoots occur on lands leased by dove clubs that pay a farmer to plant and maintain the fields. Others are invitational hunts, where the landowner invites friends over for a morning or an afternoon shoot.

I have been present on dove shoots, either officially or as a guest, where there were a hundred or more hunters scattered around large cultivated fields. Occasionally dove shoots are the centerpieces for large political events with socializing going on before and after the hunt, often accompanied by a meal of barbeque, fried fish, or Frogmore stew. Former governor Robert McNair's annual fall dove shoot is a famous political gathering, nearly rivaling the crowd at the Galivants Ferry Stump Meeting.

At many of the larger events, hosts announce that the game wardens have been invited and will be checking hunters in the field. The host cautions his guests to abide by the laws and observe the courtesies: no shooting at low birds and vacating your stand once you have gotten your limit.

When I first started with the department in 1978, a dove shoot was traditionally an afternoon affair. At some point the small-game biologists determined that morning shooting was also allowable. I was once in conversation with a perfectly law-abiding person who said he had been to a terrific shoot that morning, taking a limit of birds in fewer than thirty minutes, and that he was looking forward to a good afternoon shoot at a friend's farm on one of the nearby islands.

I asked him if he realized what he had just admitted. He seemed a little disturbed when I told him that the law allowed only twelve birds per day, not twelve birds at each shoot. Several people I know have had the misfortune to be checked on two separate dove shoots by the same game warden, who remembered how many birds they had when he checked them earlier. I am glad to say that most dove hunters observe the courtesies and obey the laws, but there are enough who don't to keep the game wardens busy.

One November our District Nine unit received information that people on Edisto Island were shooting over several baited dove fields, a practice prohibited in state and federal laws. Observing the usual formalities, we passed on that information to the District Five headquarters in Bonneau, whose chief responsibility was enforcing the inland game and fish laws. Their district included Charleston County.

A week later, the interested party informed one of the officers in our unit that the baited field he had reported had been hunted again on Saturday, that many birds had been shot, and that there was not a game warden to be seen anywhere. Further, he said, the field had just been rebaited and there was to be another shoot on the forthcoming Saturday, just three days away. He was concerned about the situation and was, according to the officer who took the call, frustrated that nothing had been done to act on his previous information.

Doubting that the District Five officers could be pried away from the Francis Marion deer hunters, our unit leader dispatched two of us to investigate the field and to document it, which involved getting samples and photographs of the bait and the general layout of the area. After documenting that a section of the field was baited with cracked corn, a unit meeting was called to devise a game plan.

We went in three separate patrol cars early Saturday morning and met in a patch of woods near an old tenant house well behind, and at a discreet remove from, the baited field. The plan was to wait until some shooting had gone on and then quickly drive around the field to where the hunter's vehicles were parked, dropping off officers along the way.

It was a crisp and frosty morning. After all the officers were assembled at the meeting place in the hidden glade, we warmed ourselves with thermoses of hot coffee and munched on doughnuts and Nabs until well past noon. At last our lookout, peering through binoculars from just inside the

*Sergeant Moïse
in winter uniform,
1996*

edge of the woods, reported that cars and trucks were beginning to arrive at
the far end of the field near a solitary oak tree.

Each of us was beginning to get a little antsy, as much from the anticipation of the event as from too much black coffee. Our unit leader went
over the carefully crafted scenario once again and reminded everyone of
which magistrate on Edisto to write the citations to and of the date and time
of court. Hunters continued to arrive, and we expected them to enter the
field somewhere between two and three o'clock.

By that time we were all gathered in a knot close to our patrol cars—
talking in whispers, chewin' and spittin', and waiting for the first shots to be
fired—when suddenly the first truck in a veritable parade of trucks loaded
with hunters and dogs, violated our little sanctuary and passed slowly in

review right in front us, headed to another field some distance away from the baited field.

As they drove past us in their dusty caravan, a few hunters faintly waved; most, however, just stared with sullen countenances, at least until they cleared the little patch of woods. Then they made little attempt to muffle their hootings and howlings of laughter.

Our unit, our little green band, was not laughing and managed to look at each other with dumbstruck and hollow-eyed expressions. We found out later that the other field was not baited. We were too embarrassed to go and check them that afternoon.

Another memorable dove-baiting case also began with a phone call. The caller related to me that a committee member of Ducks Unlimited had invited him to become a sponsor, touting that one advantage of being a sponsor in their chapter was that they had two or three sponsors-only dove shoots a year. The committee member said that the first shoot was a little more than a week away and that the field had been "sweetened," so it should be a great shoot. The caller said, "Ben, I don't know what 'sweetened' means to you, but I know what it means to me." I got information from him on the location of the field and the date and time of the shoot.

Early the next morning I went out to look at the layout. I parked the patrol car some distance away behind a hedgerow and walked around three separate fields. I found nothing in the first field nearest the road, but as I crossed a shallow drainage ditch into the next field, it became immediately apparent that there was a problem. Visible down the middle of that field were vehicle tracks, and between the tracks were fresh piles of wheat obviously pitched by the double handfuls from the back of a truck.

It was apparent that the same method of "sowing" had been employed there before because there were green dots of sprouting wheat running down between the tire tracks for the entire length of the field and the larger field beyond it. I took a few pictures of the baited area and bagged a generous sample of the freshly applied wheat to document its presence. I also sketched a rough chart of the fields, indicating the location of the access roads and where I thought the parking area would be.

After returning to the car, I called George Hines, the federal game warden in Columbia, and asked him to meet with me the following day, explaining what I had found and what I knew of the pending hunt. The next day Agent Hines and I reentered the field, took more pictures, and obtained more samples of the wheat.

From what I had been told, it was likely that there would be a good many shooters in the field, so we arranged a meeting with several other wardens in my unit in an effort to come up with an effective plan to cover all the fields adequately. By this time the scheduled hunt was only about five days away.

The state and federal wardens got together on the morning of the scheduled hunt and were dropped off at several areas near the field where we could find cover and observe the shooters when they arrived. The officers who dropped us off were to go well out of the area, wait until we called, then drive to where the shooters' vehicles were parked, and collect the licenses of anyone coming in from the field.

In our earlier meeting we had agreed that, when we gave the signal to enter the fields, we were going to go rapidly from hunter to hunter and collect their hunting or drivers' licenses, instructing the hunters to meet us at the main gathering spot, where appropriate tickets would be issued. We had decided that we were not going to wait around to see if anybody shot over the limit, that once it appeared that the shooting had begun in earnest, we were going to give the signal to move in.

When entering the area that morning to find our observation spots, we observed that the fields had been turned under with a plow within the last several days. The piles of freshly applied wheat and the sprouted spots were no longer visible on the surface. Even so the field was still considered illegal to hunt over for ten days following the complete removal of the bait. We saw several men walking around checking the field before the hunt began.

At one thirty hunters started arriving and taking positions around the field. A sprinkling of shots began shortly before two. There was still only sporadic shooting at three, and we made the decision enter the fields. We called the wardens in the patrol car to begin heading to the gathering spot. Three other wardens and I began walking into the fields to approach the hunters and collect their licenses.

We were going to cover the smaller field and work toward the larger one. As luck would have it, we had not even gotten one third the distance into the big field when the bottom fell out of the clouds. The hunters in the far end of the field fled pell-mell across the furrows to their cars to escape the deluge. The game wardens who were to have intercepted hunters coming in to the gathering spot fled to the safety of their car. The downpour did not last long but it cleared the field of hunters before they could be confronted with guns in hand. Probably only about one third of the hunters who were on the field got ticketed.

When the deluge was over, we called together the hunters whose licenses we had collected. As the tickets were being written, there was a general protest, and some of the hunters stoutly denied that the field was baited. Some were genuinely insulted at the notion of being given a ticket for shooting over bait. One fellow said that he had walked the fields and had not seen even one seed of wheat. I quelled some of the outcry by showing them the pictures I had taken of the piles of wheat between the tire tracks.

We issued tickets to those we encountered with guns in the field and to those who admitted that they had been hunting, around thirty-one in all. We exited the area leaving behind a gaggle of unhappy and angry people. If looks could kill, there would have been a bunch of dead, if not thoroughly mutilated, game wardens.

It didn't take long for things to hit the fan. I received a call early the next morning from Earl Driggers, my sergeant, who was upset that he didn't know anything about our intervention. He said he was getting a lot of phone calls from the Columbia office wanting to know what was going on. I explained to him that I had the full written report and all the documentary evidence in hand and that I would meet him at the Fort Johnson office in an hour. When I got there, he was clearly not happy and complained about not being informed. I carefully explained to him that I had apprehended violators over baited duck ponds and baited dove fields several times before this, and since he had not seemed too interested in getting advance notice then, why the big deal now?

I was soon to find that the bust had caused a storm of complaints to the Columbia office, to just about every member of the Charleston County delegation, and even to the governor's office. The complaints even appeared in news articles, editorials, and letters to the editor in the local paper. One letter writer asserted,

> The arrest of 31 members of a conservation organization for shooting doves over a baited field on James Island was a regrettable incident. It degraded the state's respected Wildlife Department and compromised an internationally acclaimed conservation organization.
>
> The laws pertaining to baited field shooting are at best confusing, but the manner in which the game wardens enforced them in this incident was ludicrous.
>
> Instead of conserving game by preventing what the wardens had predetermined to be an illegal shoot, the wardens resorted to entrapment at the expense of some 50 doves.

Our organization and the state Wildlife Department believe in conservation, practice conservation and spend millions of dollars to assure that there will be good shooting today, tomorrow and for future generations of sportsmen.

The state Wildlife Department has to enforce federal migratory bird game laws (even bad ones), but it doesn't have to employ wardens who resort to entrapment to do it.

Every letter of every word in my investigation and report was minutely scrutinized. The "why didn't you's" and Monday-morning quarterbacking started in full cry. I got the drift that the law-enforcement hierarchy was distressed by my cases and regarded them as hot potatoes.

All but two of the hunters, Frank Ford and Billy Ford, who had been apprehended and written tickets, wanted a jury trial. The Fords sent their fines to the magistrate, saying that they were satisfied that the field was baited and did not wish to participate in the trial as defendants. George Campsen, a trial lawyer and a defendant in the case, represented himself and the others. A date was set for the trial, and the jury was selected.

I thought the case was all cut and dried. The code of federal regulations clearly stated that it is illegal to take migratory birds by aid of bait and that a field is considered to be baited for ten days following the complete removal of any exposed grain. The law further stated that anyone in the field with the means and opportunity to take migratory birds over a baited area was liable for the charge of "taking migratory birds over bait." We had samples of the bait and photographs of the field showing the bait, and we could identify the people who were hunting in the baited field and who had been issued tickets.

Those who were in the gathering spot near where the vehicles were parked were not charged, only those who were approached in the fields with guns in hand and the few who admitted they had been hunting were cited.

The Columbia office sent down a department attorney to prosecute the case, but I got the distinct impression that he regarded the whole thing as a huge nuisance. Any prosecutorial zeal on his part seemed to me to be substantially subdued. The trial was conducted in what could best be described as a highly charged atmosphere. All the defendants were tried together.

The department attorney put me on the stand and asked a few perfunctory questions. I began to testify about the status of the field when I first investigated it. I was going to present my drawings indicating the locations of the bait in the fields and show dated photographs of the piles of wheat dumped between the tire tracks. At some point before the trial began, however, the trial attorneys agreed to stipulate that the field was baited, thereby precluding the presentation of any photographs or documentation of the bait or any further mention of the bait, and I was not allowed to proceed with my testimony.

I remained on the stand for cross-examination by the defense attorney, who asked me to describe what game wardens did and why they did it. I think I painted a pretty glowing picture of our responsibilities in protecting the natural resources of South Carolina.

My graphic depiction gave the defense attorney a pretty good hook for his line of defense. Mr. Campsen went on at some length about the fact that, if baiting was bad for the resource, then why did we allow any doves to be killed before we entered the field? If we were in the business of protecting the resource, why didn't we just stop the hunt at the outset or post the field before any birds were killed? He even raised the specter of entrapment, painting a picture to the jury of wardens lurking in the bushes to pounce on his innocent unsuspecting clients, all of whom were outstanding conservation-minded gentlemen.

To the best of my recollection, I groped around for satisfactory answers to Mr. Campsen's questions, but my responses certainly did not appear to have any favorable resonance with the jurors. I was getting no help from our attorney, who seemed to have the attitude that I had made my own bed and now must lie in it. I was getting more and more education by the minute.

Mr. Campsen produced a dated memorandum with a South Carolina Wildlife and Marine Resources letterhead. He asked me to read the sentence that he had underlined. The sentence read roughly, "It is not the policy of the Wildlife Department to make marginal cases on baited dove fields." The memorandum contained other qualifying sentences, but I was forbidden to read them or to make any qualifying statements of my own.

He referred to the name of the person who wrote the memo and asked me to read it from the bottom of the page. I said that it had been written by Pat Ryan. He asked if I knew who Pat Ryan was. I replied that Pat Ryan was the director of the Wildlife Department Law Enforcement Division. The attorney said, "Officer Moïse, Mr. Ryan is your boss, isn't he?" I replied that he was. He then asked, "Now, Officer Moïse, if the director of Law Enforcement sent out a memo saying that it is not the Wildlife Department's policy to make marginal cases on baited dove fields, would you have any reason to take exception to that?"

Talk about being boxed into a corner. I said, "Of course not." I was going to add, "But this is not a marginal case, here is the evidence." All I got out was, "But—" before Mr. Campsen told the magistrate, "I am through with this witness, no further questions." Our attorney did not undertake any redirect examination to clarify the issue.

The department attorney's closing argument was a dry recitation of the facts. Even I began dozing, and I could clearly see that the jurors did not exhibit one scintilla of sympathy. Mr. Campsen's closing had the jury hanging on every word, nodding their heads in agreement, and looking over at me with stern glances whenever he mentioned my name. If I had been eviscerated, there could not have been more blood on the floor. Someone told me that my face was so red, it looked as though I was going to catch on fire. The jury departed to deliberate and shortly returned to the courtroom with the verdict of not guilty for all twenty-eight defendants, including Mr. Campsen.

For years after that, whenever I gave a talk on the enforcement of the Migratory Bird Treaty Act to a civic club or hunting group, I was cross-examined or lectured about the strict-liability nature of the hunting over bait law, where knowledge or intent were not requisite for a finding of guilt. I admitted that it was a tough regulation, one that imposed a lot of responsibility on the hunter to ask questions about the field he was to hunt on, but it was a law designed to protect the resource and had been upheld in every judicial circuit in the country.

To further complicate things, South Carolina at the time allowed hunting over top-sown grain, viewing such a sowing method as within the practice of a "normal agricultural operation." The problems arose over differences about how much grain could legally be scattered. That which one game warden would find within tolerable limits in one county might be considered excessive and illegal by a warden in another county. It was bad policy and generated considerable confusion and ill will.

Since that time the strict-liability nature of the federal and state baiting laws has been changed. Now a warden has to prove that the person caught in a baited field knew, or should have known, that the field was baited, and the practice of shooting over top-sown grain has been prohibited.

If any good thing came from the case, it was that early in my career I earned a reputation for being tough on violators whoever they might be. As a consequence I received many phone calls in the years ahead from people reporting blatant hunting violations. I learned time and time again that there is no more effective bulwark against wildlife violations than a concerned citizen willing to get involved and make a phone call.

In the early 1980s a few areas close to the city of Charleston were still farmed, and several large tracts had fields that were cultivated and managed for dove shoots. Some fields were leased by dove clubs, which had regularly scheduled shoots during the season. A few areas were the scene of large annual events combining a dove shoot with a fish fry or barbecue.

An annual weekend-long dove shoot off Riverland Drive on the Dill property was called the Acuff Shoot and generally occurred in mid-September. Discreet inquiry revealed that the shoot was to occur on consecutive Friday and Saturday afternoons. I was not able to check the Friday shoot, but I drove by the field on Saturday. Hearing gunfire, I drove in and parked under the spreading branches of a live-oak tree. I could see that there were a considerable number of cars and trucks parked up and down the road in the shade of the overhanging branches. The hunters were in fields to the left and right of the road.

As I walked down the line of vehicles, I saw a man standing near the back of a station wagon with a gun in his hand. I approached him, identified myself as a game warden, and asked to see his hunting license. The man looked genuinely startled and flustered and said that he wasn't really hunting. I carefully explained to him that if he was at a dove shoot with a loaded shotgun in hand that he was required to have a hunting license and that, if he didn't have one, I was obliged to issue him a citation for it.

He continued to try and explain as I wrote him a ticket, saying he wasn't there to hunt. I could tell that he was a little agitated. I handed him the ticket and explained to him the nature of the charge, and where and when he was to appear in magistrate's court for trial.

My admonition was, "Either your warm body or your cold cash should be in court on the day and time set." I then headed out to check the other hunters. Out of the entire crowd, the man by his car was the only one who was issued a ticket. After he did not appear in court as instructed, East Cooper magistrate Jeanette Harper sent him a stern note urging him to take care of the matter promptly.

The hunter was Dr. George Nelson, a professor at the Medical University of Georgia, who then sent a one-hundred-dollar check, the amount of the requested bond, along with the following handwritten letter to Magistrate Harper:

Nov. 12, 1985

Dear Judge Harper,
Thank you for your letter of Nov. 5, 1985. I would like to take this opportunity to explain to you what happened.

I came to Charleston to pick up a mattress and box springs that my daughter had loaned to the daughter of a friend of mine. His daughter and my daughter had roomed together at The College of Chas. and my daughter transferred to Clemson and left the mattress and box springs and now she needed them. Anyway, my friend told me he was going on a dove shoot Fri and Sat and they were having a big party Fri. night and a barbeque after the shoot on Sat. He invited me to go. I told him I didn't want to shoot but I would like to go to the party on Fri. I got down there about 4 on Fri and went to the field where they were shooting. I stood around a pickup truck on the edge of the field drinking a beer while they were shooting. I own a gun and did not bring it because I had no intention of shooting. We all went to the party Fri. night. On Sat. I went into town (from James Island) and picked up the mattress and box springs (and other stuff) and went back to my friend's house before coming back to Augusta. He talked me into staying and going to the barbeque. I said OK since I didn't have to be back until Sunday. About 3 o'clock or so he said why don't we go out and shoot a while before the barbeque (I think the hunt started at 2 and the barbeque was supposed to be about 6). I told him I didn't want to shoot. He said that he didn't feel right going to the barbeque without participating in the shoot. I said OK. When we got out there it was probably between 4 & 5 o'clock. We pulled his car off the road near a field where they were shooting. We got out and he shot a few times (knocked down one that stuck in the top of a tree) and I sat on the cooler. It got kind of boring so I went back to his car and got a gun out of the back of his car (he had brought 2 guns). I had to fool with his gun to figure out how it worked (it was an automatic and my gun is a double barrel, I have never fired an automatic). Anyway, soon after I figured it out, out of the woods walked the game warden straight toward me. I thought to myself that Hollywood couldn't have set a fella up better than I had set myself up. He asked for my hunting license, which I didn't have. He then asked me how many shells I had in the gun. I told him I had no idea because it wasn't my gun (he checked it and it was OK). He then asked for my driver's license and wrote me out a ticket. I asked him if I had been sitting on the cooler without the gun when he walked up, what would he have done? He said, "Nothing." He said what made the difference was the fact that I was holding the gun.

Now to get to your letter. You state that I was "hunting doves" without a license. I think that is a questionable point. It all depends on the definition of the term, "hunting doves." If "hunting doves" is defined as "standing by a car off a road near a field in which several hunters were shooting doves and holding a gun," then I was "hunting doves." If "hunting doves" is defined as "shooting a dove," then I was not "hunting doves." If "hunting doves" is defined as "being in possession of a dead dove while in a field with a gun," then I was not "hunting doves." If "hunting doves" is defined as "getting your gun, buying shells, transporting them into a field with the intent of shooting doves," then I was not "shooting doves." Therefore, in my opinion, to say that I was "hunting doves" is debatable. At any rate, I don't think that what I did was worthy of a $100.00 fine. It seems to me that the least break I should get is to call it a donation and make it a tax deduction. I have donated several times in past years to The Georgia Wildlife Association and have listed it as a deduction (obviously not under similar circumstances).

At any rate, I appreciate the opportunity to inform you as to what happened and I apologize for missing the hearing date.

Judge Harper and I thought that the letter was a hoot. In one of her characteristically humane gestures and with my complete assent, she decided to find him not guilty of the charges and sent back his one-hundred-dollar check. Judge Harper suggested in her letter accompanying the check that if he wished to make a tax-deductible donation he could send one to the Harry Hampton Memorial Wildlife Fund. She also mentioned that his lengthy explanation brought warmth and humor into an otherwise dreary business. A one-hundred-dollar donation from Dr. Nelson for the Harry Hampton Fund soon arrived.

A Few Upland Adventures

Sometimes you bite the bear, and sometimes the bear bites you," is one of the colorful metaphors I often heard in describing some of the game wardenly exertions that didn't go according to plan. One such incident occurred off Little Britton Road between Adams Run and Dahoo Landing, near Edisto Island. I had received several reports about night-hunting activities there.

After scouting the area, I decided to set up a patrol one night to see if any culprits could be rounded up. One carload of game wardens took a position behind a tomato-packing shed off the main road to Edisto Island. Officer Martin North and I set off to find a spot from which we could observe a large soybean field and signal the others over the radio if we saw any suspicious activity. On the signal they would dash out and block the head of the road.

I found a good hiding spot that offered a clear view near the field. We parked the patrol car in a narrow woods road that connected two large fields and covered the car completely with a camouflaged parachute to eliminate any telltale reflections. We could see out, especially if a spotlight happened to be working the field we were watching. Many hours passed. It was getting around one or two in the morning. We had been telling war stories and had consumed so much black coffee that we were practically bug-eyed.

Around two thirty we saw the lights of a slowly moving car coming down the road. As it moved across to our right, the lights passed out of view behind the treeline. Several moments later we saw the light over to our right. Scant moments later, we realized that it was coming down the edge of the field on the same road we drove in on, and before we had a chance to get a grip on this enormity, the vehicle turned in on the very road where we were waiting in ambuscade.

We scarcely had time to react. As the car proceeded into the narrow confines of that little road with his bright lights pointed directly at us, its driver probably did not know what to make of the camouflaged obstruction ahead of him. At that point all I could think of was a head-on collision. In an instant I turned on my own headlights, plus the blue light on the dash, and hit the ignition key.

We must have looked like Captain Nemo's *Nautilus* right there in the middle of the woods. The approaching vehicle abruptly stopped and commenced backing at high speed toward the field behind him, just about the time my foot hit my accelerator. The parachute, which was supposed to stay put as we drove out from under it, instead wadded up around the windshield wipers, completely obstructing our forward view of the rapidly disappearing vehicle. To add to our mounting difficulties, I had an accoutrement to a bad habit of mine, a spit cup for chewing tobacco, sitting on the dash.

As I blindly lurched forward toward the fleeing vehicle, the contents of the spit cup fell into the ashtray, where we had placed the microphone for the radio, which we had planned to use to summon the other officers to block the road. The drenched microphone made radio transmission impossible, not to mention creating a huge stinking mess. Our half-empty coffee cups were launched to the rear also. I overshot the end of the road and plunged into the ploughed field with a partly billowing, mostly wadded parachute still across the windshield.

The question of visibility at that point became moot as it became apparent that we were not going anywhere. The car was bogged to the frame. We sat there looking rather piteous, dripping with tobacco juice and tepid coffee, as our culprit speedily disappeared into the darkness of the night.

The parachute, along with various limbs and other debris we could find, provided traction under the rear tires. At length we managed to extricate ourselves and get back to the paved road, where we used two rolls of paper towels to clean up the car and ourselves.

The microphone did not survive its immersion. To our good fortune, there was a hand-held mobile radio in the trunk with sufficient charge to make contact with our fellow officers, who were still patiently waiting behind the packing shed. I radioed that it looked like a quiet night and that it was time to go home.

Perhaps one of my scariest moments brought home the fact that being in the same field with a night hunter carrying an automatic shotgun could result in a life-threatening dose of buckshot. This revelation occurred while I was working on a night-hunting case near Seabrook Island, across from where Bohicket Marina is now located. After we had received several reports of gunfire late at night, around some of the large tomato fields there, my sergeant, Earl Driggers, and I decided we would stake out one of the fields and see if we could get lucky.

We scouted the area just before sunset and found a good place to hide the patrol car. It was one of those dark nights where you could barely see your hand in front of your face. We were standing next to a wind row of wax myrtles growing on either side of a deep ditch. A dirt-track road pierced the center of the fields from the paved road on one end to a tree line beyond another field.

We stood there in the dark engaging in small talk for almost two hours until we observed a vehicle stopping on the Kiawah road at the far end of the dirt-track road that accessed the fields. A door slammed in the distance, and the vehicle drove away. A few moments later we saw the beam of a spotlight come on, shine across the field, and then go dark. Later the beam came on again and searched the field. This was repeated several more times, and each time it was getting closer to where we were standing.

Sergeant Driggers said he was going back to the car to call for backup. Taking the only flashlight, he headed back to the patrol car, which was parked behind some trees almost one hundred yards away. The person in the field continued his intermittent shining, each time closer to where I was standing. I remember that, during one of the periods of darkness, I began hearing footsteps scrunching on the dirt.

All of a sudden, the light came back on. It was pointed directly at me. In the beam of that light, I could see the muzzle of a shotgun aiming straight at me. Staring into that beam, I shouted, "South Carolina Wildlife, Captain. You are under arrest!" At that announcement the light went out, and all I could hear were the rapid footsteps of the culprit booking it across the dark field.

I ran over to the road but could not see a thing. My sergeant came walking up a few moments later asking what all the shouting was about. Pointing out toward the field, I glumly informed him that our night hunter just got away. We trotted back to the car and, in a futile exercise, drove around the perimeter of the fields a few times, shining our spotlights, finding nothing. After I got home, I stayed awake the rest of the night thinking how close I had come to being a "hunting accident."

Another night-hunting adventure occurred over on Edisto Island in a joint effort with officers from District Five and the Columbia-based department airplane. We had been receiving an unusual number of complaints in the District Nine office, about shots being fired at all hours of the night at various locations around Edisto Island and along Parkers Ferry Road between Highway 17 and Willtown Plantation.

Night-hunting enforcement was not normally considered to be among the duties of District Nine officers; yet our officers' lack of response to complaints about night hunting did not sit well with callers, who did not understand, let alone appreciate, the administratively established separation of duties.

We knew the best way to patrol the large area involved was to use the department airplane, and the only way to accomplish that was to involve District Five in a joint effort by claiming that our officers knew the area roads well and could facilitate rapid movement to properties when shining activities were spotted.

When the time came for the night-hunting patrol I was riding with Conservation Officer Ivan "Boss Hawg" Holden of Georgetown. He and I later served together on the Wildlife Department's Investigative Team. No one could fault his enthusiasm for the job. When we were taking the investigators' course at the Criminal Justice Academy in Columbia, he could figure out the scenarios set up by the instructors and solve the problems almost immediately.

His driving prowess was legendary, and on all occasions being a passenger in his car was bound to be a jaw-clenching, white-knuckle experience. I was constantly comforted, however, to notice that there were no dents on his car.

We parked on a dark side road off the main highway leading to Edisto Island. Six officers in three other vehicles were within fifteen miles of us, also parked and hidden. The pilot and one of the local game wardens, acting as an observer and wearing night-vision goggles, were in the airplane. Night vision goggles could detect a person lighting a match more than a mile away, so headlights or spotlights were dramatically visible.

In an effort to keep radio traffic to a minimum, the observer was to transmit only when a target was sighted. He was looking for any unusual headlight or spotlight activity around cultivated or wooded areas. He spotted a light sweeping back and forth in a field not too far across the Mc-Kinley Washington Bridge leading to Edisto Island, on our side of the surveillance area. He reported that the vehicle had no headlights on.

Our rapidly approaching headlights could be seen from the plane, and we were guided through the turns until we neared the area where the shining had been spotted. Officer Holden used a special switch to turn off his headlights, leaving the taillights burning, so the warden in the airplane could continue to track our movements. We came to a long fence and then a gate. The observer reported that the shiners were about two hundred yards in from us. The gate had a lock and chain, which Officer Holden quickly severed with a bolt cutter, the "universal key."

We entered the field, closed the gate, and refastened it using one of our own locks. By that time Officer Holden had switched off the taillights, and we continued completely in the dark. We could see the tall leafless branches of a pecan orchard over to our right. We followed the faintly visible outlines of the two-track sand path leading into the fields ahead of us. As we slowly inched our way in, we saw in the distance the glow of a spotlight moving back and forth.

Holden got a good bead on that light and roared off toward it in a great cloud of dust. When we were within one hundred feet of the car, on came the siren, the blue light, the headlights, and my hand-held spotlight. The vehicle ahead of us came to a stop, and we jumped from our patrol car instructing them to exit their truck with their hands up.

Keeping the spotlight on them, I ordered them to produce some identification while Officer Holden checked the cab of their truck. It contained a loaded .30-30 rifle, a handful of .30-30 bullets on the dash, and a hand-held spotlight plugged into the cigarette lighter.

One of the hunters was a juvenile. The other was twenty-four years old. Both of them had Edisto Island addresses. They were searched, handcuffed, and placed in the back of Holden's car. At the Charleston County Jail, they were photographed and fingerprinted. The older hunter spent the night in the Charleston County jail, the younger at the Juvenile Detention Center.

Early the next morning I was still completing the paperwork and the inventory of the seized vehicle when I received a phone call from John Horlbeck, a Charleston lawyer I knew well. He related that he had been asked to represent the boys and wanted to know what the charges were. I explained that they both were charged with night hunting for deer, and the older boy was also being charged with contributing to the delinquency of a minor, a serious big-court offense.

He asked if we could get together in his office to discuss the cases. Since we were well acquainted, I agreed to come by later in the morning. Before the meeting, I spoke to the solicitor and told him what we had. I informed him that I had been called by the defendants' attorney, who wanted to talk, and that I thought, when presented with the facts, he would agree to have them plead guilty to the charges without all the entanglements that stem from a jury trial. The solicitor asked me to see where the conversation with Mr. Horlbeck led, but not to make any deals until I cleared them with him.

Mr. Horlbeck was a somewhat stiff, but courtly, gentleman. I gave him the facts of the case and informed him of the gravity of the charges. He said that the older boy had been driving his father's truck without permission and inquired whether there was anything we could do to secure its release. He also asked, if his clients pled guilty to the night-hunting charges, would I consider dropping the charge of contributing to the delinquency of a minor? He told me that the older boy had posted bond that morning, and the younger boy had been released into the custody of his parents.

I related it was necessary to obtain the solicitor's approval and said I would call him the next day. When I met the solicitor the next afternoon and informed him of Mr. Horlbeck's offer, the solicitor said he would order the release of the vehicle, but the gun would have to be confiscated. He said he would accept a guilty plea from the older defendant on the night-hunting charge and agree to drop the "contributing" charge; however, the juvenile's case had to be handled in Family Court.

The juvenile was put on a probationary status where he had to have no unexcused absences from school, maintain passing grades, and report to a county juvenile offender officer once a month. He actually had a more difficult time of it than his older friend, who had only to pay a fine and lose his rifle.

There was another time when our whole unit was out on a night-hunting patrol near Willtown Bluff. We were in three different vehicles hidden in the woods at various locations along the Parkers Ferry and Willtown Bluff roads. It was a moonless night, an optimum situation for night hunters, but as the hours passed, there was no sign of any sort of activity. We had been informed that this location had been the scene of constant gunfire, but it appeared it was not to happen on this occasion.

Along with us that night was Officer Martin North, who had retired from the U.S. Air Force and had worked for a time for the Marine Resources Division before coming on with law enforcement. He was full of enthusiasm and constantly looked for opportunities to impress us with his vast store of knowledge about the great outdoors. This was his first night-hunting patrol.

In our mounting boredom we decided to implement a plan that we had earlier concocted in order to have a little fun at the expense of Officer North's dignity. At a prearranged radio signal, one of the officers, who was located some distance away from Officer North's vehicle, was to fire his pistol twice into the air. An officer in another vehicle was to come on the radio and ask, "Did you hear that?" and say that he thought the shots came from near the dirt road entering Grove Plantation and he was on the way there. The instant the signal was transmitted, the shots were fired, and the patrol cars were roaring to the scene with sirens wailing and blue lights spinning.

The officer riding with North later explained that North had immediately picked up on the shots and was beside himself with excitement as he heard the radio exchanges. We were parked on the shoulder of the road, shining spotlights into the woods when Officer North and the officer with him arrived.

They lurched to a stop, Broderick Crawford style, and jumped from the vehicle. One of the officers shouted, "He went thataway!" pointing to the direction of the woods. He directed several of the officers to guard the road and directed Officer North to run through the woods in pursuit of the fleeing culprit and try to chase him out to the road.

North, with a walkie-talkie in one hand and flashlight in the other, immediately flung himself headlong into the thickness of the brush and was quickly out of sight. We could hear him thrashing through the woods and would occasionally shout that we had heard the culprit running over to the left near the dirt road and then later that we had heard him over to the right heading toward the paved road. We were whooping and shouting to one another making it sound like a royal chase was on.

We gathered near the patrol cars, turned off the lights, and waited to see how long it would take for Officer North to reappear. He was gone for a good twenty-five minutes when we saw a light emerge from the edge of the woods a considerable distance up the road. When he returned, he was bleeding from scratches and wheezing heavily from his exertions. Between gasps he inquired if we had seen any sign of the culprit. One of the officers offhandedly responded, "Well, I guess he got away." Everybody silently headed back to their vehicles and began driving back home.

The officer riding with Officer North said that it took half an hour for him to get his breath back. North kept complaining that we had given up the chase too soon, and with a little more time he was certain that he could have flushed the culprit out of the woods. He was genuinely dumbfounded at our reaction that night and didn't believe us for the longest time when he was told that it was all a ruse.

Occasionally I got to do a little hunting myself. Over the years I have been a guest on countless deer drives throughout the lowcountry and have witnessed sweeping changes in much of the landscape. Many of the hunts took place right where the main commercial center of Daniel Island now stands and in areas around Mount Pleasant that are now densely populated subdivisions.

The two main methods of hunting deer in South Carolina are still-hunting and dog drives. Still-hunting is typically a solitary activity where the hunter shoots from an elevated stand, often employing bait to attract the deer. I have done that only once and was so far up a tree that I was reluctant to shoot the gun for fear of being displaced from my precarious perch.

Dog drives are group hunts where hounds are used to flush the deer out of the woods within gunshot range of standers who have been placed at safe intervals around the woods. Hunting with dogs is an ancient tradition in South Carolina, and many deer-hunting clubs take great pride in their trained packs, which are directed in their pursuit by riders on horseback using the signals from hunting horns and the snaps of bullwhips.

For years I have been privileged to be a guest of John Maybank of Lavington Plantation, which was where I finally killed my first whitetail deer. It happened on November 24, 2001, on a stand in a section called Big Hog Crawl. It was 8:45 in the morning as the hunters were still being distributed among the stands and before the dogs were cast.

My younger daughter, Sarah, and I had left the city just before sunrise and driven south to Jacksonboro, the temporary seat of the state government during the American Revolution. At the time of the hunt, it was the home of Toomer's Restaurant, a small eatery that offered mugs of steaming hot coffee and some of the best breakfast fare you could eat outside of home.

As Sarah and I entered the restaurant, we were greeted by a stalwart crowd of Lavington hunters already seated around a table and engaged in lively conversation. We were shortly followed by others, including Dr. Tommy Leland and his new fiancée, Gwen Brown, who were loudly serenaded with a basso profundo rendition of "Here Comes The Bride."

With breakfast plates polished clean and the last gulps of coffee taken, a sated procession of deer hunters headed toward the plantation as a bluebird morning unfolded complete with dew on the grass and low shrouds of miasma hanging suspended, ghostlike, over the bordering fields.

As we arrived at the gathering place—after driving down a long dirt road and through the twin rows of white-painted slave cabins—we could see that a large crowd had assembled. Among them were old friends and new acquaintances, fathers with sons, grandfathers with sons and grandsons; these hunters included Frank Ford, then in his ninth decade of deer drives; Edward Lowndes, horseman and houndsman without peer; and our host, John Maybank.

As is the custom, Mr. Maybank welcomed the camouflaged assembly, made several personal observations, and reiterated the rules of the hunt: no pigs were to be shot, except in self-defense; guns were to be unloaded when we were going to and from the stands; and no one was to leave his stand until the hunt was "blown off" by three long blows of the horn. Sarah and I loaded up in the back of a pickup and rode in a train of trucks and SUVs while standers were placed at safe intervals around Big and Little Hog Crawl, a huge section of woods in the heart of the plantation.

I wished Sarah "good luck" as I departed the pickup and headed to my stand, which bordered a finger of swampland that drained into the nearby Ashepoo River. There I set up my chair; slipped my two double-ought buckshot shells into the chambers, relaxed, and reviewed the scene. I had settled into a quiet reverie in that leafy setting with the warm rays of the morning sun on my back, when I caught the movement of a dark shape some one hundred feet away, silently and slowly walking across to my left through a thicket of small saplings.

I quickly determined that it was a deer and an instant later saw that it was wearing antlers and was well within gunshot range—a brain-clearing moment! All those past deer drives, all those out-of-range bucks, all those ticks and mosquitoes, and all those occasions of sharing the joys of other hunters' successes flashed across the screen of my mind like the final vision of a dying man.

My life was to be forever changed. I was, in a scant instant of time, going to raise my gun, take aim, and fire at that buck. He continued to move slowly through the shadows around to my left. I remained seated, still, scarcely breathing; shotgun shouldered, the sight moving along, steady on the deer. I pushed the safety off with an audible click; the buck stopped and looked back straight at me, his ears up and alert.

I fired one shot from my seated, twisted, off-balance position and was promptly knocked loose from the seat of my chair onto the leaf-strewn forest floor, helpless to fire off a second round at the rapidly departing animal. I gathered myself up, somewhat thankful that there were no witnesses to this undignified spectacle. I knew that I had taken careful aim before I fired and could not have missed.

As I walked in the direction where the buck had stood only moments before, I began noticing with increasing alarm that a number of trees and saplings had absorbed an ever-mounting count of buckshot pellets. By the time I got to where the deer had commenced his departure, I had accounted for nine of the pellets in assorted tree wounds. That left only three shot to get to the deer.

I saw the disturbance in the leaves at the place where it had wheeled and fled. From there, leading off in the direction of its flight, was a distinct blood trail, which I followed for about one hundred feet before heeding the caution about not wandering off my stand. I sat for more than two hours contemplating this fine turn of events before hearing, at last, the distant sounds of three long blows of the hunting horn, signaling the end of the drive. I was thinking of this venerable lowcountry tradition in which I found myself a participant, and how it was an event that allowed intervals of socializing, time for individual contemplation in the fastness of the forest, and moments of tense excitement at the advent of the chase with the huzzas of the mounted drivers, the cry of the hounds, and periodic gunshots that announced success or failure.

We followed that blood trail after the hunt. The Lowndes boys—Edward Jr. and Rawlins, with woods acumen and better eyes than most tracking dogs—found that buck, hammer dead, pierced by two well-placed pellets, not one hundred yards away from where I had fired. I could no longer say that, in all my years of hunting, I had never taken a whitetail deer.

I was reminded of the enduring nature of the traditions of this ancient sport by receiving a full frontal ablution of deer blood, as close as you can get to total immersion while standing on your feet on the hard ground. William Elliott, in his *Carolina Sports by Land and Water* (1846), recounted a similar experience at Chee-ha Plantation probably not ten miles distant as the crow flies from where I stood, my face masked with the blood of my first deer. Elliott described a similarly blooded, young hunter's face as "glaring like an Indian Chief's in all the splendor of war paint." At the time there was apparently an attendant dictum that required the hunter to wear his grisly livery to the very end of the day. Elliott wrote that "sooth to say he returned to receive the congratulations of his young and lovely wife, his face still adorned with the stains of victory. Whether he was received, as victors are wont to be, returning from other fields of blood, is a point whereon I shall refuse to satisfy the impertinent curiosity of my dear reader." My fragile flower, Sarah, herself initiated years before with blood from the entrails of Virginia and Irish foxes, looked on with interest and delight, gave me a big hug, and told me how proud she was.

I can think of two memorable incidents in which I apprehended men who were illegally setting steel traps. The first began with a Saturday-evening phone call from the father of a small boy who lived on the Isle of Palms. The father first asked me if using steel traps on the island was legal. I informed him that it would be highly unusual for trapping permits to be issued there since it was largely a residential area. I knew my friend and fellow game warden Officer Locky Freeman occasionally set traps on the islands when residents contacted him about problems with coons, but he generally used box traps that do not kill the animal, and I was certain he had none set in the area where the father and son lived.

The father asked me to speak with his son and gave him the phone. The boy said he and a friend had been out walking around that afternoon and heard some disturbance, "a thrashing around," as he described it, in the bushes near a house construction site. They went over to investigate the source of the noise and found a crow whose leg had been caught in the jaws of a steel trap. He and his friend pried the jaws of the trap open and released the bird. He said a chain attached to the trap was nailed to a tree and that they could not get it loose. I asked him if he could find it again, and he replied that he could.

I met him at his home early Sunday morning, and we walked from there over to the construction site, where he led me straight to the location of the trap. It was a number two, double-spring Oneida leg-hold trap, a popular model used in the fur trade.

With the assistance of the little boy, I carefully searched the area around the half-built house and found another trap with a coon in it. I walked the boy back to his house, complimented him on his powers of observation, and thanked him for getting involved enough to ask questions and call the proper authorities. I told him I would let him know what happened and then returned to the site to dispatch the coon.

It is difficult to release a live coon from a leg-hold trap, and I was pretty sure that the poor beast would be held there until Monday morning when the construction crews returned to work. I wiped out a swath around the sprung trap to make it appear that a struggle had taken place and the animal had escaped. I repeated this with the trap the boy had found and searched around for some place to hide.

The lot had been cleared, but it had a shrub fringe between the house and the street that contained a number of small low-lying palmettos. I cut a stack of fronds from around the outer edge of the lot and brought them to a point at some remove from the house site but with a clear view of the two trap locations. My idea was to arrange the palmetto fronds in a big pile so I could burrow underneath them, a scheme that was about all I could think of given the somewhat open nature of the lot.

I planned to arrive around four thirty the next morning. The gate security had told me that the construction crews generally arrived between six thirty and seven in the morning. Some seventeen hours later I was driving over the bridges to the islands in the middle of a torrential downpour and was wondering how things were going to pan out with the added difficulty of the deluge.

The only rain suit I owned at the time was a heavyweight, bright yellow, commercial-fishing outfit in no way designed for invisibility. I parked my patrol car in the back of a golf-course parking lot some distance from the scene and struggled into my rain gear while sitting in the car. At the construction site I checked the traps again by flashlight and crawled under the nearby stack of palmetto fronds. As I waited there in the darkness, hidden underneath that pile, I was thinking that raindrops falling on palmetto fronds make an awful lot of noise.

Just before first light the rain abated somewhat, and, right on schedule, a pickup truck appeared and drove up to the house. I inched back into my pile as far as I could go without sticking out the back. A man, later identified as Lonnie Williams, exited the truck and threw an empty Styrofoam coffee cup onto the ground. He reached into his truck, grabbed a claw hammer, and walked unsuspectingly in the direction of the first trap. As he approached the first trap, he stood there a moment and seemed to be studying the scene. Kneeling down, he unfastened the trap from the nail, moved toward the second location, and disappeared from my line of sight. Just as

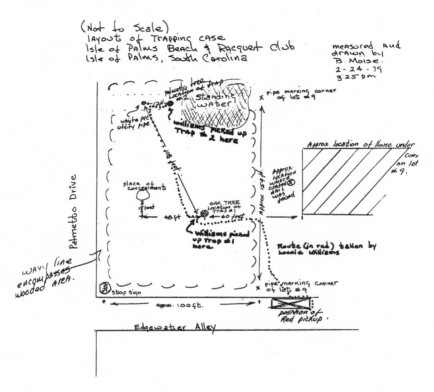

Crime-scene drawing used in a magistrate's court trial for illegal trapping on the Isle of Palms

I was beginning to become a little concerned that he might hide the traps or take another route back to his truck, he reappeared heading straight toward me. I could see that he had the traps in his hands. When he got around thirty feet away, I jumped up, throwing the palmetto fronds aside, and assertively declaimed, "South Carolina Wildlife, Captain, you are under arrest!"

I don't know what he thought when he saw that pile of fronds erupting from the ground to reveal a chrome-yellow form who was making loud noises directed at him. Whatever his thoughts may have been, he screamed like a scalded cat and flung the traps some distance. It later took some effort to retrieve them. I think he realized that there was nowhere to run and no place to hide, so he just stood there breathing heavily as I approached him.

I identified myself again and informed him of the charges: two counts of trapping out of season, two counts of failure to tag his traps, and trapping without a license. As we sat in his truck while I wrote the tickets, he barely spoke a word. I found out later that the game wardens in Dorchester County had been after him for similar offenses for years.

The other trapping incident happened over on Cainhoy Plantation in Berkeley County. I was in my patrol car near Awendaw when I got a radio call from Jake Wilson, one of the plantation managers.

Mr. Wilson asked me to meet him at the plantation gate on Clements Ferry Road. He said he had something he wanted me to see. That section of the county was then isolated and lightly populated. The paved road leading from Highway 41 ended about where I-526 now crosses and became a dirt road that entered a small African American settlement on Thomas Island.

Mr. Wilson explained that he was driving in the back section of the plantation near a tidal creek called Old Joe, a tributary of Yellow House Creek, almost opposite the Naval Weapons Station, and had spotted an animal that appeared to be in distress.

Being a keen observer of the landscape, he had found a possum held firmly in the grip of a leg-hold trap. He took me over to the edge of the creek and showed me where a boat had pulled up to the bank nearby and where the leaves had been disturbed from the bank over to the trap holding the possum. I took a few pictures of the scene. As we were discussing a scenario for setting up surveillance, we heard an approaching boat that sounded as though it was slowing down.

We barely had time to scramble into concealment behind the roots of a large overturned tree. Peeping through the roots, we saw a man exit the boat holding a rifle. He was not an attractive sight. He was wearing quilted overalls and a black stocking cap. He walked toward the trap leaving another man sitting in the boat. We were no more than forty feet away.

I was afraid that the trapper might hear my heart beating. He strode over to the trap, cocked his .22 rifle, and shot the possum. About that time the other man left the boat and walked over to join his partner, who was his son, and helped remove the possum from the trap.

All I could think of was, here I was with a camera in hand, an eyewitness, and the two culprits in camera range holding a trap, a gun, and a dead possum. A case doesn't get any better than that! I jumped from behind the stump and announced, "South Carolina Wildlife, fellows, don't move!" and snapped the picture. Playing a hunch, I told them that I knew where their other traps were, and if one of them went and fetched them, I would just issue them tickets and not lock them up in jail. The son got in the boat and in about a half hour's time brought back fifteen more traps. The father and son were issued tickets for trespassing to trap, failure to tag traps, trapping without a license, and trapping out of season. Since I had a witness, pictures, the traps, and the possum carcass, it was a slam-dunk case.

Until the advent of modern video equipment, it was rare to be able to photograph violators in remote locations with the evidence in hand, especially in such convincing detail. That was a fairly dramatic situation for me and proved the theory that violators have to be lucky every time they go out to break the law, but the game warden has to be lucky only once.

The Duck Hunters

Duck hunting is the annual reenactment of an ancient tradition, one with many devotees along the South Carolina coast and waterways. Although my early experiences with the sport were few, I grew to like duck hunting and duck hunters. Some of my colleagues wryly observed that I really preferred hunting duck hunters, especially the ones who violated the law.

The duck-patrol scene included the salt marshes of the coast and the brackish-to-freshwater rivers that pierce the coastal plain. Scattered around that landscape were managed plantation impoundments, broken rice fields, and riverine swamps. At night many of those areas appear to the uninitiated as formidable darkened mazes. In duck season the gloom may eventually give way to one of those incendiary fall sunrises and reveal the full extent of the coastal panorama.

During twenty-four waterfowl seasons I probably met most of the duck hunters who plied the rice fields, salt marshes, and rivers along the coast. They covered the widest social range imaginable, from wealthy plantation owners to day laborers from the mills around Georgetown. Duck hunting, I think, is one of the real exemplars of American democracy.

The short season of the duck patrols wound my clock every year, and I eagerly looked forward to duck season every fall. I prepared my decrepit, but serviceable, 1976 johnboat and thirty-horsepower Evinrude motor with new camouflage designs and arranged a marsh-reed lining around the sides. Sometimes midway through the season, I repainted the boat in a different

*Camouflaged and
ready for action
on duck patrol in
Hope Creek near
the South Edisto
River*

pattern and replaced the marsh reed with palmetto fronds so I wouldn't be instantly recognizable as I approached coastal duck hunters.

I had found my johnboat sitting forlornly in the fenced lot at the Styx facility in Columbia, which held all the old patrol cars, trucks, and boats awaiting auction. The compound was also used to store equipment seized in night-hunting or drug offenses. I was told that the old johnboat had been confiscated from a convicted night hunter apprehended on the Congaree River.

The story goes that two game wardens returning from a late-night patrol near Orangeburg stopped in the middle of the I-77 bridge over the Congaree to answer the call of nature. As they were standing there, they noticed the glow of a light moving in the treetops at some distance down the river. They finished their business and drove their car to the other side of the bridge. They walked back onto the bridge and were watching for activity down the river when they heard a gunshot coming from the direction of the light.

They knew that the nearest landing was behind them some distance up the river. They began to hear the sound of an outboard engine and soon saw the boat pass under the bridge, running with no lights. The officers ran to their car and headed to the landing upriver. When they arrived they saw an old pickup with an empty boat trailer. They backed out of the landing, keeping their car out of sight.

When the driver came around the bend in the road heading out of the landing, he was suddenly confronted by bright headlights and a flashing blue light. The officers jumped from their car and ordered the man out of his truck. They found a freshly killed doe in the floor of the boat. That violator's boat became my favorite marsh-hen and duck-patrol boat.

It was not uncommon in some areas to be able to see as many as seven boatloads of duck hunters from the position where I was sitting. Sometimes there were hunters to the left and right of me and across the river, all in clear view. I found out early in the game that the best way to see what was actually going on was to be right in the middle of the action. I wore camouflage and had a camouflaged boat. I took along my wonderful Boykin, Belle, and I threw out a set of cork decoys wherever I stopped to set up. I wore a leather lanyard that held several duck calls, a concealed badge, and a small ring magnet. I used the magnet to check shells for lead shot. With the magnet I detected quite a number of steel-shot shells that had been reloaded with lead shot, which had been prohibited because it was toxic to waterfowl. A few hunters went to the trouble of reloading shells with lead shot in the belief that it was more effective than steel shot. When that little magnet dangling from the lanyard didn't kiss the crimped end of the shell, it was time to break out the ticket book.

The most common duck-hunting violation is shooting before or after legal hours. Except for the early teal season, the legal time begins one half hour before sunrise and concludes at sunset. Perhaps the competition generated by the sheer numbers of duck hunters is the reason for the frequency of this violation; there were a lot of people hunting very few ducks.

On duck patrols I launched my boat between three and three thirty in the morning. Most of the landings I used were private, where I could leave my trailer and patrol car without fear of vandalism. I had quickly discovered that marked patrol vehicles left at public landings were a target for angry duck hunters who had been given tickets, and some of my old cars and trucks bore the marks of their displeasure. One time an obviously disgruntled hunter climbed on the hood of my car and committed an unspeakable nuisance on my windshield. There were people gathered around my car gawking at it as I appeared back at the landing. They scattered like a covey of quail as I stepped out of the boat. From then on I took measures to hide my car out of sight.

Sometimes when I left the landing well before sunrise I motored straight to a spot where I had seen concentrations of hunters the day before or to an area where I had heard early shooting the previous morning. Frequently I just crossed the river to a point opposite the landing. There I concealed the boat behind stands of marsh grass and waited to see where most of the boats leaving the landing were heading. Then I got in among them. I found that spending a little time observing and listening could tell me a lot about what type of hunter I was going to be checking.

It was always amazing to me how the stillness of the morning before the arrival of the first boats at the landing could concentrate one's thoughts. I often imagined omens of a good morning to come on sighting the occasional meteor flashing across the predawn sky. I replayed old encounters and thought of different ways that they could have been handled. Sometimes I lay back against my engine cover and just snoozed. On hearing the distant rattle of vehicles and boat trailers coming down the dirt road to the landing, I went to full alert.

When I was working out of Willtown Bluff Landing, I always looked forward to visiting with retired banker Hugh Lane after the conclusion of an early morning duck patrol. When I arrived at his back porch, he was usually in the kitchen of his 1809-vintage home, in his bathrobe reading the paper, and he would call for me to come on in when I tapped on the door. He would invite me to make a cup of instant coffee in his microwave and was always eager to hear of the morning's activities on the river. Mr. Lane was an imposing man, and even though he had become a little creaky with age, he still had a sharp mind. I admired his genuine conservation ethic and was deeply impressed with the fact that not only did he think and talk about conservation issues, but he made them a reality.

He was one of the frontrunners of the Ashepoo-Combahee-Edisto (ACE) Basin conservation initiative, an exemplary land-conservation project that combined the efforts of private landowners, private conservation organizations, and state and federal agencies. If Mr. Lane was convinced that a project was worthy, he proceeded with getting the people and the resources together to make it happen.

A johnboat running through a narrow creek in the Santee Delta

Even more noteworthy, he passed on his sportsmanship and his land ethic to all his children, who have in turn been deeply involved in many noteworthy and productive conservation efforts locally, nationally, and internationally. They are passing the torch on to their children. Mr. Lane died at the age of ninety-one in the spring of 2005.

One of my last magistrate's court jury trials involved an incident of early shooting, which took place near Mr. Lane's plantation. My written account of the event, which was used in the pretrial hearing, describes the issue at trial:

> In the pre-dawn hours of November twenty-seventh, 1998, a small boat, later determined to be carrying defendant "A" and his shooting companion, "B," came down the Edisto River from the direction of Willtown Bluff Landing and took a position near the rice field dike of Willtown Bluff Plantation on the east side of the river.
>
> I was positioned against the Dodge Plantation dike on the west side of the river directly opposite the boat occupied by the defendant and his companion.
>
> I saw and heard multiple shots from the boat occupied by the defendant and his companion. I saw muzzle flashes every time they fired their

shotguns. Their shots commenced at twenty-seven minutes after six A.M. and continued for four minutes, at which time I began approaching their boat.

Legal shooting time is one half hour before "legal" sunrise, which is published in newspapers, the Federal Migratory Bird Regulations and other publications as well.

One half hour before sunrise in that area came at thirty-five minutes after six A.M.

My watch is accurate to within five seconds of the U.S. Naval Observatory time. I synchronize with them as many as two times a week and had just synchronized with them days before.

Upon approaching the defendant and his companion, I identified myself and inquired if either knew what the legal shooting time was.

Neither professed to know.

The defendant's companion said they shot after hearing the earlier shots up the river, which had been going on some five minutes earlier.

As I was checking them for other requirements such as licenses, stamps, plug and steel shot, my wrist watch alarm set to the legal time began alarming. It was then thirty-five minutes after six. I informed them, "THAT" is the legal shooting time.

This law has been in effect since 1918 to prevent the killing of waterfowl, which cannot be accurately identified because of restricted visibility due to darkness.

Proper identification is necessary because of the many restrictions imposed on taking certain kinds of ducks.

At no time during my encounter with the defendant or his shooting companion or during several subsequent hearings has either ever denied they shot.

Most of the time early-shooting cases were pretty simple and straightforward as this case report shows. There was occasional confusion when hunters went by the time of sunrise published in the Charleston paper because, in the area south of Charleston, official sunrise occurs four minutes later than in Charleston and the area northward from that city. It was because of the time issue that I ensured the accuracy of my watch to the millisecond using the U.S. Naval Observatory time service.

If a hunter said that he had relied on the time printed in the paper and if he had not shot more than five minutes early, I wrote him a warning ticket. If a hunter made no such claim—and especially if he was not in possession of a watch and claimed he was relying on other shots up the river —he got a real ticket, as was case on that early November morning.

The hunters I caught that morning were summoned to appear in magistrate's court in Mount Pleasant in mid-December. When I arrived on the date set, I found that one of the hunters (identified in my statement as the "companion") had come by the magistrate's office and paid the fine, indicating that he did not want to contest the charges. The other hunter (identified in my statement as "A" or "the defendant") said that he wanted a jury trial. This was only the first of many months of delay.

In early January 1999 Lee Cope, an attorney representing the defendant, wrote to the East Cooper magistrate requesting a change of venue. In late January a change of venue hearing was conducted, and Mr. Cope's request was granted. The trial was switched to a magistrate on Edisto Island.

In February Mr. Cope requested a pretrial hearing, which was set for a date in early March. When I appeared, I thought that I was merely going to be required to present what evidence I had against his client. My statement contained all the facts, which I recited to the judge.

Mr. Cope said that his client had been charged with "taking waterfowl before legal shooting time," but that he hadn't actually taken anything. The attorney said he had checked the code section his client was charged under in the South Carolina Code of Laws, and all it said was that the state adopted in whole the Federal Migratory Bird Treaty Act into state law. Thus, Mr. Cope said that there was no specific reference in the South Carolina code to "taking before legal shooting time" and that he wanted me to produce the law then and there, or the case should be dismissed. In a sudden brain-numbing moment, I pictured my whole case going down the tubes because I had overlooked the obvious. It never occurred to me that the existence of the law would be challenged, or that anyone could possibly think he could shoot all night and not be charged until he actually hit something.

Mr. Cope made an assertive argument, and I thought for a moment that he actually had the judge won over. Almost blithering, I explained to the judge that it was common knowledge that its was illegal to shoot ducks in the dark, and I certainly didn't realize that I was going to have to come to his court and have to prove the existence of a law prohibiting it.

I told him that there were published definitions of what the word *taking* meant in this context and that there were well-defined and specific laws regulating how waterfowl could be hunted, including the specified legal shooting time. The judge said he was going to take Mr. Cope's request under advisement and told us to send him documents to frame the charge the defendant was facing. Several days later I sent the judge a package of information, including copies of the state and federal laws regulating the taking of waterfowl, as well as a letter framing the charges. I wrote:

> Dear Judge Bligen, this comes in response to your order to frame the charge pending against Mr. "A" since November 27, 1998.
> My recommendation is that Mr. "A" should have the charge against him read as follows:
>
>> Mr. ["A"] is charged with taking waterfowl before legal shooting hours on November 27, 1998 between six twenty-seven A.M. and six thirty-one A.M. (legal shooting time was six thirty-five A.M.), under the South Carolina Statute 50–11–10, which states that the Federal Migratory Bird Treaty Act and its implementing regulations are the law of this state.
>>
>> The implementing regulations are described in the Code of Federal Regulations (50–CFR-20) and the shooting hours specifically in 20:23, where it is stated, "No person shall take migratory birds except during the hours open to shooting as described in subpart K which states in part that hunting of migratory birds is prohibited unless a state establishes regulatory schedules for seasons, daily bag limits and shooting hours."
>>
>> The definition of "Taking" for the purposes of 50–CFR-20 and S.C. 50–11–10 is contained in the expanded version of the Federal Code. . . .
>>
>> I have asked that a copy of it be sent to you from our legal department in Columbia. It will be sent without comment and it should clarify the legally accepted definition of the word "Taking" as used in the charge.
>>
>> I am also sending a copy of it as well as a copy of this communication to Mr. ["A"]'s attorney.

In late March the judge denied the motion to dismiss the charge and granted the defendant's request to have a jury trial, which took place on a blistering July afternoon in a small courtroom on Edisto Island. Our case was simple. I testified to what I had seen that morning, almost nine months before. The defense lawyer quizzed me about some of my statements regarding the accuracy of my watch. How, he asked, could I allege that I knew precisely at what times his client had fired his gun?

Mr. Cope had apparently forgotten statements made during the pretrial hearing regarding the accuracy of my watch. In response to his question, I reiterated that, since it was a matter of law, time was important and that during the duck season I frequently synchronized my watch with the U.S. Naval Observatory time service. I added that I had the long-distance phone records to prove it.

It became a little sticky at times because I had to avoid any mention of the defendant's friend having been in the boat with him, nor could I reveal that his friend had pled guilty to the charges in the same incident. Both sides had been deftly skirting around the issue, until I was asked how many shots had been fired. Then my truthful answer revealed that there had been two people in the boat. My reply caused some quizzical looks among a few of the jurors, but it didn't lead anywhere. Mr. Cope quickly steered the questioning down other avenues.

When the jury left to deliberate, the only real issue was whether I was lying or the defendant was lying. The jury was out for slightly more than forty-five minutes and returned with a verdict of guilty. Whew!

Until the late 1980s there were significant numbers of bay ducks: blue bills and canvasbacks, that were drawn to the large bodies of open water in the South Edisto River between Jehossee Island and Bear Island, which had been an attractive area for generations of duck hunters. Several elaborate blinds had been built overlooking those stretches on the fringes of marsh around the tip of Jehossee Island, known as the "fishtail" or "whale's tail." The blinds had been standing there long before I began working the area.

I could invariably count on finding a number of serious duck hunters along the river during the worst weather conditions. In fact the worse the weather the better it was for duck hunters. Well before daylight on a stormy morning, I launched my boat at Dahoo Landing and traveled down to where the Intracoastal Waterway intersects the Edisto River. I sat against the marsh edge there to see if any boats would come by and was not disappointed, for at least four buzzed by in the darkness, almost completely obscured by the rain and fog.

After a few more boats had run by, I pushed the boat off the bank and ran down the river in the direction several passing boats had taken. I found them near Alligator Creek, across the river from Raccoon Island. After checking them. I bucked wind-driven sleet back up river to find the sources of the shots I had been hearing in the vicinity of Jehossee. The appearance of a large array of decoys signaled an occupied blind. What happened next is written on the back of a photograph taken in 2003 by Robert Hutto of Orangeburg, an occupant of the blind. The picture is of the forlorn remnants of the old blind. Mr. Hutto wrote:

> Upper river blind built in October 1968, by Pat Fomby and Robert Hutto at Jehossee Island. Used until 1993. Diving ducks played out about 1986. At least one hundred fifty to two hundred divers were killed each season. Would not hunt until Dec. fifteenth each year. One-day hunt best total was forty-three diving ducks by three gunners in 1980 or 1981. Charlie Williams, Bob Varn and Robert Hutto were gunning. Along came Ben Moïse and Belle out of the rain. After license check, it was discovered we were using lead shot. When all the tickets were written (in the rain) Charlie Williams had two tickets, Bob Varn had one ticket and Robert Hutto had none. I got mine the following day three miles away from where we were hunting.

I had their licenses in hand and was attempting to write the appropriate tickets in the driving rain. A few of their licenses as well as my tickets began to disintegrate from being soaked through, even as I tried to shield them under my outspread rain jacket. In the confusion I wrote two tickets for the same offense to Mr. Williams, none for Mr. Hutto, and one for Mr. Varn. I handed over the sodden little stack of paper and departed.

I remember coming out of the fog that morning, through the middle of their decoys, and up to the front of their blind, where we had a short but lively conversation before I flashed my badge and began checking their guns. I was surprised to see Mr. Hutto in another blind the next day and, since I had discovered my error after I had dried out my ticket book in a microwave, I issued him the one he was owed. Just before the court date the magistrate received this note from one of the defendants:

> Dear Judge Simmons:
>
> I am writing this letter on behalf of myself Robert Varn, Charlie Williams and Robert Hutto.
>
> During a hunting trip on Dec. thirtieth we were checked by officer Ben Moïse. We all had our licenses, duck stamps and plugged guns, however we did have in our possession steel and lead shot. Subsequently we were given tickets for possession of lead shot in a steel shot only county. We asked Mr. Moïse what the fine would be. He said that the minimum he could charge us was fifty dollars each. He also told us that

if we came to court you would probably reduce the fine to twenty-five dollars each. Prior plans make it impossible for us to attend your court. We ask that you would please reduce our fines. I don't know how much you know about steel shot versus lead shot, but it is a very controversial law with hunters, but we have learned our lesson and were checked again on January first and had our steel shot which sells for seventeen dollars a box vs. eight dollars or nine dollars per box for lead shot.

There was a mix up in the tickets written by Officer Moïse. It was raining and still a little dark while he was writing. He wrote two tickets for Charles Williams and none for Robert Hutto. Included in this letter are tickets for myself and Charles Williams I am sending two checks, one for seventy-five dollars and one for one hundred fifty dollars. Please tear up whichever one you decide not to use and call me collect at the above telephone number to tell me which one to void.

The magistrate's courts were informal in those days, and in our discussion of the case the judge decided to fine Mr. Varn, Mr. Williams, and Mr. Hutto, who had already sent his money in, the lesser amount.

There were probably not more than two dozen permanent blinds scattered around the salt marshes of South Carolina. I found them in the Dale Marsh between Highway 17 and St. Helena Sound and along the South Edisto. I also found several behind Otter, Pine, and Spring islands and a few in the brackish marshes up the Cooper and Wando rivers.

There is no tradition respecting blind ownership as there is in North Carolina and Maryland and no such thing as riparian hunting rights in the marshes of South Carolina. Many river hunters believe that marshes are free and open and that, regardless of who built a blind, whoever gets to it first may use it. This attitude often led to confrontations.

Many years ago Penrod Simmons and a friend constructed an elaborate blind in the marshes of Yellow House Creek, a tributary of the Cooper River. They arrived one morning to find their blind occupied and a large array of decoys in the water around it. Mr. Simmons called over to the men standing in his blind that the blind was his and that he had come to use it. The hunters responded that he didn't own the marsh, that it was a free country, that they had gotten there first, and they weren't moving. Anybody who knew Simmons would have known immediately that those hunters had just made a serious mistake.

Well known for having a short fuse, Mr. Simmons uncapped one of the six-gallon gas cans in his boat and poured it into the water. The flooding

Throwing out a bait scrape from a log bridge in a swamp near Jacksonboro, South Carolina. The picture was staged, but the scrape came back with corn in it, and the violators were later caught.

tide conveniently floated the gasoline into the interloper's decoy spread and around the blind. The hunters yelled, "Hey, what in the hell are you doing?" Mr. Simmons shouted back, "I built the damn thing and I can damn sure burn it down!" It was reported that the hunters leapt out of the blind into their boat and got away with only half their decoys as they fled the scene just ahead of an impressive conflagration.

I made regular rounds to the blinds I knew about and threw out my bait scrape (a square, basketlike scoop) in a wide arc around them, dredging the bottom for bait. I also examined the shell casings found in and around blinds to determine if any lead shot was being used. The number of shell cases was also a good indicator of the amount of waterfowl activity in the vicinity of the blind.

If I discovered any lead-shot shells, I made a follow-up visit on the next hunting day. From experience I knew that I had to plan my approach to the blind carefully. Often when I was recognized, I heard the sounds of shells being jacked out of shotguns or the "plop" of the shells hitting the water.

One morning as I approached a blind across from Block Island on the South Edisto, I spotted a boot-clad leg sticking down in the water behind it. Pulling up in the marsh grass beside the blind, I waded through shin-deep water to the back of the blind, groped around in the muddy depth, and brought to light one of the two black ducks the hunter had killed that morning. I also found half a box of 12-gauge lead-shot shells, which happened to be identical to the freshly spent shot casings lying on the floor of the blind and floating in the water around it. I could hear the moans of the occupant inside the blind each time a new item of contraband was discovered. He was moaning even more when he saw that pencil jump out of my shirt pocket.

A similar event played out at the end of Cane Island in the North Santee River. I was running out in the river when I saw and heard muzzle blasts fired from a boat blind. I saw one bird fall from the air and land in the water right in the middle of their decoys. I quickly glanced at my watch and saw that it was still around nine minutes until the legal shooting time. While guiding my johnboat over to pick up the dead duck, I saw one of the men in the duck boat stand up and shuck his shells from his gun right into the water. As I was retrieving the duck, he got out of his boat and stomped around in an obvious effort to mash the shells down into the mud.

I was more than a little peeved at his behavior and became even more so when he started offering me a bunch of lame excuses about what he was doing. He said that he had unloaded his shotgun as a "safety measure" and that he was out stomping around in the mud "to stretch his legs." I knew that more than one participant could play the "aggravation game."

I demanded their guns, licenses, and duck stamps and began methodically examining them. Then I asked to see their boat registration and safety equipment, which required a lengthy process of rooting through the camouflage material and pulling it out of various boat compartments. Then I returned my attention to their guns, putting shells into the magazines and slowly extracting them. While I had their guns in hand, I copied their serial numbers down on my little notepad.

Continuing in that excruciatingly tedious manner, I pulled out my ticket book and slowly filled out a ticket for shooting before legal time. The

Admiring a wooden greenwing-teal decoy carved by Tom Beckham (right) of Cane Island Duck Club, North Santee River. Beckham's mother also carves decoys.

intervention lasted for probably more than thirty minutes. The beginning minutes of the legal shooting time came and went, and flight after flight of ducks—stirred into movement by other hunters' gunshots—passed undisturbed over their blind. To say that they were seething would be an understatement. I could clearly tell that they were not to become my friends.

I checked a good many hunters that morning in North Santee Bay, as well as some of the Cane Island Club members who were coming in from their flooded fields. Almost five hours later I returned to the scene of my first encounter that morning. Where they had been floating in a boat earlier that morning was now completely exposed by the low tide. I felt around deep in the mud every place I saw a foot print and managed to come up with two unfired lead-shot shotgun shells as well as two matching spent shells.

I had earlier performed an autopsy on the dead duck and found several lead shot pellets lodged against the breastbone. I washed the mud and salt water off the shells when I got back to the Santee Gun Club, sprayed them with WD-40 and stored them, along with the extracted lead pellets, in a ziplock plastic bag that joined the mounting pile of evidentiary paraphernalia in my truck.

About a week later Georgetown officer Stanley Vick called me over the radio to inform me that he was writing "my friend" for shooting early near Brown Island on the South Santee. It was the same man I had written for early shooting near Cane Island. I asked Officer Vick to check his gun and read me the serial number.

The serial number he read to me was from the same gun the hunter had been using the week before. In a migratory-bird violation, it was legally permissible for game wardens to seize a gun used in a violation and hold it as evidence until the trial. I asked Officer Vick to seize the gun and give the man a receipt for it.

The following Monday morning, I carried the gun and shells to the South Carolina Law Enforcement Division (SLED) crime lab in Columbia and asked one of their technicians to see if a match could be determined between the extractor marks on the edges of the shells I had found in the marsh mud and the extractor on the gun we had seized.

About ten days later the SLED technician reported that he had linked the shells to the seized gun. When the man came to court on the charge of early shooting, he was issued an additional ticket for shooting ducks with lead shot.

In 1997 I used the services of the SLED lab again in a case against that same hunter, who was charged with "trespassing to hunt waterfowl." It was a big complex case, which began on a duck patrol in the same general area where I had caught the man before. I had periodically heard shots coming from the direction of the back dike at Moreland Plantation on the Santee Delta, an area that I knew could be accessed only by Atchison Creek, a narrow, winding watercourse bordered by tall reeds, that entered from the North Santee River. Moreland was accessible only by boat and was hunted only several times a year by its owners, who were from North Carolina and up-state South Carolina and were members of the Santee Gun Club.

The Moreland clubhouse was built within the circular brick walls of one of the remaining antebellum storm towers that formerly adorned many of the coastal rice fields. The towers were twenty to thirty feet in diameter, capped with conical roofs, and originally had floors elevated ten feet above ground level. The ostensible purpose of these storm towers was to protect the slaves who toiled in the rice fields from hurricane-driven floods. The ruins of most of the towers were long ago pillaged for their bricks.

One afternoon while checking out Atchison Creek, I noticed several areas where palmetto-frond boat blinds had been set up against the wall of marsh reeds. Such blinds were not an unusual sight, and they were sited in legal locations. Further up the creek, however, I observed a couple of spots that appeared to be entry points of well-beaten trails leading from the water's edge through the tall marsh grass over toward the Moreland impoundment. One path led right past a "No Trespassing" sign. Those paths appeared to lead to trouble.

Following each path through the marsh up to the dike, I found a profusion of spent shells on both the inner and outer edges of the dike and along the top of it. I collected the shells in zip-lock bags with tags indicating where and when they were found. I repeated this routine at least two more times as the duck season progressed. I decided with one week left to dedicate the remaining days of the season to catching the trespassers on Moreland.

I entered Santee River early in the afternoon, and drove around to Atchison Creek. After a little exploration, I found a deep side creek where I could sit unseen, not too far from the entrance to one of the well-trodden paths. Several hours later I began to hear the sounds of several outboard engines coming up the creek. One stopped about a hundred yards away in the wide expanse of water where two smaller creeks came together. The other boat continued running and came to a stop not seventy-five feet from where I was hiding. I could hear this boat idling, the sound of decoys hitting the water, and the hunters' conversation as they brushed their boat over with palmetto fronds.

One problem I dealt with constantly was the numerous leaks in my 1976-vintage johnboat. It was so bad that I had an electric bilge pump installed, which more often than not was running just as fast as the engine. As Belle and I sat there listening to the muffled conversations of the nearby hunters, the bilge pump suddenly started running with a buzzing noise that probably could be heard on the moon. I had manually switched on the pump several times earlier during my wait, as the water level rose on the deck inside my boat, but I had completely forgotten about the automatic feature that engaged the pump when the water rose to a certain level. The conversation in the duck boat immediately stopped. A moment later I heard, "Is that you Mr. Ben?" I quickly realized that I had to give some thought to implementing "Plan B."

The next day I towed one of the old cypress skiffs owned by the Santee Gun Club across the river, hauled it over the Moreland dike, and placed it in the canal that ran around the interior perimeter of the flooded impoundment, which extended from river to river across the width of the delta. For the next four afternoons I tied my johnboat to a dock piling in a small creek near the Moreland camp and poled the skiff through the canal around to the opposite side, close to where the illegal entries were occurring. The first three afternoons were completely uneventful and the season was fast running out.

I was on location in the canal on the last day of the duck season, January 20, 1997, when I began to hear boats arriving in the creek from the river. I heard one slow to a stop further back while three ran past where I was sitting inside the impoundment and continued some three hundred yards.

It is difficult to describe the feeling I got when my plan finally seemed to be coming together. I could feel the tension. I was on full alert, totally tuned in to every sound. I knew that each movement I made would have to be slow and deliberate to avoid making sounds that would give away my presence. The marsh reed growing on the edge of the canal was dry and brittle. I had to inch through it, looking carefully to avoid stepping on the jumbles of stalks.

It took me more than forty-five minutes to move a hundred yards. I knew that I had a hot case because, just before I had stepped out of the skiff, I noticed in the distance what appeared to be several decoys floating in the inner perimeter canal. For a moment I got a little worried because I heard two boats start up and come back down the creek headed out toward the river, but I remembered three boats had earlier passed me.

I began to hear a few gunshots down the dike. The sun was sinking lower on the horizon, and I knew that I was going to have to think fast because the hunters could easily escape in their boat. I had walked to where the top of the dike was a little more open and was able to move a little faster. As I closed the distance to the shooters, I saw a man with his back to me, holding a gun, and standing atop the dike. I also heard a couple of volleys coming from a little further down the dike. The first man I encountered was startled when I walked up behind him and said in a firm but low voice, "South Carolina Wildlife, Captain, you are under arrest and don't say a word!"

Speaking barely above a whisper, I asked for all the shotgun shells he had in his pocket and directed him to hand me his gun. I also took his hunting license, leaving him with firm instructions to stay right where he was until I called for him and reiterating my warning about not saying a word. That first encounter was with Bruce Taylor of Georgetown.

Moving briskly, I approached the other shooters in the deep shadows of the fading sun. As I arrived, holding Taylor's shotgun, a man sitting on the outer edge of the dike between two children called out, "How'd you do?" He was genuinely surprised when I replied, "South Carolina Wildlife, you are under arrest for trespassing!" I demanded his license, shotgun, and shells and called for the other hunter to join us. As I studied the man's name on the license, Charles Bass of Georgetown, it seemed familiar, but I couldn't quite remember why. It was only later I realized we had met before.

Stepping down the embankment while carefully avoiding the fresh muddy footprints on the edge of the canal, I found the three mallard decoys I had seen earlier. They were expensive burlap-covered solid decoys. I dragged them in and saw that one had a nameplate with the name and phone number of my hunter stamped on it. Yet he denied knowing the decoys were there in front of him.

Since it was getting dark and I had neglected to bring a flashlight, I told them to take the children who were with them home, but I was going to keep their licenses, guns, and decoys with me and would meet them in two hours in the parking lot at a filling station south of Georgetown. I also instructed each of the men to come with five hundred dollars in cash or check to satisfy the amount of the bond.

Since it is both unprofessional and rude to exult in the face of another's misfortune, I waited until well after I had heard their boat depart before I allowed myself to give voice to a brief moment of celebration. I then carried my armload of evidence back down the dike to the cypress skiff and poled back across the delta in the mounting darkness.

I was so pumped up that I wasn't even tired when I finally got to the camp and began loading everything in my johnboat for the trip back across the river. As I arrived at the Santee Gun Club landing, several of the staff there were preparing to launch a boat to come out looking for me. They helped me trailer my boat and offload the guns and decoys into the trunk of my car as I hurriedly recounted the events of the afternoon.

I told them that I was to meet the men I had caught in forty-five minutes and that I would fill them in on the rest of the details in the morning. Arriving at the filling-station parking lot a little early, I took the opportunity to write down the details of everything I could remember. I went back to the trunk and recorded the make, model, and serial numbers of the guns, and noted which shells came from which gun. Later those notes came in handy.

When the men arrived, I wrote each a ticket for "trespassing to hunt waterfowl," an enhanced-penalty violation, which carries a minimum penalty of a five-hundred-dollar fine and a one-year suspension of hunting privileges. They each gave me a check for five hundred dollars, and they departed with my admonition that they should appear in court at the date and time set, or their bonds would be forfeited.

A few weeks later when I arrived at the magistrate's office in Georgetown, both defendants asked the judge for a jury trial—not what I expected to hear. I carefully explained to them that I was prepared to offer them the opportunity to plead guilty in magistrate's court and just forfeit the bonds they had posted. The maximum penalty that could be imposed for their violation, which included six months' imprisonment, exceeded the jurisdiction of a magistrate's court. Therefore, while a magistrate could accept their guilty plea, a trial would have to be conducted in General Sessions Court. By insisting on a jury trial they were opening up the possibility of facing more severe penalties. I warned them that they should give serious consideration to what they were asking for.

The defendants were becoming more annoying by the minute, demanding the return of their guns. I told them they would get their guns back after the case was settled, and they could either settle the issue now or it could be settled later. Realizing that they were not of a frame of mind to be reasonable, I told them to call me later about their decision. They were not persuaded and left a message the next day at the Georgetown law-enforcement office that they wanted their day in court.

At the time no case of trespassing to hunt waterfowl had been prosecuted in General Sessions Court. Just about all the cases on that charge had been handled in magistrate's court, where the defendants simply pled guilty and paid the five-hundred-dollar fine. When a defendant balked over pleading guilty because the penalty included being suspended from hunting for a year, it was not unusual for officers to reduce the charge to one of simple trespass, which carried a smaller fine, no suspension, and a lot less paperwork.

At that juncture I was in no humor to play games and made a trip over to the solicitor's office in Georgetown, where I spoke to an attractive young woman who introduced herself as Elise Crosby, a Fifteenth Circuit assistant solicitor. As she questioned me about the details of the cases, she soon proved to be as smart as she was good looking. She said that she would present the facts of the cases to Solicitor Ralph J. Wilson and get back in touch with me.

About two weeks passed before she called for me to come by her office, where she explained that the solicitor did not think there was any way in hell they could ever get a conviction on a couple of "good old boys" on a duck-hunting violation in Georgetown County. He said that the work it would take to bring the case to court would be a complete waste of their time.

After devoting a few moments of thought to that unforeseen assessment, I asked her if she thought it might be possible to take the cases before the grand jury. A grand jury is drawn from the same population as a trial jury, and I thought that, if they could be convinced that the evidence was good enough for indictments, then we might stand an equally good chance at a jury trial. I told her that if the grand jury did not give us indictments, I would settle for reduced charges in magistrate's court.

She said she would run that idea by Solicitor Wilson. Meanwhile I went to my friend David Schwacke, the Ninth Circuit solicitor in Charleston, with whom I already had some experience, and asked him to call Mr. Wilson and inform him that I was not just some damn fool game warden who would likely waste his time. About ten days later I got a call from Ms. Crosby with the news that we were taking the cases before the grand jury. She asked me to come by her office the next day.

I had already taken the two shotguns and my collection of spent shells to the SLED lab to see if they could find any matches. I carried an impressive array of items into her office the next morning. I had drawings, charts, narratives, and the decoys. I also had a letter from one of the plantation owners stating that neither of the defendants had permission to hunt on their land.

We went over all the details and outlined an orderly presentation of the facts. After I went before the grand jury the following week, they gave us the indictments we sought. We were going to "big court" on the case of *State of South Carolina v. Charles Bass and Bruce Taylor.*

Mr. Bass and Mr. Taylor had hired Douglas Thornton, a Georgetown lawyer, to represent them. He was at their side when I read the charges on the indictments and served them their arrest warrants. Mr. Bass became testy and again demanded that I return his shotgun. Mr. Thornton indicated that he wanted to set up a discovery hearing. I explained to him that he should make arrangements with Ms. Crosby.

At a discovery hearing the defendant's lawyer gets to see all the prosecutor's evidence against the defendant. I had been through the discovery process before, and knew what to expect. I had also found that discovery hearings were a good opportunity for evidence overload. I presented so many little packages of evidence that Mr. Thornton didn't have a clue as to what our focus would be. I did notice a reaction from Mr. Bass when I said that the green shotgun shells on the table in front of me had come from his gun.

The trial date was set for several months later at the county courthouse in Georgetown. Before the trial the assistant solicitor and I went over the facts and the evidence on at least three different occasions. I had drawn a large diagram of the scene and had taken photographs of the beaten path from the creek through the marsh, the "No Trespassing" sign, and the area visible from atop the dike.

We figured that the most conclusive piece of evidence was the decoy with Bass's name and phone number on it. Pretty much everything else was going to hinge on the strength of my testimony. I already knew that the shells I had picked up along the plantation dike earlier in the season, some of which had been matched to a gun owned by Bass, could not be presented as evidence because they didn't have any direct relationship to the act of trespass on the day he was charged.

The "big court" experience can be quite daunting. With opposing lawyers, larger juries, bailiffs, clerks, and generally a room full of observers, it is a whole lot more formal than the magistrates' courts. This case had attracted a good bit of attention, and there were an unusual number of local lawyers watching the proceedings, which finally began just before noon on January 7, 1998.

We had our pile of evidence on the table in front of us, as well as an easel to display my large diagram and aerial photograph. Mr. Bass and Mr. Taylor had brought with them four large mesh bags packed with decoys. The jury was empaneled. When Circuit Judge James Edward Lockemy of Dillon, entered, the court came to order.

The trial began with Ms. Crosby's and the defense lawyer's opening statements. Thornton told the jury that his clients had never trespassed, that I had called them up out of the marsh, where they had a right to be, and had written them tickets for being on the dike only after I had called them there. I kept eyeing the jurors to see if they were swallowing any of that hogwash, and they did not appear to be noticeably moved by Mr. Thornton's statement.

I gave testimony about the facts of the cases under direct questioning by Assistant Solicitor Crosby. All the exhibits were marked as I brought them forward. They included the two shotguns, still in the wrappers labeled "SLED Crime Lab"; the shotgun shells I had taken out of their guns when they were apprehended; the three decoys; my large hand-drawn diagram; photographic enlargements and a big aerial photograph of the Santee Delta showing the plantation between the North and South Santee rivers and the creek that ran in behind it.

Ms. Crosby asked me questions about where the defendants were when I confronted them and what they were doing there. She asked me to point out the spots on the aerial photograph as well as on the diagram. I explained the enlarged photographs of the plantation dike, which showed the green buckets I had placed on the spots where each of the two men had been standing. I told the jury that the defendants were not in the marsh; they were fully on the Moreland dike, where they did not have permission to be, and holding shotguns with shot loads consistent with those used for waterfowl hunting.

As I mentioned the shot loads, I introduced into evidence the green and red shotgun shells I had extracted from their guns and out of their pockets. The decoys were also introduced and marked as exhibits. I pointed out on the diagram where they had been placed in the canal and where each of the defendants had been standing. I also mentioned the fact, as I turned one of the decoys over to show the jury, that the decoy had a metal name tag fastened to its keel. Ms. Crosby asked me if the tag had a name printed on it. I responded that it did. She then asked me to read the tag. I read the name and Georgetown address of Charlie Bass. As I did, I noticed a visible stir among the jurors.

At that point, some two hours into the trial, Judge Lockemy, called for a recess. As Ms. Crosby and I sat comparing notes, a long parade of orange-clad prisoners filed past the judge's bench to plead guilty to sundry felonies, apparently as a result of plea bargains. Before our jury returned, Judge Lockemy, addressing the defense lawyer and the assistant solicitor, said that he could not believe that we were wasting the court's time on a duck case and that we ought to find a way to settle it. Then he adjourned the trial until the following morning.

I knew that I was going to be cross-examined by Thornton the next morning, and the word was out in the legal and law-enforcement community. When I arrived, there were even more spectators than the day before. Before the jury was seated, the judge reiterated his opinion that the case ought to be settled. One of the defendants blurted out that he wasn't guilty, however, and the second day of the trial began.

Before Mr. Thornton was turned loose on me, Ms. Crosby went back over some of the details of my testimony the day before, just to make sure that they were fresh in the jury's mind. I knew I should respond to the defense lawyer's queries directly and without elaboration, and I should look at the jurors when I answered. It is never a good idea to give more details than are asked for.

Mr. Thornton walked me through the scene of the encounter and directed me to describe my actions at the time. Handing me one of the exhibits, a shotgun shell I had taken from Mr. Taylor, Mr. Thornton asked me to read the inscriptions printed on the red plastic casing. I read "Winchester, three inch magnum, number four steel."

He then said that in my testimony, I had reported that the shell in evidence had come from the gun of defendant Taylor, the first person I had approached. Mr. Thornton picked up the shotgun, still sealed in the clear SLED Lab envelope, saying to the jury that I had just testified that the shell I had described had come out of the gun he was holding. He walked over to the jury box holding out the gun and said that he was going to show them that I was wrong (that is, lying) because the shell I was holding would not fit in that gun.

Mr. Thornton began removing the gun from the envelope, an act that set the judge astir. Mr. Thornton explained to Judge Lockemy that to prove his assertion that I was wrong, he would have to have me put a shell into the gun. The judge didn't like the idea of having a loaded gun in his courtroom and insisted that the demonstration be effected with the gun barrel pointed out of a nearby window.

As a bailiff was struggling to raise the large window sash, I was handed the semi-automatic gun, which was wrapped with black electrician's tape from forward of the trigger guard halfway up the length of the barrel. I was directed to read the inscriptions stamped on the receiver of the shotgun. I read "Sears, Model 300, 12 gauge." He asked, "Isn't there a number on the back of the receiver?" I responded, "2¾."

He asked if I knew what "2¾" inscription meant. I said that it meant the length of the chamber. I could sense the mounting tension as he exclaimed to the jury that I had earlier testified "under oath" that this particular shell was removed from the gun I was holding. Then he asked me if that was correct. I affirmed that it was.

He motioned me over to the open window. The jury's attention was riveted on my every move. Mr. Thornton asked me to load the shell in the gun. As I shoved the shell in the magazine, he was looking over his shoulder, telling the jury that the shell would not fit. On seeing the shell disappear into the gun, Mr. Thornton momentarily paused in his steady commentary, seeming a bit confused, and said, "Oh, now load the shell in the chamber."

I pulled the bolt back and let it go. The shell fully loaded into the chamber. Mr. Thornton stepped over to examine the gun and saw that the bolt was firmly forward. He looked genuinely confused and asked me how that could be. I said that it was probably because the chamber and barrel assembly were not original to the gun. We repeated the demonstration and produced the same result. Mr. Thornton seemed almost addled, and I could see that a few of the jurors were smiling over his self-made dilemma. Shortly after that debacle, he even caused some of the jurors to laugh when he explained that the 2¾-inch shells I had taken from Bass's gun, a Browning 2000, definitely would not fit because it had a 3-inch chamber.

Finally, I was off the hook, and Mr. Bass took the stand. Mr. Thornton coaxed him through the usual revelations that he was a hardworking family man who was just sharing a wonderful outdoor experience with his grandkids until he was rudely interrupted by the mean old game warden. Mr. Bass went on to repeat the assertion that he, the children, and Mr. Taylor were out in shin-deep water in the public marsh when I called for them to come over to me, and when they stepped up on the dike, I then told them they were trespassing on it and began to write them tickets.

I knew that they had to explain the presence of the bags of decoys sooner or later. The whole time I had been testifying, the mallard decoy with Bass's name on it, had been lying on its side on the front rail of the witness stand, where I was sitting, with the tag in clear view of the jury, and it was still there beside Mr. Bass, similarly exposed, as he testified on his own behalf.

Mr. Thornton asked him if the decoy was his, and he responded that it was but that he didn't know it was in the water right in front of where he was hunting. I could see a few jurors rolling their eyes.

Then I found out what the four huge sacks of decoys were all about. Mr. Thornton asked Mr. Bass if all the decoys in the sacks were his. Mr. Bass replied that they were and launched into a long story about how he was a really serious duck hunter and that when he went hunting, he put out large numbers of decoys. He said occasionally other duck boats would run through his decoys and that some would get cut loose and drift off. He speculated that someone had probably picked up those three decoys drifting with the tide and had put them in the canal before he got there.

The defense lawyer created additional confusion when he insisted on introducing a video he had made near the site of the arrests, showing that shotguns being fired in the marsh close to the dike could actually eject shells some distance, onto the top of the dike. I could see that he had gone to a lot of effort, carrying video equipment and a variety of guns across the marsh in an attempt to make his point. All he did, however, was confuse the issue because we had never introduced into evidence during the trial any of the spent shells I had presented at the discovery hearing. The jury, therefore, did not understand how the video of shells atop the dike was relevant to the issue of trespassing because the only shells we introduced into evidence were the ones removed from the defendants' guns. All the jurors saw were people standing in the marsh and firing guns outside somebody else's property. It also illustrated the scene better than I could describe it.

After closing arguments and instructions from the judge, the jury departed for the jury room. The instant they left to deliberate, some of the visiting attorneys present began the usual speculation about how the length of time the jury was out was an indicator of what their verdict would be. One attorney said that, if they reached a decision quickly, it would most likely be a not-guilty verdict. After only thirty minutes, which seemed like only moments, the jury sent word that they had reached a verdict. They found both defendants guilty of the charge of trespassing to hunt waterfowl.

Judge Lockemy called both defendants and me before the bench. He asked Mr. Bass and Mr. Taylor if they had anything to say before he pronounced the sentence. One of them continued to maintain that he was not guilty. The judge replied, "Son, you are guilty. You are guilty because those twelve people over there said you are guilty. Now go sit down."

The judge then asked me if I had anything to say before he imposed the sentence. I told him that the defendants were obviously still unrepentant. I said that landowners spent a lot of time and effort managing their impoundments. If there were no consequences for trespassing, the landowners would quit managing their lands, which could have a bad effect on overwintering waterfowl populations in the whole area—a consequence that would be bad for everybody, river hunters and plantation owners alike.

The judge called Mr. Bass and Mr. Taylor back to the bench and instructed them to go home, get packed, and be prepared to serve ninety days in the county jail, a sentence that would be suspended on payment of $1,100. They were also told that they would lose their hunting privileges for one year.

Mr. Bass was truly a hard-core case. He was apprehended in North Dakota three or four years later by federal wardens and charged with taking hundreds of mallards over the legal limit. I was told that he had so many ducks that he had them ground up and processed into sausage. I was informed that the U.S. attorney in North Dakota substantially reduced the charges and fines in return for Mr. Bass's cooperation with federal agents bring charges against a hunting outfitter from Louisiana who was promoting and booking those hunts with the promise of such excesses.

Other than the Santee Delta and Dale Marsh, the South Edisto River between Dahoo Landing and West Bank and Willtown landings got the heaviest numbers of coastal duck hunters. The heavy traffic there was facilitated by the proximity of the nearby landings, and it was not unusual to find as many as three hunting parties within a hundred-yard stretch. That reach of the river and its adjacent rice fields was the scene of many law-enforcement encounters until I "officially" retired there, just off of Matthew's Canal, at sunset on January 20, 2002.

Just before the 2001–2 duck season began, I arranged an airplane flight over a wide expanse of the coastal area to look for any constructed blinds or unusual concentrations of ducks in the salt marsh. I was also curious to see what was going on in the plantation impoundments. I had noticed over the last four or five seasons that a significant number of the plantations had evolved from managing for indigenous moist-soil vegetation to planting row crops, usually corn, and flooding them just before the season opened. That practice attracted and held large numbers of ducks.

Wherever I spotted unusually large flocks, I wanted to find out why they were there. In the past I had observed fields from the airplane that appeared to have orderly rows of corn, but on checking a particular field on the ground I found that the plants had not borne ears of corn or had made very few. These were the fields to keep an eye on in case the owners yielded to temptation and brought cobs of corn into the field to make up the deficit of the poor crop in order to attract ducks.

As I was flying over the South Edisto area, I was startled to see in one impounded field, what appeared to be deep random loops cut through the corn rows. It is not illegal to harvest all or part of a crop, then flood the field and hunt ducks over it. It is illegal to manipulate a standing crop in order to expose and scatter corn over the ground for the purpose of attracting waterfowl, just as it is to introduce corn and scatter it over the field. After landing at the Johns Island Airport, I went home, hooked up my johnboat, and drove to Willtown Bluff Landing. I was soon down the river and walking up the dock to the cornfields in the Block Island impoundment.

I was even more astounded at what I found on the ground. There were wide swaths where rows of corn had been harvested in areas around the blinds. But for every four rows that had been harvested, there were four rows of plants that had just been flattened with the ears still attached. Throughout the field I found evidence that the harvester had made wide arching turns tangent to the rows, knocking over the stalks in a path the width of a tractor. When I got home that night, I called a federal game warden, who agreed to come with me the next morning to further document the field. Instead of taking the johnboat from the landing to the plantation as I had done the day before, we decided to drive to the location to save time. We parked behind the Springfield House at the back end of the Bear Island Management Area and walked a considerable distance to Block Island. We examined the entire impoundment, and the federal officer agreed that in its current state it would be illegal to hunt. Because knocking down rows of corn is an illegal manipulation of a crop, hunting ducks over such a field is prohibited.

As we were walking through the field, we heard a vehicle approaching and jumped to the side in the standing corn, but it was too late. We had been busted. We confronted the man, who was one of the owners, and told him that if his group hunted ducks on the area in its current state, it would be a serious violation.

There were around two weeks before the season opened, so we told him if he got a crew to come in and pick up all the ears of corn that had been knocked over, we would return and redocument the field. The man called the next evening saying that he had picked up around five truckloads of corn and that he thought that the field was okay. I went back in the morning and saw where trucks had been driven through the field, but there were still a huge number of ears of corn lying around in clear view all over the ground.

In an attempt to illustrate the abundance of corn, I picked up every ear of corn I could find within about a seventy-five-foot circle and stacked them in a pile. I repeated that up and down several of the large strips in the field, took pictures, and drove home. I called the man and explained that the field was still illegal. I said he would see what I meant when he went back.

He called three days later and announced that the field was finally "right." I returned the next day to find that he had taken a disc harrow and attempted to turn the exposed and offending ears of corn under the soil. Everywhere I walked there were still whole ears of corn, as well as ears that had been broken and scattered by the harrow.

I then informed him that he had only made the situation worse. If he had removed the ears of corn, as I had advised earlier, he would have been a lot better off. I explained why I was not going to give him the go ahead to flood and hunt the field, reminding him that a field was considered baited for ten days following the complete removal of any bait.

One of the owners began calling politicians, a waterfowl organization's executive director, and various members of my department. I explained to each of them that the act of knocking over rows of corn was not a normal agricultural operation and that, for the purposes of hunting ducks, it was an illegal manipulation. The law was clear.

A biologist from the South Carolina Waterfowl Association called and tried to convince me that the corn left after plowing should be considered an acceptable amount of spillage resulting from a normal harvesting operation. I told him that, since he had not seen the field and only had the report of the complaining owner, I did not think that he was qualified to make such a judgment, and besides, I said, the spillage did not result from a normal harvest but from an illegal manipulation of the crop.

The owners had missed any opportunity to hunt the impoundment legally during the short first season. I told one of the owners that they should go ahead and flood it in the hope of attracting enough ducks to consume what remained scattered under water, but that it would remain illegal to hunt until the tenth day after I ceased finding significant amounts of corn there.

I had to wear chest waders for my subsequent checks of the flooded field. I noticed in my knee-deep watery forays through the field that large numbers of deer ran splashing off through the cornstalks at my approach, so I had to take into account that they might be knocking some ears of corn off the stalks. The plantation remained closed through the early season and was finally cleared for hunting by the beginning of the second season. It didn't take long for the word to get out that hunting over managed row crops came with certain responsibilities and that the game wardens were checking to see that those responsibilities were met.

One morning I got a call from J. P. "Butch" Pendarvis, one of the Wildlife Department board members, who reported that he thought the Cut, a private impoundment adjacent to his duck club, was baited.

After I met him at his camp at the Bear Island Club, he took me to the other club's dike in his all-terrain vehicle. Pulling up near a row of johnboats on the Cut embankment, he jumped off the four-wheeler, reached in near the transom of one of the boats, and brought out a wet handful of small black seeds, which he held out for me to examine.

I checked the boat myself and observed a considerable quantity of the seeds scattered over the deck. They were much smaller than thistle seed, and I didn't have the faintest clue what kind of plant produced them. I poled one of the johnboats out to several of the blinds and found the seeds floating everywhere on top of the water. Several casts of the bait scrape yielded no trace of anything incriminating on the bottom around any of the blinds.

I had seen some unusual baiting scenes before, but this was a complete mystery to me. I told Mr. Pendarvis that I would have to identify what kind of seeds they were before I could take any action. On the way back to Charleston, I stopped by the Clemson University plant laboratory and showed the seeds to one of the botanists. He checked through two or three volumes of plant taxonomy, and finally admitted that he could not identify the seeds.

I drove for another hour up Highway 17 to the Santee Coastal Reserve and went into the office of district biologist Tommy Strange, who took a quick glance at my little bagful of seeds and said, "Scirpus robustus, it grows everywhere." He explained that it was native sedge common in the brackish and salt marshes up and down the Atlantic Seaboard. He thought the seeds probably got into boats as they brushed past the plants on the way to the blinds. That night I contacted Mr. Pendarvis and told him that the seeds were naturally occurring and that we could not make a baiting case.

Over the years I discovered many inventive and clever ways to bait duck impoundments that were far more creative than just pouring out the corn. On one plantation I found dye vats where corn and soybeans were dyed black or dark purple to help disguise their presence in the shallows around blinds.

I discovered another imaginative scheme while scouting a pond and finding massive numbers of acorns floating around the water's edge. I knew that hunting had been going on there because I found shell casings at intervals around the pond. Walking the entire perimeter of the pond, I did not find a single oak tree, only eastern red cedar and wax myrtles. Expanding my search further back in the woods, I found the area where the hunters parked their vehicles and spotted a stack of wooden bushel baskets off to the side, several of which still had an acorn or two stuck in their cracks.

I had to do some illustrative photography to show the absence of any nearby oak trees, which would have accounted for the acorns. After interrupting their Saturday morning wood-duck shoot, I showed the photographs to the hunters, who were convinced by the pictures to admit their misdeed and pay their fines. They confessed they had paid some young boys to sweep up five or six baskets of acorns from downtown streets.

Other creative baiting occurrences included the use of whole sweet potatoes and stale bread rolls, which had been obtained from area restaurants. One case involved the use of small floating feed troughs containing corn, which were removed the day before the pond was hunted. Perhaps the most inventive of all was the combination of molasses and corn, which I discovered as I was scouting around a few deserted duck camps during the middle of the week. I spotted a barrel of molasses, as well as a number of empty paper sacks that had once contained whole-kernel corn, a curious combination that attracted my interest.

I kept an eye on the place as the duck season neared and found out through the grapevine that before the season the landowner put out corn mixed with molasses. Just before duck season, he discontinued the corn but kept on applying the molasses, apparently to the delight of the many ducks seen flying into his field. During the cold months the water was cold enough to keep the molasses from rapidly dissolving, and it was like duck taffy.

I have to admit that it was devilishly difficult to obtain any convincing samples of it in a bait scrape. I could tell it was mixed in with the muddy mass, but I never could get enough to carry to court as evidence. Since it appeared that my chances of making a case would be fairly slim, I decided to try public relations and left one of my business cards on top of the molasses drum at the duck camp. On my next pass through the camp the drum had disappeared.

Violators frequently think that they are invisible or that their gunshots will not attract any official attention because of the relative remoteness of their location. I happened to be cooking oysters at a Saturday evening party on the point of Sullivan's Island when I began to hear gunshots from across the channel on Morris Island. The shooting went on intermittently for around two hours and stopped just as it got dark.

The duck season was open. I knew that there were several small ponds on the eastern side of the island and that there was a huge spoil area on the far end. The next morning I began checking a couple of access points to the area to see if there were any signs of recent traffic. I found one well-used path leading through dense spike rush. Following it over to the first of the two little ponds, I investigated until I found freshly spent shotgun shell cases lying around a dense clump of reeds.

Continuing my search, I reached another spot with a profusion of shells and determined that the hunters had been using lead shot, probably on the day before. The brasses were still bright and the smell of burned power still strong. I had on knee boots, and as I walked around in the shallow pond, I discovered grains of corn scattered everywhere. I walked over to the windward side, where I saw a handful of corn chaff and bits of broken up corncobs floating in the grass.

Checking the area again in the middle of the week, I found plenty of corn left, but it was disappearing fast. I took another sample of the corn and shot a few pictures. No one had been there since I had last checked it, but I figured that there was a good chance the hunters would return the following Saturday.

I was in position near Fort Sumter at first light Saturday morning, listening for gunfire. When nothing materialized, I decided to come back that afternoon. It was a blustery day, so in the afternoon I stayed in the lee of Sullivan's Island until I began hearing gunshots across the channel.

I bucked my way over to Morris Island as the tide was beginning to ebb and entered the little drain off Clark Sound that led to the edge of the path. As I idled in, I saw a small boat tied to a pole on the bank. Pulling up to the boat, I removed the cover on the motor and pulled the spark plug wires. I didn't want anybody escaping on me.

As I was crossing the channel I had heard a constant barrage of gunfire. Since it sounded as if there were more than two guns, I altered my initial direct approach, going instead through the tree line behind the ponds so I would have time to observe where each hunter was standing. I hung back in the shadows of a stand of palmettos and observed them for around twenty minutes. They were shooting from two different areas around the pond. Two hunters were standing together; the other was directly across the pond from them. Even with all that firepower, they didn't appear to be hitting many birds.

When I determined the time was right, I walked straight out from where I had been watching and splashed into the middle of the pond. They gaped at me with their mouths open until I held up the badge hanging from my lanyard and waved it around conspicuously while introducing myself. At that point their expressions of incredulity turned into ones of extreme consternation.

I asked them to join me in the middle of the pond and to bring their guns along. Two walked toward me, but the other said that he wasn't wearing boots. I told him that I wanted to show them the corn all over the bottom of the pond. He glumly said he would take my word for it.

I pointed out the many grains of corn visible to the two standing with me and emphasized that there was simply no way in the broad daylight that they could not have known it was there. I checked their guns and found they contained lead-shot shells. One of them had no license and no stamps. I felt a bad case of writer's cramp coming on.

It was getting late and I knew the tide had turned, so I directed them to follow me back to their boat, where I reattached their spark-plug connections. We exited the little drain, and they followed me around to the back beach of the island, where I sat on the bow of my boat with a flashlight under my chin writing and passing out paper.

I found those little ponds on the east end of Morris Island full of corn quite a few times over the years. They always seemed to be baited by people who were in a hurry. Their type of duck hunting entailed a brief trip across the harbor when the tide was right to access the little path, a quick shoot as ducks came into the bait, and then out again before the tide got too low.

I found that people in a hurry tended to take short cuts and didn't appear to take the time to think about the consequences of their behavior. The orderly cadences of the judicial process generally afforded sufficient intervals for a hunter, then known as "the defendant," to reflect on the error of his ways.

Baiting was more than a way to take unfair advantage of wildlife; it was also used for settling scores with other hunters, an act I called "grudge baiting." That practice started to raise its ugly head some years before I retired. It typically took place in any spoil area that held enough water to float a duck.

An act of grudge baiting usually resulted from competition for public hunting areas. A savvy hunter would scout around and find a spot that offered good shooting opportunities; then after a few successful and undisturbed hunts, he would find his spot invaded by other hunters. Sometimes the original party had already put out his own bait and was really chapped that someone else was enjoying the fruits of his labors. It is a lot of work lugging those heavy corn sacks around.

Territorial disputes varied in intensity, ranging from mere expressions of disappointment to heated exchanges of harsh words and threats. Grudge baiters took the issue further, expressing the attitude that if they couldn't hunt the area undisturbed by interlopers, then nobody would hunt it.

Whichever hunter considered himself the chief aggrieved party would pour a conspicuous amount of corn all over the face of the dike around the access point and then call a game warden. Sometimes if a spoil area that had become an attractive hunting site had more than one point of access, grudge baiting could ensnare completely unknowing hunters who entered the spoil at some distance from the display of corn.

To me it was a pretty obvious setup whenever I found it, and I did not waste my time sitting on the baited sites to make a case that might satisfy someone else's need for revenge. Instead, I usually made a few cardboard signs announcing that the area was baited and put my name and phone number on them. Then I would visit the area occasionally to make sure my posted notices were being heeded.

Another form of grudge baiting took place when plantation owners—angry at the constant barrage of gunfire from the river hunters lining the perimeter of their impoundments—baited their fields, put signs up announcing that they were baited areas, and then expect a game warden to watch them for the duration of the season. I counseled those who did this to discontinue the practice because, during those times when no game warden was present, ducks would be drawn in for the slaughter.

Scattering bait around a pond and hunting ducks on it is a conscious commission of a crime, but hunters also created problems for themselves by not doing things—crimes of omission such as failing to purchase a hunting license and waterfowl stamp or not making sure repeating guns were legally plugged. Some hunters made bad situations worse by committing another violation while attempting to lie their way out of the first one.

While checking hunters one morning in Rock Creek and the Ashepoo River, I heard a good bit of gunning going on within an impoundment on Hutchinsons Island. After I had checked the last of the river hunters, I steered my boat to their dock on the Ashepoo River opposite Bennetts Point. I asked a person standing near the clubhouse dock if the hunters were still in the field. He replied they were on their way in. I began walking past the clubhouse toward the flooded fields.

Just a short distance away I encountered two men carrying guns and ducks. I introduced myself and asked to see their hunting licenses and duck stamps. I knew I had a couple of live ones when they looked at each other with glazed expressions, making no effort to produce the requested items. Moments later, two other hunters, Tony Brown and Buddy Kronsberg, came walking up and I also asked to see their licenses and stamps.

Looking imploringly at Brown and Kronsberg, one of the first two hunters said that I had just requested their licenses and did they have any idea where they might be. Their story was they had successfully bid on the Hutchinsons Island hunt at a Ducks Unlimited auction in Tennessee, where they lived, and had paid a huge amount of money for it. They were assured all the details would be taken care of, and they had assumed "details" meant the licenses and stamps.

Mr. Brown and Mr. Kronsberg seemed to be a little embarrassed. As they were searching for their own licenses, I checked everyone's shotguns for plugs and their shell bags and pockets for any prohibited lead shot. The visitors showed me their Tennessee licenses and federal duck stamps, and everyone was looking at each other with sheepish expressions on their faces. Brown pulled me aside and asked, considering the circumstances, if I would give them a break.

I responded that the only break I was going to give to them was not requiring them to post a cash bond for the two tickets I was going to issue each of the two visitors for hunting without a nonresident license or a state duck stamp. Brown asked me to give him their tickets, and he would pay their fines.

Before we departed, I left a phone number where I could be reached and cautioned the men who were issued the tickets that they were responsible for making sure the bonds were paid. I also informed them that, if the state charges were not settled, I could just as well make federal cases of the violations. As I departed, heading back to my boat, I could feel that I was leaving a rather tense scene.

Three days later Patty Brown, the wife of Tony Brown, contacted Richard Wood, the chief magistrate of Colleton County, who was to hear the cases, and told him that she had purchased the licenses and stamps for the out-of-state hunters the day before they were apprehended and that they did have licenses and stamps in their names at the moment they were cited. She went on to say that she had neglected to give them to her husband to pass on to his guests. She asked that the charges be dropped or at least substantially reduced. I made arrangements to meet with Mr. Brown so he could show me the licenses. I indicated that, if his guests had been issued the requisite paperwork before the time of their apprehension, I would ask the judge to find them not guilty, and the cases would go away.

When we met, however, something just didn't ring true. I don't remember if he said something slightly at variance with what his wife had explained to the judge or if I just had a feeling. I took his guests' licenses and informed him that I would get back in touch with him soon regarding the disposition of the cases. I went over to the Limehouse gas station by the Ashley River bridge, where the licenses had been obtained, and asked to see their hunting-license records. It did not take long to check the order in which licenses had been issued to determine that the dates on the licenses Mrs. Brown had claimed to have bought were out of sequence. Subsequent investigation revealed that the license agent's signature had been forged. She wasn't even working at the date and time indicted on the licenses. The state duck-stamp forms were similarly misdated.

I called Mr. Brown and told him that we had to get together because I had made a decision on the license cases. We met the next day at his West Ashley office where I confronted him with the results of my investigation. I explained to him that he and his wife were facing some serious charges. Without hesitation he admitted his culpability and begged me not to involve his wife because he had put her up to making the phone call to the judge. I explained that I was going to write him two tickets for postdating a license, for which he was going to pay the maximum fine. I said that I needed a check made payable to the magistrate for his two tickets and the four tickets issued to his guests, also for the maximum fine. Along with the sting of the substantial fines, he suffered his friends' cruel taunts for months over his self-made predicament.

The area near Price Inlet behind Bull Island was the setting for a duck case that involved multiple infractions. On several afternoons in early January 1981, I heard gunshots coming from that area. I scouted around but didn't find anything. I made note of the days of the week and the time of day that I had heard the shots and decided to go work on it. I figured the shooting stopped when I came into the area because the shooters could hear my engine running.

A colleague, Officer Terry Cumbee, and I decided to wait in the Intracoastal Waterway until we heard shooting and then approach the inlet at idle speed until we figured out where the shots were coming from. From that point we would be close enough to pole and paddle in the direction of the shooting. As we waited with the bow of the boat on the edge of a mud bank, we began to hear distant shots.

We idled out Price Creek, occasionally pausing to try and get a better bearing on the location of the shooting. As we approached the junction of

Bull Narrows, a long winding creek that threads through the marsh behind Bull Island, we cut the engine. We were not going to take any chances on running any closer and being heard.

As the shots continued, we were able to drift with little effort further up the narrows with the incoming tide. We knew that we were in the right territory because the shots were getting louder and louder. The sun was only minutes away from sinking below the western horizon. We came to a fork where one side ran out into Hickory Bay and the other fork continued its course all the way out to Bull Bay. We had closed to within about seventy-five yards of the shooting, which continued until well past sunset.

As we sat there wondering how much longer the shots would go on, we heard an outboard engine crank up and the hollow rattle of decoys being retrieved. By that time we had pushed away from the bank into the middle of the creek. Suddenly we could hear the engine throttle up, and it was coming in our direction. I lowered my engine, hit the ignition, and was thankful that it started on the first try.

From a small side creek emerged a small duck boat carrying two people, which turned heading straight to us. Officer Cumbee flipped on the beam of a flashlight, and we quickly were alongside them. The expressions on the

With Terry Cumbee (right) and twenty-four ducks seized from two men charged with shooting more than the limit, after legal hours, and over bait

hunters' faces were instant indicators that bad things had been going on, and I immediately recognized them, both friends.

We collected their licenses, duck stamps, and shotguns, and asked to see their ducks. Officer Cumbee impatiently began rooting around under their seats and decoy bags, dragged two burlap sacks into our boat, and started pulling out ducks, twenty-four in all, including three black ducks and a mallard-pintail hybrid. Further investigation revealed they had been using lead shot. We also felt the crops of several of the ducks, and then opened them to find kernels of corn, which confirmed my suspicion about how they could have taken so many ducks in the salt marsh.

The hunters were issued a separate ticket for each duck taken over the legal limit. They were also cited for shooting after legal hours and using lead shot. I think that Cumbee and I used every single ticket in our ticket books. The men had brought their duck boat inside a larger boat, which they had left anchored in a small creek further up Bull Narrows. We followed them to that location and watched them grimly load their boat and guns, haul in their anchor, and depart into the mounting darkness.

I went back the next morning on the low tide to the little creek they had come out of. It had a high shell rake all the way across its mouth, making it impossible to enter except at high tide. I slogged across the top of the marsh until I located their blind and found lead-shot shell casings lying in profusion around it. As I climbed down the creek bank, I could see corn scattered all over the area and picked up a good handful to use as evidence. Two days later the hunters were issued additional tickets for shooting over bait.

A lawyer soon became involved and tried to get all the over-the-limit charges consolidated into a single charge, but we weren't budging. Following their appearance before a magistrate, where they pled guilty to all the charges and paid substantial fines, their lawyer tried to get the date changed on the tickets charging them with shooting over bait, which were issued two days after our initial encounter.

His reasoning was that he did not want it to appear that his clients were charged with violations stemming from more than one hunt, as if such an appearance could possibly injure their reputations more than was already the case. His request was denied. The much-chastened hunters, embarrassed over the public nature of their judicial ordeal, thereafter became model sportsmen.

On several occasions just prior to my retirement, during the quiet hours of the duck patrol just before sunrise, I had time to reflect on some memorable past events, and it occurred to me as I raised my eyes to the star-lit sky in a spontaneous gesture of silent prayer, that I had much to be thankful for.

One such occasion was set in motion 103 years ago when the Santee Gun Club was formed as a duck-hunting club by a group of eleven men from New York, Charleston, Georgetown, and Santee. Seventy-seven years later, their successors, the 1975 membership, donated the club's more than twenty thousand acres—lands that had formerly been twelve different rice plantations—to the Nature Conservancy, which in turn, after imposing restrictive easements, gave the land to the State of South Carolina to be managed by the Wildlife Department.

The quid pro quo was that the members would retain exclusive waterfowl-hunting rights for twenty-five years, after which such rights would revert to the public. The state would manage the impoundments and the club property, which included the 1902-vintage clubhouse. All expenses for club management, club staff, maintenance of dikes, boats, and equipment were paid for by the club membership.

By the year 1999 the Santee Delta had been my "office" during the duck season for more than twenty years, and I had formed enduring friendships with most of the Santee Gun Club members. I had been invited over those years to hunt with them frequently during the season. I was humbled when I got a call from club member Lee Bryan of Winston Salem, North Carolina, inviting me to hunt with them on the final duck hunt of the Santee Gun Club, twenty-five years after that momentous deal with the Nature Conservancy.

The wake-up call that last morning came as a gentle tap at the door. "Four thirty, Mr. Moïse." This act was repeated at eight more doors up and down the second story hallway of the Santee Gun Club lodge. The call signaled the beginning of a fine day as a guest in a truly magnificent setting, which bordered the old rice fields of the South Santee River, with as fine an array of dedicated waterfowlers as could be found in the state of South Carolina. The call signaled that in one half hour, I was to be dressed and ready to be seated at the large table in the dining room for a hot and hearty breakfast designed to lift from bleary eyes the fog created by the previous evening's festivities.

As I rolled out from under my thick and warm down comforter, in my small room with its own wash sink and corner fireplace, I was remembering that the wake up call on this twentieth day of January 1999 was the last, as was the breakfast, and as was that day's hunt in the flooded fields of the Santee Cape. Being part of this event was a great privilege, almost a reverential occasion, and I savored every moment, enormously glad to be there yet sad in the knowledge that there would be no more such events to follow.

The night before we had drawn blind numbers that were inscribed on small white marbles poured from a leather-covered bottle. I drew Vaughn Stand Trunk, one of the closest blinds to the lodge, and Joe Robinson was assigned to be my guide. That evening we had gathered in the large main room bordered by a wide porch that spanned the width of the building. The gunroom was on one side and the liquor room and dining room on the other. Centered on the back wall was a huge fireplace with blazing pine logs atop large brass andirons. Over the brickwork mantel hung a Richard E. Bishop painting, a marsh scene of descending mallards, wings cupped, landing gear down. Next to it was a small slate chalkboard that announced wake-up time, the time to leave for the blinds, and the legal shooting time for the following morning, 6:53 A.M.

The art of the raconteur was in full flower on that night before the final day, as various potent brews—accompanied by an array of savory offerings —fueled lively conversations. Monte Cristo Number Twos and Cohibas added an additional pungent atmosphere to the sharp scent of the burning pine logs. At length, with the realization that the four thirty wake-up call was going to come all too soon, the weary and much-contented assemblage repaired to the sleeping quarters above.

After consuming an ample breakfast, the hunters arose from the huge communal table and began to assemble the necessary garb and gear, which was arrayed about the large gunroom. This space also had its own fireplace and contained banks of individual wooden lockers filled with duck calls, dog collars, chest waders, shotgun shells, down parkas, and other sundry items considered essential equipment for conducting a successful duck hunt.

At six o'clock hunters, guides, and dogs boarded the vans parked near the front porch and went forth into the dark, chilly morning to that section of the club called the cape. The other areas of the club are Murphy and Cedar islands where hunters had to be delivered by boat. Joe Robinson and I disembarked from the crowded van, unloaded the sectioned canvas bag that held my six treasured twenty-five-inch-long cork black duck decoys, my 20-gauge over-and-under Beretta shotgun, and Belle, my faithful little brown companion. I wished the remaining passengers good luck, and they slowly departed into the distance down the long dike road.

We loaded the gear into a fourteen-foot cypress skiff that awaited us on the bank, and Joe Robinson poled us into the rice field—past a maze of drains and quarter drains—with no light and with no hesitation until we arrived at the blind called Vaughn Stand Trunk.

In the steadily emerging light of sunrise, I carefully placed my decoys in what I judged to be an enticing pattern in the large open area of water that surrounded the blind. We pushed the skiff between the sides of the blind, which had been heavily brushed with tied bundles of marsh reed. We climbed in, shared a cup of coffee and a chocolate bar, and looked with anticipation at the ever-brightening horizon as we heard the peeps, whistles, and quacks of nearby waterfowl, still on the water from their night's rest.

Belle was on full alert as ducks began to circle, marveling at those six big boys sitting on the water in front of our blind. At the advent of legal shooting time I removed my little twenty from its case and loaded it with a couple of bismuth number fours.

As my carefully set alarm announced from deep within my sleeve that the moment had arrived, there were a number of teal swimming in the decoys. Other birds were checking out the scene. Two drake pintails approached and hovered over like kites tied to a string. This was it! The first shot of the last day. I would like to say that Miss Belle retrieved it, but she had never picked up a duck where she could stand up. She had made water retrieves only when she was swimming. She tried to pick up that big pintail by the wing, but the rest of it was still down in the water. She looked thoroughly confused as I came to "help" her fetch it. She did seem to get the hang of it with the remaining five, somewhat lighter and more compact teal, bluebill, and gadwall. With my sixth bird in hand, it dawned on me that the hunt was over, really over.

While the state continues to maintain the property as a waterfowl management area, the Santee Coastal Reserve, and while the public may hunt there, now it is just a duck hunt with a lot of strangers. The faces of the hunters returning to the lodge later that morning—and as they emptied their lockers of years and even decades of accumulated paraphernalia—reflected a sense of loss and sadness. Their conversations were muted and subdued. The knowledge that this fine event would not be repeated; that this grand chapter in the history of South Carolina sports was now played out, caused not a few moist eyes.

When I go back now, the lodge stands in its moss-draped grove of live oaks as a gray monument to all the members of the Santee Gun Club who formerly animated it and gave it life and spirit. I felt privileged over the years to be invited to hunt there and to have among the many members so many kind and generous friends. Whenever I think about ducks, duck hunting, and duck hunters, the Santee Gun Club is always at the very top of the list.

I was reminded how fragile and important the elements of the gun club's remoteness were when they came under siege in the early 1990s by a Charleston member of the South Carolina House of Representatives, Jimmy Bailey, who was trying to do a favor for a friend. His friend Robert Knoth then owned nearby Moreland Plantation, which he leased to a duck-hunting club. The only way to get to the plantation was by boat. By informal arrangement hunters who were going to the plantation were allowed to drive through the Santee Gun Club property and launch at the ramp on the South Santee River, which was otherwise closed for public use. The Moreland Club members were required to park their vehicles and trailers at a designated spot some distance away from the ramp.

This was one of those "don't ask, don't tell" type of arrangements that permitted a use not available to other members of the public. Over time the issue of the arrangement was forced as some of the members arrived at the landing in a hurry, leaving their vehicles and trailers in the immediate area of the ramp, which impeded the ability of Santee Gun Club members and law-enforcement officers to use or park at the ramp. A furor ensued after the gun club manager instituted strict rules requiring the plantation hunters to park in an area even further away and stipulating that only one of their boats could be launched from the ramp. They were expressly forbidden to park anywhere on the access road to the ramp or near the ramp itself.

Mr. Bailey pushed measures to make the landing on Santee Coastal Reserve a public boat ramp, which meant that there would be public access through the gun club at all hours to use a small ramp and a tiny parking area. The outcome of such an intrusion would have been a total disaster, but Mr. Bailey was persistent, especially when it became apparent that his decision was being challenged by a state agency, which he felt should show more deference to his political status.

I singled out two House members in the Charleston County Delegation, Harry Hallman, now mayor of Mount Pleasant, and Don Holt of North Charleston, who I thought had good sense, and took them on a boat tour of the Santee Delta to give them some perspective on the issues. I carried them on timed runs from Pole Yard Landing, the nearest public landing on the North Santee River at Highway 17, to the dock at Moreland Plantation on the South Santee.

I explained to them that every other river hunter had to run the same distances or even further, that the real issue at hand was mixing people in a hurry with a leisure activity. Bailey had described the issue as the Wildlife Department forcing the fine upstanding members of the Moreland duck club to risk life and limb in all sorts of weather and in the darkness of night. I drove Representatives Holt and Hallman in my patrol car down the long dirt road into the Santee Gun Club to the small boat ramp, showing them what an intrusion constant traffic would be and explaining to them how difficult and expensive it would be to keep such a road maintained if traffic on it became heavier. I also pointed out the limited space at the landing and showed them how the only possible expansion of the landing would be at the expense of wetlands in the middle of such an important waterfowl habitat. They were suitably impressed, and Mr. Bailey's effort to establish a public boat landing there ended quietly. This close call illustrated how, on a mere whim, the entire character of an area can be severely compromised.

That was not my only encounter with misguided and uninformed legislators only too willing to use the weight of their political offices to make an end run around established law. Another encounter happened in the mid-1990s over the questionable legality of the new Benelli shotguns beginning to show up in dove fields and duck blinds. I routinely checked them for plugs just as I would any other repeating shotgun: shucking out the shells and reloading them in the magazine, which legally should hold only two shells (with the third being in the chamber). One morning on Santee Delta I encountered a duck hunter who was using a Benelli, and in the process of checking his gun, I unloaded four shells. The hunter was adamant that his gun was plugged. When I repeated the process, sure enough, it would hold only two shells in the magazine. I checked to make sure that it was not an issue of 2¾-inch shells inconveniently fitting into a tube plugged for 3- or 3½-inch shells. Further investigation revealed that not to be the case, and I decided to let the matter slide as some sort of anomaly.

Later, while talking with another game warden about the Benelli incident, I heard that the Benelli mechanism allowed a shell to be held on the carrier behind the chamber. He said that highway-patrol officers were taught how to load the extra shell in their state-issued Benelli shotguns. That meant that two shells could be loaded in the normally plugged magazine, one in the chamber, and one on the carrier for a total of four, which—according to the uncomplicated language of the Migratory Bird Treaty Act—made the Benelli an illegal gun to use for hunting migratory birds, unless it was plugged so that it was capable of holding only three shells.

I took descriptive data on the Benelli shotgun to the honorable Falcon Hawkins, one of the federal judges in Charleston, and asked him if he thought the gun violated the federal law. After some discussion he said that, if the gun could hold and fire four shells in succession, it was illegal to use, even with a plug, for hunting migratory birds, according to the wording in the U.S. Code of Federal Regulations. Saying that the law was sure to be controversial, he cautioned me to be prudent in how I went about enforcing it. I then had a lengthy phone conversation with one of the senior agents with U.S. Fish and Wildlife in Washington, who said that the enforcement people there had also been looking into the issue, but nobody there wanted to put his head on the chopping block.

I told a few of my fellow wardens of the judge's opinion and explained to them that I was initially going to issue warnings to those I found using the Benelli, except when I found one with four shells in it. Hunters with those guns would be handed real tickets. The first few warnings ignited a firestorm of criticism. There were letters to the editor, newspaper articles, blog-site commentaries on the internet, and irate calls to the Columbia office. Even the anti-gun-control element got involved.

The hoopla attracted the attention of a Charleston politician well known for his knee-jerk reactions to local controversies. House member John Graham Altman charged ahead with highly public threats to introduce legislation prohibiting state game wardens from enforcing the three-shot law when a hunter was using a Benelli shotgun.

If Altman's legislation had passed, it could have had the unintended consequence of a federal prohibition on hunting migratory birds in South Carolina. At length the Columbia office sent out an edict telling all officers that we were to leave the Benelli issue alone. I went on about my business, and the issue quietly subsided.

Passing the Torch,
Spreading the Word

It was always gratifying to see children enjoying the outdoor experience with their fathers, grandfathers, or uncles, whether they were hunting, fishing, shrimping, or camping. I was confidant that those shared moments out under the sky would foster a continuing tradition of stewardship and instill a genuine regard for the lands and waters of our lowcountry heritage. I had many occasions over the years to be not only a participant in but also a witness to such deeply rooted feelings in countless duck blinds, deer stands, and fishing boats and around many campfires. In my professional capacity I was sometimes able to help pass on that tradition to a new generation.

One morning while patrolling in the upper reaches of the Wando River near Paradise Island, I spied a small boat with two people in it coming down the middle of the river. As I drove my boat over to them, I saw the occupants were an old man and a young boy. There were a few palmetto fronds in the front of the boat, and they were wearing camouflage clothes.

After introducing myself, I asked the man if they had been hunting that morning. He reported that this was his grandson's first duck-hunting trip. I could see that they had only one single-barrel shotgun in the boat and asked to see his license and federal duck stamp. The old man produced the requested items and proudly exclaimed that his grandson had shot his first bird, a goose, that morning. I immediately expressed my interest in seeing it. I was curious because I had never seen geese in that part of the river before and the season for shooting Canada geese was closed east of Interstate 95.

The old man reached into a sack lying under the palmetto fronds and pulled out a very large male loon.

Pride beamed in the faces of the old man and the boy, and I did not have the stomach to be the one to break the bad news. I figured that justice would be served when they put that loon in the pot. I departed, leaving them with a copy of the migratory-bird laws and a duck-identification booklet.

A similar situation occurred in North Santee Bay as I was checking a man and his young son. The little boy, visibly shivering, sat close to his father as I checked their guns and licenses. When I asked if they had had any luck, the man said his son had shot his first duck and produced a fine drake pintail from the folds of a towel. He explained that he had it wrapped up because he was going to have it "taxidermied."

After a moment of deliberation, I asked the man if he would mind stepping over into my boat for a brief conference. I backed away a short distance and informed the man that the season on pintails was closed, and I knew that his son would be embarrassed and disappointed if he was told that his duck had been taken illegally. Without going into a lecture, I explained to him that under normal circumstances I would seize the bird and issue a ticket, but I didn't feel this was a "normal" situation.

I explained that I did not want him to go back to the landing with the illegal bird and said I would meet him later at the crossroads at McClellanville, where I would return his duck. I told him to tell the boy that it was so pretty that I wanted to take it and show it to somebody. Weeks later, after transferring the duck, I ran into him again, and he said that his son had hugged that duck in the towel all the way back to Charleston and that it was in the hands of a taxidermist.

In December 1979, after a patrol where I had checked three young boys who had been duck hunting in the Wando, Dr. James A. Timmerman, the director of the Wildlife Department, received the following letter from Eddie Walker of Charleston:

> It is not often, as a matter of fact, very, very seldom that I take my time to write public officials and when I do, it is to complain and gripe in no uncertain terms. However, I believe that a few words of praise and thanks are due in this case.
>
> My son Eric (age 14) and two friends went up the Wando River to try their hand at some jump shooting for ducks. My son has been hunting with me for two years and has been along since he was eight or nine years old. As my grandfather and father did, my son has heard many

stories of "how it used to be." Me and my contemporaries' stories on jump shooting finally got to him and he and two of his friends took off at the usual everyday hour to try their hand at it, my wife objecting and me going along with the idea that they have to learn sometime. I also think that I learned more about ducks, weather, cold, misery, fun and fellowship during my jump-shooting days than I have ever since.

At any rate, after a totally unsuccessful trip, the boys were heading home, when they were stopped by Mr. Ben Moïse. My son told me that he checked their guns, life preservers, asked how they did, where they went and in general did the job he is paid to do. After doing the above Mr. Moïse proceeded to give the boys tips on what to do and what not to do. I think Mr. Moïse went the extra step in that he did not explain what his job was and the negative part of hunting, but went about these young people's heritage and how they might properly handle it.

After hearing my son's story, I was impressed to the point of that I called Mr. Moïse to thank him for not only doing his job, but for taking the time to spend with these young boys and doing what he did. It was a pleasure talking with Mr. Moïse, but mainly my son feels that Wardens are not the enemy of the hunter but are friends of all hunters who abide by our laws.

All of those young boys are now grown men, and from time to time I still see a few of them, including Eric Walker. They are fond of recalling their first encounter with a game warden, but the story seems to have grown somewhat in proportion to the actual event.

I was often called on to participate in career days at several of the area public and private schools. I enjoyed telling young people about what game wardens do. I have even been invited to do a "show and tell" for kindergarten classes. At one preschool gathering—which included my niece Bracey Moïse, who had asked me to talk about my African safaris—I brought along a box full of African items, including horns, feathers, skins, and a group of carved African animals. On the way out of the house, I also grabbed a mounted alligator head to add to the collection. In my talk to the children I showed them on a map where South Africa was and told them a little something about each of the things that I took from the box.

When I got to the alligator head, I told the class about the large crocodiles that inhabit the African rivers and handed the toothy head over to be passed around. One small boy, who was probably around five years old, said, "Why this isn't a crocodile head. Its snout is too wide, and its teeth are not incurving." I quickly got a grip on the situation and said, "You are quite right. That is an alligator. I must have picked up the wrong one by mistake." With the *National Geographic, Nova,* and *Animal Planet* programs on television, children are far more knowledgeable than I was at their age.

Sometimes the children's questions can be quite amusing. One of the marine-division biologists told me that once she was giving a program to a second-grade class and explained to them that a single shad could produce several hundred thousand baby shad. One little girl raised her hand and asked her how many little shad would the married ones have.

For three years I was involved with the eighth-grade mentor program at Buist Academy, a Charleston County academic magnet school. In this program a student accompanied a mentor one morning a month for seven consecutive months beginning in November. I tried to expose my students to a variety of experiences and carried my camera along to record the law-enforcement situations they encountered.

Their experiences included attendance at magistrate's court trials and visits to Waterfowl Management Areas or regulated mariculture operations. They also went along on water patrols while I checked hunters and fishermen or visited the docks to check on shrimpers, crabbers, or oystermen. I even took them to several law-enforcement district meetings at Fort Johnson. Each student was required to keep a journal of the day's outing and give a report to his class. One morning I took one of my students to visit the Santee Coastal Reserve to assist in the duck-banding program, and he wrote the following report:

5th Mentor Visit
March 6, 1996

In the morning I got dropped off at my mentor's house at around 7:50 A.M. He was waiting there as usual. This time he said we were going to band ducks. It took us about an hour to get there. Once we got there we met a biologist technician that worked there. He got some corn and we loaded everything into the truck and we were off to go check the traps. We got to the first trap and the technician and I got into the little man made boat. It was pretty small. We paddled out to the spot and baited it with corn since there weren't any ducks inside it. The second trap we looked in didn't have any ducks and even the third trap we checked didn't have any. Finally on the fourth trap we caught about eight ducks and one kook [*sic*]. He got inside the trap and handed me them one by one. They were very nice. They didn't even try to bite me. I put all the ducks into the crate and then we paddled back to land. My mentor took a lot of pictures of me with the ducks.

We were going to shoot a net over the ducks to catch them, but it was way too windy out there. It would have flown right back at us. There were also alligators everywhere. It was alligator infested waters.

On the way back we picked up lunch and headed back to school. He dropped me off at school at about 12:30. We were right on time. When I came back into school I met with a couple of friends. We talked about what we did at mentors. I usually have good stories to tell. I also had some shark's teeth to show them. I had a great time!!

I loved to read copies of their journal entries to understand their perspective on the particular outing and to see what they found interesting or exciting. Their teachers said that my students' papers were real adventure stories and that the other children were always envious. I was pleased to note that the most common expression all three students used to describe their experiences was "cool."

Teaching Cub Scout "Ree" Ravenel of Mount Pleasant about the Wildlife Department's wood-duck nesting-box program

I was a member of Ducks Unlimited, a conservation organization in which I served in various capacities. My favorite position was that of chairman of the state Greenwing program, which was designed to involve children in the organization's conservation efforts.

Each Greenwing chapter throughout the state usually sponsored an event where dog trainers, shooting instructors, fishermen, and sometimes even game wardens gave demonstrations for the children's amusement and education. As in all Ducks Unlimited events, the participants were well fed.

I had the idea of creating a statewide Greenwing event, inviting each Greenwing chapter chairman from throughout the state to bring a child from his chapter to the lowcountry for a weekend stay at one of the Wildlife Department's Waterfowl Management Areas. The criteria for receiving an invitation were that a chapter had to have a Greenwing program with at least ten children and that the chapter had to host at least one Greenwing event during the year. Fifteen qualified to receive invitations. I was given permission to use the Bear Island Waterfowl Management Area, which had several buildings that could accommodate the crowd.

I put together a program designed to hold the attention of children as well as the adults. The Wildlife Department biologists gave presentations on waterfowl identification, building wood-duck boxes, and banding and releasing teal; they also had show-and-tell sessions with snakes, lizards, and small alligators. Other department personnel gave hunter-safety classes and allowed the children to shoot at targets. Santee Coastal biologist Tommy Strange brought an airboat and gave the children rides around the impoundments, excursions that were also popular with the grownups.

Volunteers helped with dog demonstrations, transportation, and the acquisition and preparation of food and refreshments. I found out one thing the hard way; never give children full-strength caffeinated soft drinks. Between the sugar and the caffeine we almost never got them to go to sleep. The next year they drank apple juice and bottled water.

The weekend event was well received and drew favorable comments from throughout the state. I have always remembered what a profound influence my early wildlife-conservation-camp experience had on me, and I worked to pass along a little of the same experience to the next generation.

I became not only an ardent supporter of Ducks Unlimited but also a dedicated believer in its conservation mission. From my observations it has done more for effective wetlands management and for fostering awareness of the value of such efforts than any other conservation organization. I served for

District Waterfowl Biologist Tommy Strange, sportsman-conservationist Sam Hiott, and Officer Moïse riding on an airboat in the Bear Island Management Area

years on local and state committees and remain active as a life-sponsor member. Many members and staff of Ducks Unlimited were of great help to me throughout my career, and many of the organization's members became my eyes and ears in various duck blinds along the length and breadth of the lowcountry.

Matt Connolly, the executive director of Ducks Unlimited asked me to give a program on law enforcement for a meeting of the organization's regional directors at its 1988 national convention in Nashville, Tennessee. I fine-tuned a slide program I had already developed on the enforcement of the Migratory Bird Treaty Act and asked to have it listed on the program as "War Stories 101." I had created this slide program in response to many requests that I speak to civic clubs and sportsmen's groups about what I did as a game warden. I have never considered myself an organized extemporaneous speaker and was never completely comfortable giving a speech in front of a room full of people. The Wildlife Department produced a tape-recorded narration to accompany a slide show designed to educate viewers about the duties of the game warden, and I fulfilled my early speaking obligations by bringing that program along and answering a few questions after it was over.

That program, however, spoke little about what I actually did. There was very little story to it, and it contained absolutely nothing that would add to anyone's understanding of the regulatory process, which—I knew from experience—was an important topic. I was always asked a lot of questions about it at every meeting I attended.

In the mid-1970s I had developed several slide programs on the subject of historic Charleston. One of the programs, illustrating the value of historic preservation, was created for the Preservation Society of Charleston. Another was produced as an independent effort and traced the influence of the design books of Robert Adam on Charleston architecture. I gave this slide show to the Historic Charleston Foundation for use in their docent-training program. My third excursion in this media format was an art piece on Charleston, using two slide projectors that were synchronized with a tape-recorded narrative. That program made the rounds of every organization in Charleston and many others throughout the state before I gave it to the South Carolina Historical Society.

Having some experience in this form of public presentation, I began to develop several slide programs on what I did as a game warden, trying to make them entertaining as well as educational. It took several years to get a representative collection of slides depicting the environment, the people, and the variety of situations that I confronted on my daily "routine" patrols. Many of those slides are reproduced in this book.

I produced two separate programs, the "War Stories 101" version and one on the enforcement of the coastal-fisheries laws, "War Stories 102." I presented the coastal-enforcement version at a meeting of the Wildlife Commissioners in Columbia and at its conclusion; many of the commissioners approached me and professed to have had no idea that our responsibilities were that far ranging.

I found that by getting the conservation message out in this manner, I could make a lot of friends for the department. The effort also established a valuable base of concerned and informed people willing to get involved in constructive conservation efforts, especially in discouraging or reporting violations of the law. Shortly after showing one club my program, which included a few grim slides illustrating piles of doves and ducks taken in excess of the legal limits, one of the members came up to me and related an interesting story. He said that at the social gathering following a recent afternoon dove shoot near Charleston, the club steward had called out one of the members in front of the assembled hunters and berated him for shooting more than the law allowed. The steward gave him a check returning his membership money and sent him on his way. I have always thought that people who would do something like that were worth a hundred game wardens.

Wildlife in the City

The city landscape was a never-ending source of "wildlife moments." Several wildlife cases happened right in the city limits of Charleston. One afternoon I was enjoying a convivial oyster roast at a friend's house near the Ashley River up beyond the Citadel. A good number of people were standing around the oyster tables in his backyard when their attention was attracted to periodic shots ringing out from across the river near Orange Grove Creek.

More shots were heard as the evening progressed, and the guests began to ask me questions about what could the gunners possibly be shooting at and whether it was legal to shoot in the city limits. They also asked if I could tell from the frequency of the shots if the guns were plugged and if people in that section of the river ever got checked.

Enough of that! I exited the party, dashed home across town, grabbed my johnboat, and sped to the boat ramp at the City Marina. From there I was soon running up the river. I went to the fork where Orange Grove Creek branches off Old Town Creek, and found a spread of decoys in front of two men in a small boat. They were not even a hundred yards away from several waterfront homes. When I pulled up in the marsh grass beside their boat, I could see a neat little pile of hooded mergansers on the seat between them. I politely informed them that they were legally allowed to have only one of those birds apiece and that they were violating a municipal ordinance by discharging firearms within the city limits of Charleston. I checked their "particulars" and found no other violations. (Game wardens did not enforce municipal ordinances.) Instructing them to pack up their gear, I wrote them several tickets each for their excesses, seized their birds, and returned to the party where I was welcomed as a conquering hero. There were plenty of war stories told around the fire that night.

Another downtown "hunt" took place in January 1982, off Lockwood Boulevard near the Charleston Coast Guard Base. My dispatcher contacted me on the radio to inform me of a phone call from the Coast Guard base in downtown Charleston reporting shots fired at a flock of ducks swimming in the open water between the street and the base.

Being not too far away, I drove over to investigate. As I was coming down Lockwood toward Broad Street, I saw a pickup pulled over on the side of the road and a young boy at the edge of the marsh directing a black lab to fetch a duck floating belly up some distance out in the river. I walked up to the boy and asked him what he was doing, and he said that he just happened to be driving by and saw the dead duck and just happened to have his dog along and was sending it out to retrieve it.

When I asked if I could look in his truck, he opened the door. I checked behind the seat and under it. There was no gun or shells, and since I really didn't see anything that tied him with the ability to shoot, there was no case. I told him that the duck had been shot in the Charleston Bird Sanctuary and in the city limits, so if the dog returned with the duck, I was going to have to take it. That dog made an amazingly long retrieve and brought a canvasback right to the feet of its owner. I left after taking his name, address, phone number, and the bird. I stored the duck in my freezer, which was already bursting with plastic bags of frozen birds and beasts of every description that I was holding until they were needed as evidence. (That freezer full of critters became a large and nasty problem years later, in 1989, when the power was out for the better part of a week in the aftermath of Hurricane Hugo.)

A day or two after the duck shoot by the Coast Guard Base, someone told me the true story about what had transpired. My informant said that the boy I had interviewed on Lockwood and a friend had been watching that flock of canvasbacks just about every day. The two boys had concocted a scheme whereby one—after determining that the coast was clear—would shoot a duck from his car window and drive off. Then the other, unarmed friend would just "happen by" a short time later and send his dog to retrieve the duck. I had a grudging admiration for the ingenuity that went into their plan, but I knew they had been bragging about it, a weakness that led to their downfall, and I didn't think that they should get away with it.

I called them and made arrangements to talk to each one separately. I told them that I knew all about what had gone on, that there had been a witness, and that I was going to give them the opportunity to confess and get a ticket for a minimal fine rather than face going to court with the possibility of a large one. Each confessed, admitting that he just couldn't resist what appeared to be a slam-dunk opportunity to take one of those monster canvasbacks and have unlimited bragging rights to the experience. Throughout the years I found that the lack of restraint was the downfall of many a good hunter.

I occasionally hunted those canvasbacks myself, but legally, much further up the river close to the Cosgrove Bridge. Other than the impressive size of the ducks, I never found the Ashley River canvasback shooting to be too sporty. If they saw even one decoy while they were flying down the river, they would come streaming in. The canvasbacks and mergansers were the only things flying in that section of the river, and the legal limit was one of each.

I got frequent calls from city residents that involved me in such problems as catching a Canada goose that was strolling down the sidewalk on Murray Boulevard; relocating a small flock of mallard ducklings that were living in a South Battery fish pool; and capturing marauding possums from several downtown backyards.

I even made a steel-trap case on the Cooper River waterfront. I received a call from the dispatcher of a tugboat company, who said that an otter appeared to be caught in a trap at the Mosquito Fleet dock next to their office. (The Mosquito Fleet was the name given to a number of small rowboats and sailboats owned by African Americans who fished, crabbed, and caught shrimp in the waters around Charleston. The fleet had largely disappeared by the early 1970s.) When I arrived at the tugboat company's dock to investigate, I looked through my binoculars and spotted the writhing, squealing otter, which appeared to have one of its toes caught in the jaws of a steel trap that was nailed to a float at the end of the dock.

I knew that I could not just grab an excited adult otter and cuddle it as I gently extracted it from its painful situation. Some have learned the hard way that otters are strong animals and have sharp teeth. As I was standing there pondering this dilemma, I saw a man unlocking the gate at the entrance to the Mosquito Fleet dock. I stepped behind some pilings and watched the man walk down the dock to the float. As he neared the trapped otter, it began furiously thrashing about and spinning around, violent movements that succeeded in twisting off the caught toe, which remained firmly gripped in the trap. As the otter disappeared from sight, the man leaned over and unfastened the nail to retrieve the trap. While he was occupied, I moved up near the tugboat company's office. As the man was closing the gate, I stepped over and asked if I could see the trap he was holding. The otter's toe was still in it. I asked a question to which I already knew the answer: "Do you have a license for the trap?" I then told him that setting a trap without a license was against the law and wrote him a ticket for it.

It took forever to get him into court. I had to go with a bench warrant in hand a couple of times into parts of uptown where the atmosphere was clearly hostile to anyone wearing a badge. The fine was difficult to collect, but persistence paid off. I finally cornered him and carried him to the magistrate, who gave him a choice of paying a fine or going immediately to jail. He had to call three different friends to come up with the amount of the fine.

As I was coming down the Town Creek channel of the Cooper River by the old coal-tipple dock late one evening, I spotted a johnboat pulled up on the shore of Drum Island. A quick investigation revealed an empty gun case in the bottom of the boat, a discovery that immediately attracted my attention because Drum Island was within the Charleston Harbor sanctuary, and hunting was prohibited.

I ran my boat to the other side of Town Creek tying off to one of the pilings near the coal tipple. About an hour later I saw a large tugboat steaming down the river in my direction. I untied my boat and headed out into deeper water to ride the enormous wake as the tug went by.

When it had passed, I looked across the channel and saw that the wake had flipped the johnboat upside down. A red gas tank and an orange life jacket were drifting nearby. There was still no sign of the boat's owners, so I went over and retrieved the gas can, life jacket, and other items and carried them to the overturned boat.

I righted the johnboat, pulled it up on the bank, placed all the items back inside, and returned to my observation spot across the creek. The sun was beginning to set, but I knew that the hunters eventually had to return to their boat, so I sat straining to hear any sound of gunshots over the traffic noises of the nearby Cooper River bridges.

After another forty-five minutes of waiting in dwindling light, I finally saw two people come over the top of the dike and begin walking down to the johnboat. I waited for a few minutes before I slipped my line from the piling and slowly eased across the creek. As I approached, I saw one of the men standing on the bank holding a rifle while the other was in the stern of the boat attempting to hand start the engine. I introduced myself and asked the man with the gun to unload it and hand it over to me. I also explained to them why their boat was not likely to start.

When I inquired about what they had been hunting, they said that they had seen deer in the middle of the spoil while riding over the bridge earlier in the week and that they had come to see if they could shoot one. They both produced proper hunting licenses as I explained to them that Drum Island was a posted sanctuary and that it was illegal to hunt there. I also explained to them that the violation carried a pretty serious fine.

After numerous attempts to start their engine, it became apparent to the hunters that it wasn't going to run. I instructed them to get into my boat and took them and their boat to Remleys Point Landing. During the short trip I quizzed them further about their hunting expedition. After helping them get their disabled boat on the trailer, I wrote them each a ticket for hunting in a sanctuary. I also pointed out that they had only one life jacket and no running lights, cautioning them to be more attentive to those details in the future. Their fines were paid to the magistrate by the time I got to court; they had left word that they didn't want a trial.

Whether the victims of man or of nature, a never-ending parade of wounded birds that appeared around downtown Charleston had to be corralled or chased down and carried much against their will to veterinarians or rehabilitation volunteers. I remember pursuing one reportedly wounded egret all around Marion Square to the amusement and cheers of onlookers. The bird rewarded me for my efforts by befouling my clothes and a considerable portion of the front seat of my patrol car.

The Canada goose that I herded into a driveway on Murray Boulevard also did not submit willingly to its capture or to being stuffed into the back of my patrol car. When I arrived at Hampton Park to release it in the lake, I found that it had expressed its displeasure by decorating the entire backseat, which after a number of bird rescues quite resembled a Jackson Pollock painting, a design that stayed with the vehicle as long as I had it.

Other urban intrusions included the poodle-eating alligators that inhabited the decorative lagoons scattered around just about every lowcountry subdivision and golf course. Until a Wildlife Department–regulated alligator management team took over the task, it was one of the responsibilities

Giving a sick egret a free ride to the veterinarian after a spirited chase around Marion Square in downtown Charleston

of the game wardens to catch and remove them. Some of the wardens were better at it than others. Victor Lincoln, a Berkeley County warden could stand on the edge of a pond and call an alligator in close enough to get a snare over its head. Other officers resorted to building bait stations on which a snare was set. Every now and then we managed to pounce on one that was high and dry.

In the early days, when alligators were still counted as a "threatened species" in South Carolina, they had to be captured alive and relocated to an area where they posed no threat to timid suburbanites—or to little dogs, which seemed to be the alligator's snack of choice. Sometimes relocation seemed a complete waste of time because many alligators found their way back to where we had caught them. We knew they were the same alligators because, after we captured one, we attached a numbered plastic tag to one of the big scales on its tail. Later, as alligators became more numerous, they were shot at the scene and removed.

Shooting an alligator had to be done with the greatest of care, however, for considerations of public relations as well as safety. It became unofficial department policy that, if one of the beasts had been given a name by local residents, it would be removed from the area alive and tended to later out of sight. The department made that policy after a storm of controversy following the public demise by gunfire of a huge alligator named "Lake Boss."

In the several times I became involved with alligators removal, I found that it was a lot easier to catch them than to turn them loose. By the time they had been snatched from a pond, hog-tied, and jolted around in the back of a truck, they were really mad.

One time I caught several three-footers that had apparently washed down the rivers after a period of torrential rains and were found crawling around on the front beach of Sullivan's Island. I brought them downtown in the trunk of my car and released them in a small pond near the Charleston City Marina. In less than a week I was getting calls about those two alligators.

With Officer Terry Cumbee (right), capturing a "nuisance" alligator from a suburban pond

Holding a three-foot alligator caught on the Sullivan's Island beach. After it was released in a Charleston pond, concerned citizens reported that it had grown more than three feet in one week.

which had somehow miraculously grown to enormous lengths. One caller reported that an alligator at least six feet long had hissed at her. I wound up having to catch them again and relocate them out of town. That ended the hissing problem.

I answered the phone one evening, as I was attired in a tuxedo, ready to walk out of the house with my wife to attend a formal gathering at South Carolina Society Hall. The caller identified himself as a television reporter and said that he had called the Wildlife Department several times earlier in the day to report that a duck's legs were frozen fast in the ice on a pond in North Charleston.

He said that no one had called him back, that the duck had been there all day. He was going out with a camera crew to film a nightly news report on the plight of the duck and the obvious official indifference of the Wildlife Department. At that point, since he knew my name, I was certain he would be heaping blame on me, the "indifferent official," as he wrung his hands before the television camera.

I informed the reporter I would come and fetch the duck, but added that I had never heard of one being frozen by its feet before. He assured me that was indeed the case, and I went upstairs to change back into my uniform.

When I arrived, I found that the pond was in the middle of a large graveyard. It was frozen over with a thin layer of ice, and I could see in the beam of my flashlight, later aided by the bright television camera lights, a white domestic duck out in the middle. I radioed the dispatcher to call the funeral home that owned the cemetery and inquire about the depth of the pond. After about half an hour the dispatcher called back and reported the pond was said to be only about a foot and a half deep. I donned my hip boots and carried along a hatchet to break the ice as I walked out to get the duck. I chopped ice, pushing it aside as I neared the hapless beast, all the while dreading the prospect of the ice puncturing my waders. As it became clear that the estimate of the pond's depth was incorrect by at least a foot, I found that the water was numbingly cold.

When I finally got to within six feet of that duck, it stood up and ran away quacking and flapping its wings across the top of the ice. With clenched jaws I slowly made my way back lugging hip boots now filled to the top with freezing water. I walked straight to my car, pulled off the boots, dumped the water out of them, threw them in the trunk of the car, and departed without uttering a single comment. I did give the reporter a bad dose of the "stink eye." I heard that my stunned expression when the water came over the top of my boots made some interesting news footage. We were only about an hour and a half late to the party, but my feet were far too numb to dance despite generous infusions of "antifreeze."

Feathered Disasters

One day I was patrolling in my boat along the docks on Shem Creek and spotted some activity on the deck of Captain Lewis Porcher's green-painted trawler, the *Miss Glena,* which was tied to the dock on the west side of the creek. Captain Lewis and his crew were on the stern of his shrimp boat cleaning out the nets and tidying up after a day of trawling.

I pulled alongside and stepped up on the bow of my boat. Holding on to the port rail of the *Miss Glena,* I began asking Captain Lewis about how things were going in the business—the price of shrimp, the amount of shrimp they were catching—and just making general conversation.

A man possessed of a gentle nature and a quiet dignity, Captain Lewis was one of the few African American trawler owners in the Shem Creek shrimp-boat fleet. He was knowledgeable about the business and much respected by others in it. I used to enjoy hearing his comments and his laugh on the marine VHF in the predawn hours as they lowered the outriggers and readied the nets for trawling just offshore of Morris Island.

As I stood there talking with him, one of several brown pelicans that were perched atop the outriggers turned itself wrong side out and let fly with a voluminous and vile downpour that managed to wash over me from head to toe. If I had been dipped in a bucket of whitewash, I could not have been more covered. I don't know who was more surprised, me or Captain Lewis.

His crew, who had been busily at work on the deck, quickly exited the scene and stampeded through the wheelhouse door. I could hear their squealing, hissing, and muffled laughter emanating from within. Captain Lewis just stood there mute, appearing absolutely stunned. I could tell that he was trying desperately to contain his amusement over my predicament. Knowing him to be a good Christian, I was equally desperate to refrain from abusing the King's English. In a sudden burst of lucidity, I asked Captain Lewis if he had a water hose handy, and he replied that there was one on the other side of the deck. I asked him if he would mind dragging it over to me. He stepped across the deck, pulled the hose across to the rail, and started to hand it to me. I said, "No, I want you to hose me down." By this time the situation had attracted the attention of many people on the raised deck of the nearby restaurant, and the rail there was beginning to become quite crowded.

I asked Captain Lewis to just give me a good, thorough hosing down to get all that stuff off me. After a little initial reluctance, he aimed the nozzle and proceeded to wash me down from top to bottom, a spectacle that created quite a stir among the onlookers, who by that time were beginning to cheer and clap and attract even more attention to my dilemma. I also saw several of the crewmen peering through the cabin windows, wide eyed and wheezing thorough their teeth in a feeble attempt not to be too obvious in their mirth.

After that public ablution, I took the hose from Captain Lewis and washed down my boat, thanked him for his help, started my engine, and slowly exited the creek, still listening to gales of raucous laughter receding behind me in the distance. Belle did not seem impressed, sneezing and snorting at the odoriferous residue of pelican.

Not too many years later, I exacted an accidental revenge of sorts on a—if not *the*—pelican. I had been giving my friends Danie Malan and Johan Spies, both professional hunters from South Africa, a midwinter boat tour of the Santee Delta and Cape Romain and was heading south down the Intracoastal Waterway. They were seated forward of the console in my fifteen-foot Whaler, and I was pointing out the fauna and flora of the passing marshscape. There were numerous flocks of oystercatchers, semipalmated sandpipers, cormorants, wimbrels, and pelicans arrayed on the white oyster banks bordering the waterway.

As we approached the intersection of Price Inlet and the waterway, I noticed a large flock of pelicans standing atop the shell bank. To give my friends a closer look, I steered the boat over, running parallel to the bank, explaining over the noise of the engine that, not too many years ago, the pelican was listed as a threatened species in South Carolina because the widespread use of DDT had affected their reproduction.

Just as I approached the flock they took to wing in a dramatic display right in front of the boat. Most swooped up and over us; however, one unfortunate bird flew low, right in the path of the boat and disappeared under the bow. In an instant the engine came to an abrupt halt, and the boat went dead in the water. I restarted it in idle, but as soon as I put it in gear it cut off. I pushed the trim and tilt button to raise the foot of the motor and was mortified to see that poor mangled pelican completely wrapped around the prop of my engine.

I poled over to the shell bank and got out of the boat in order to extract the gruesome remains from around the propeller. I could not help but notice the smirks on the faces of my friends as they witnessed my discomfiture and embarrassment at causing of the demise of the unfortunate bird, which had gone from "threatened" to "extinct." From then on I gave those bird banks a wide berth as I passed by, the ghost of that poor pelican a constant reminder.

I became involved a number of times over the years with some of our department biologists who were conducting studies on the life cycle of the eastern brown pelican. Most of the time my involvement consisted of helping them to herd flocks of immature pelicans still in their island rookery into a corral fashioned of netting fastened to poles stuck in the sand. There they would be caught, weighed, checked for parasites, and banded. Some had blood samples taken to test for the presence of toxins. The young pelicans did not cooperate willingly when being handled, and everyone involved in the roundup was scratched and bloodied by the end of the day. The birds had sharp claws as well as vicious hooks on the end of their long beaks.

Determining whether they were infected with parasites was easy because in all the scuffling the bugs would often jump ship, and we could clearly see on our arms and legs the nature of the infestation. Most of the time they were just bird mites, but on one of the trips to the rookery, we found that the pelicans were plagued with ticks. A significant number of the newly hatched were pitifully infested, and a plan was rapidly implemented to apply insecticide on and around all the nests. A later study, however, proved that dusting the nests had no measurable effect on the tick population and that the tick infestations did not seem to harm the birds. We had just assumed that they had to be as uncomfortable as we would be if we had that many ticks. Even though the crew had heavily doused themselves with tick repellant before disembarking from their boats, they still found numerous ticks firmly fastened to various tender parts. I had been suspicious of ticks ever since I had a serious bout of Lyme disease some years before as a result of a tick bite and did not enjoy the experience one bit. Over the years I could see the gradual recovery of the pelican population, and now they may be seen in great numbers throughout the coast. More recently the eastern brown pelicans have been joined in the summer and fall by flocks of large white pelicans, whose numbers seem to be increasing every year.

In addition to assisting department biologists, I worked with ornithologists from around the country over the years on projects ranging from surveys of nesting least terns, egrets, and ibis to exploratory trips around the marsh to study or photograph migrating wading birds. On one such mission I took the well-known nature and bird photographer Tom Blagden and his wife, Lynn, to Capers Island to camp for the weekend.

I dropped them off on the west side of the island on Capers Inlet and left them with the understanding that I would pick them up late Sunday afternoon at the same spot. It was a hectic weekend with a lot of boating activity and calls for enforcement presence from one end of the county to the other. I was worn out by late Sunday afternoon and went home, ate supper, and crawled into bed.

I was just putting my head down on my pillow when I sat bolt upright and shouted, "Good Grief!" I leaped out of bed and dashed down the stairs, pulling on various parts of my uniform. I ran out of the house to my car and sped over to the Isle of Palms Marina. When at last I arrived at the darkened inlet beach, I shined my spotlight around and saw their tent in the dunes.

Presently Tom opened the tent flap. Talk about being covered with embarrassment! He said that they had waited until well past the appointed time to be picked up, and then set their tent back up. They seemed relieved at my arrival, however late, because their stocks of water and food were exhausted. I think Tom went out and bought his own boat shortly after that little misadventure.

For many years one of the largest heron, egret, and ibis rookeries in the Southeast was located just under the Cooper River bridges on Drum Island. The rank growth of mulberry trees there appeared to be covered with snow every

Viewing nestling egrets on the Drum Island wading-bird rookery in Charleston Harbor

spring as huge numbers of white-feathered birds congregated there to nest. I was frequently called on to take wildlife photographers to this rookery and noticed that the older nestlings, particularly on the lower nests, became alarmed at our approach—however careful our movements—and went running up a limb, sometimes falling out of the tree. Usually it was impossible to replace them in the nest, so I discouraged any further intrusions.

Before the next nesting season began I constructed a burlap-bag-covered observation area in the middle of the rookery with a camouflaged access path leading from the river's edge. From this hiding place the birds could be studied and photographed without scaring them.

One morning I saw a familiar crabber's boat tied up near the edge of the Drum Island rookery on Town Creek and stopped to investigate. Just as I tied my boat up the crabber emerged with a basket full of dead baby birds. He said that he just went around and gathered up the ones that had fallen from the nests, most of which were already dead, and that he used them to bait his crab pots.

I told him he had to discontinue that practice because, even though they were dead, they were a protected nongame migratory bird. I learned later that in the old days before wire crab pots came into use, crabbers baited their trot lines with the baby birds. I could not even begin to imagine the howl such a practice would cause if it happened now.

Hook, Line, and Sinker

I got a phone call late on one of my free Sunday afternoons from Jim Smiley, the public defender in the Ninth Circuit solicitor's office in Charleston. He said that he and some friends were on the east end of Bull Island at the Jacks Creek dike and had seen a boat with four men in it hauling in spottail bass hand over fist. He said that he had seen several of them put six or seven fish in the boat. He told me he had called down to them that they were supposed to keep only five fish each and was given a good cussing and the finger in response to his cautionary advice. He reported that, while he was there the tide was pretty low and still seemed to be going out, so he thought the fishermen could not get out of the creek until better than a half tide, which was several hours away. He gave me a description of the boat and motor but said that, from where he was standing, he could not read the boat's registration number.

Telling him I would check it out, I immediately pulled on my uniform and headed over east of the Cooper to look around. I decided to check the most distant landings first, so I drove to Awendaw, where I checked Buck Hall Landing and found no vehicles or trailers there. I checked several other smaller private and public landings on the way back to Mount Pleasant finally winding up just after sunset at the Isle of Palms Marina parking lot, where I found two vehicles with trailers attached as well as several cars without trailers. One trailer was obviously meant for a small johnboat, and the other was configured to hold a larger boat.

I called the dispatcher in Columbia and got him to run the vehicle license-tag number. It came back as belonging to an individual with an

Taking data from a stranded bottlenose dolphin on Sullivan's Island

Awendaw address. I asked the dispatcher to check for any boats and motors registered to the person at that address. They came back with an exact match to the description of the boat and motor that Smiley had given me earlier. I parked my patrol car out of sight of the ramp on the other side of the marina store, and took a position on the darkened porch behind the marina office, where I had a good view of the boat ramp.

About an hour later I saw the distant running lights of a boat coming from up the waterway. As it entered the marina, I moved deeper into the shadows of the porch and observed, as it neared the lighted area at the end of the ramp, that the boat contained four men and that it fit the description of the boat I was looking for. I waited until they got the boat on the trailer and on the way to the top of the ramp before I came around the building to introduce myself. I could tell right away that they were not pleased to see me. As I was checking the boat registration and fishing licenses, I tried to be pleasant and asked them how they had done with the fishing.

Two of the men, who were from out of state, quickly responded that they had not done any fishing, that they had just been along for the ride. The other two reported that, while they had caught some fish, they had not kept any of them and confirmed that their companions had not been fishing. "Methinks the lads doth protest too much," I thought, as I informed them that I would like to examine their boat and check their safety equipment.

Climbing up in the boat with my flashlight, I started opening coolers, bow compartments, and the storage areas near the transom. I was pulling out life jackets, fire extinguishers, and boat cushions, all the while looking with carefully restrained anticipation for the fish I was certain I would find and periodically studying the expressions of the fishermen standing around the boat. I could see fish blood and scales all over the deck and smeared over the inner sides of the gunnels, and there were five or six fully rigged fishing rods stacked over to one side.

Searching the boat, using the beam of my light to focus on every little detail, I suddenly caught a glimpse of the corner of a deck-hatch cover, barely visible under the large cooler sitting in front of the console. I lifted the cooler by the handles and moved it up on the bow, fully exposing the closed hatch. I could clearly sense the mounting agitation of the two locals, who had said they had not caught any fish. As I lifted the lid of the deck compartment, I could see that it was filled completely to the top with spottail bass.

Saying something like "Hey, you must have forgotten about these," I told them that I would have to check the sizes of the fish I had found. Even after discovering the lie, I made no accusations and tried my best not to be cute about the discovery. I knelt down and began removing the fish, placing each of them lengthwise on the calibrated measuring device I had brought along.

After measuring ten fish, the legal limit for two people, without finding any of illegal size, I informed them that, if they were the only ones fishing, any others found in the compartment would be over the legal limit. I told them that I was going to hand down to them the additional fish and that they were to put them in a row on the grass by the ramp, and I also asked them to help me keep an accurate count. They were grudgingly accommodating.

I started measuring fish as I removed them from the compartment, then handing them down, counting each one out loud. I kept counting and kept counting, asking them at intervals if my count was correct. I brought out a total of forty more fish, in addition to the ten I had set aside as their legal limit.

After climbing out of the boat, I rearranged the fish in rows of ten to reconfirm the number. The two who claimed they didn't fish, seemed nervous as cats and asked if they could leave. I explained that what we had here was a pretty serious violation and that I wanted to write down some information from their drivers' licenses. I saw that they were from Tennessee. I asked them again if they had caught any of the fish, and they stated that they had not. I got the information I needed from their licenses, and they hastily exited the parking lot.

Going over to the floating dock of the marina, I removed the large plastic liners from several of the trashcans, bagged up all the fish, and put them in the trunk of my car. The two remaining fishermen and I sat under the light at a picnic table on the back porch of the marina store, where I calmly and carefully detailed to them the gravity of their situation. I informed them that it was possible to write them a ticket for each and every fish in excess of the legal limit of five per person. I didn't tell them that at that moment it was impossible for me to write them the forty tickets they deserved because I had only eight tickets left in my ticket book.

I informed them that I was just going to issue them four tickets apiece for the offense of taking over the limit of spottail bass and that I was going to ask for the maximum fine, which I think was around four hundred dollars on each charge. I further explained that in addition to the fines, a finding of guilt would result in the suspension of their recreational saltwater licenses for one year. When we parted company, I had the distinct feeling that they thought they had been treated fairly and that they felt they had gotten a good deal out of what could have potentially been a much worse situation.

I showed up for court in Mount Pleasant expecting to find that the defendants had posted bond, but I was met by Barry Krell, a criminal defense attorney from Charleston, who told me that he was representing both defendants and wanted to propose a deal. Responding that the deal had already been cut, I explained to him that they could have been issued a separate ticket for each fish over the limit.

He seemed to act as though this were no big thing. He was wearing one of those Cheshire cat smiles when he said he wanted me to drop three of the charges on each defendant, and then they would agree to plead guilty and forfeit their bonds on the one remaining charge. I told him that his proposal was out of the question, that his clients had committed a gross violation, and that he had better go back and talk to them. I told him I would return to court the following week for his answer, and I walked out.

When I arrived at the magistrate's office a week later, Mr. Krell met me at the door of the courtroom and asked me to come into the small jury room to discuss the case. He told me that he had read the law and said that he had found that under our regulations a third and subsequent offense carried an enhanced penalty, which placed his clients beyond the jurisdiction of the magistrate's court, so they could only be tried in General Sessions Court for the third and forth violations. He further stated that, if I persisted in being unreasonable, he would ask that two of the charges be tried before a circuit judge, and he would then move for their dismissal on the grounds that the result would be two trials stemming from the same offense.

Not really knowing if that little maneuver could be done or not, I had heard all the theories of justice I wanted to hear from him and said so in a loud and totally unprofessional manner. It was loud enough for the magistrate to come out of the door to her office to ask if everything was all right. I apologized for the fuss, left the court, and headed straight for the Ninth Circuit solicitor's office in North Charleston.

I got an audience with the solicitor, David Schwacke, and explained to him what was going on. I told him I had the evidence in hand as well as a witness, Jim Smiley, his public defender. I think I conveyed to him my total outrage that Mr. Krell seemed to be trying to manipulate the judicial process to his clients' advantage and appeared to be almost contemptuously dismissive of the gravity of the offenses. I left the solicitor copies of my report and the tickets as well as photographs of the seized over-the-limit fish. He said that he would look at it and give me a call.

The radio dispatcher called me early the next morning with the message that I was to be at the solicitor's office that afternoon. When I arrived I was taken to a young assistant solicitor, Keith McCarty, who went over the details of the cases with me and considered all the applicable laws in play. Mr. McCarty said that he would study the issues and come up with a game plan and for me to do nothing more on the cases until I heard from him.

Several weeks later he called me to come over to his office. He said he wanted me to go to the magistrate's office and have the four charges on each of the defendants dismissed. Once that was done I was to come to his office the following day, and we would take out warrants charging each of them with twenty counts of taking over the limit of spottail bass. Saying that he was sending the case before the grand jury, he informed me that I would have to appear before them in a couple of weeks and show that there was sufficient evidence for an indictment.

I was asked to present the charges and the supporting evidence. Various members of the jury panel asked questions about the law and why it was enacted as well as questions about why I had dismissed the original four charges on each defendant and was now taking out a warrant for those and sixteen more charges. I explained the circumstances of the warrant and impressed on them the serious nature of the offense.

Mr. McCarty called me a day later, and told me that the grand jury had "true billed" the indictments. A week or so later he called to tell me to pick up the warrants and to serve them the following day. I rounded up a few of my colleagues to help with serving the warrants and transporting the defendants to the county jail, where they would be booked and held overnight for a bond hearing. One defendant lived in an apartment complex in Mount Pleasant and the other in the rural reaches of Awendaw.

Officer Wiley Knight and I were going to serve the warrants in the early evening and decided to pick up the defendant in Mount Pleasant first. When we knocked on the door of his apartment, it was opened by his wife, who called for him to come to the door. When he appeared he was informed that we had a warrant for his arrest and that he was to come with us now. We read him the warrant, gave him a copy of it, searched him, handcuffed him, and put him in the back of a car, which carried him to the county jail to be booked.

We then headed to the other defendant's house in Awendaw. When we arrived the house was in total darkness. As we drove into the yard, we could see where vehicle tires had torn up the dirt in the front yard. We shined a flashlight through a darkened window. On the kitchen table we saw plates full of still steaming food and forks with food still on them. We figured that, after we had made the first arrest, a phone call was made to Awendaw, and our culprit had fled the scene.

We drove back to the county jail in North Charleston and filled out all the booking documents on the defendant we had in hand. He was photographed, fingerprinted, and divested of his shoelaces, belt, and other personal possessions. We told him that we would see him at around ten o'clock the next morning for the bond hearing, and left him to be someone's cellmate for the night.

The next morning, as we were walking up to the courtroom, we were confronted by the men's angry attorney, who was accompanied by the missing defendant and his mother. Noticeably annoyed, Mr. Krell accused us of outrageous conduct. Ignoring his outburst, I informed him that I had a warrant to serve on his client and that he could remain with him while I read it if he wished. I read the defendant the warrant, gave his attorney the copy, and informed him that he would have to be booked before we went into the bond hearing, which again sent Mr. Krell into a torrent of uncomplimentary remarks directed at our professionalism.

His client was taken to the booking cell, where he too was frisked, photographed, fingerprinted, and divested of his shoelaces, belt, and other personal possessions. he was then handcuffed to a rail in a long line of defendants awaiting their bond hearings.

The other officer and I left the booking area and went into the bond court. Mr. Krell and the defendant's mother glared at us as we entered the courtroom and the whole time we sat waiting for our cases to come up. There is really not much to say in a bond hearing, other than what the defendants are charged with and the total amount of the possible fine. Their attorney, who got up to stand with them as they were called before the bench, began, in an obviously annoyed tone of voice, to tell the judge that his clients were being treated unfairly only because they had obtained a lawyer. The judge cut him off, said he would have to take that up with the arresting officers, and imposed a five thousand dollar personal-recognizance bond on each defendant.

Outside the courtroom after the hearing, Mr. Krell again lit into us and angrily stated that the only reason we were doing this was because his clients had hired an attorney. I replied in a somewhat peeved tone of voice that it was most likely true that the reason this situation had escalated to this point was absolutely because they had hired a lawyer and that, had he been reasonable at first, we would not be standing there now. My colleague took me by the arm and led me off to the car, saying it was never good business to talk to a defense lawyer unless he asked you a question in court.

Mr. McCarty had warned me that it could take some time for the case to come up for trial. He also told me to get hold of the necessary number of ticket books and write forty separate tickets on the over-the-limit charges, which our department would need as tracking documents to follow the charges through the court system. That was a lot of writing, and I got help from a fellow officer in filling them out.

While waiting for the trial date to be set, I got a call from Solicitor Schwacke, who asked if I could come by his office. He related to me a long story of the pressure he was under to settle this case before trial. He had received visits from two former Ninth Circuit solicitors, one of whom asked him to consider going back to the original four charges, to which the defendants would now agree to plead guilty. Saying that he did not even get this kind of pressure on some murder cases, Mr. Schwacke asked if there were anything less than proceeding to trial that I would happy with. I thought about it a minute and said I would get back to him.

I walked down the hall to Mr. McCarty's office and admitted to him that I was not happy at the prospect of going back to the original four charges, especially after all the trouble that we had gone to. He said the real sticking point was apparently the total amount of the fine, which was around eight thousand dollars each plus the additional court costs if the two men were found guilty at a trial.

I told him that the only way for them to escape the court cost, which was assessed at 80 percent of the fine, was for them to be sent to prison. I also told him that in addition to fines some states had restitution fees for the value of the natural resources destroyed. While South Carolina did not then have an official restitution policy, I told him that implementing such a policy was currently being discussed. I said I would find out what our department figured forty spottail bass were worth and if the department would be comfortable with anything less than a full-court press on these cases.

Several of the fisheries biologists in the Marine Division liked the idea of restitution because that money could be earmarked for a specific program, such as fish restocking or research, whereas fines at that time went into the general fund in Columbia with no benefit to the department. They decided on a figure of one hundred dollars per fish. My bosses took the stance that it was my case, and I could run with it however I wanted.

Mr. McCarty and I fashioned an offer. If the defendants would plead guilty to all the charges, we would recommend that the judge sentence them to serve six months in prison, which would be suspended on payment of restitution in the amount of two thousand dollars each to the Department of Natural Resources fisheries-management program, and that the judge suspend their saltwater-fishing privileges for a period of one year from the date of sentencing.

We presented the proposal to Mr. Schwacke, who seemed pleased with it, and he sent it to Mr. Krell in the form of a plea-bargain offer. I believe by this time Mr. Krell was all too happy to get this case over with and to get out of it without his clients having to pay a fine exceeding fourteen thousand dollars—an outcome that would have damaged his professional reputation.

By this time word had spread all over Charleston that a game warden was running all over a highly paid criminal-defense lawyer in a fish case. During the trial, after the charges were made and the solicitor read the plea agreement, the circuit judge looked over at me and asked me if I was happy with the arrangement. Not meaning to be cute, but responding to his query truthfully, I said, "No, I'm not exactly happy with it." WRONG ANSWER!

The judge immediately recessed the proceedings and instructed Mr. Schwacke, Mr. McCarty, Mr. Krell, and me to convene with him in his chambers. I could see that Mr. Schwacke was somewhat pained over this turn of events, and Mr. Krell just barely managed to mask his arrogance with a little touch of surprised concern.

The judge asked me straight away about how I felt about the terms of the plea bargain. I told him that an awful lot of work had gone into getting the case to this juncture. I told him that it could have been satisfactorily settled with a lot less effort, expense, and acrimony over a year sooner, had it not been for poor legal advice given the defendants.

I could see that Mr. Schwacke and Mr. McCarty were wondering where I was going with this, and I quickly got to the point. I told the judge that I would have been far happier if there had been good-faith dealing right up front, but that was over and done with. I told him that I was not entirely happy with the current arrangement, even though I was one of its authors, because I really thought that the defendants should serve some time; however, in accepting the plea bargain, I thought justice would be properly and fairly served. I could feel a sense of relief coming over the faces of the lawyers in the room, except for Mr. Krell, who continued to scowl.

We went back into the courtroom; the judge read the charges to the defendants and asked them how they pled. They both pled guilty. The judge then sentenced them according to the terms of the plea agreement, and the long saga of the fish case was over.

The case was written about in many sport-fishing magazines, newspaper articles, and national resource-agency legal briefs. It was always important to me to get the story out so that the lessons to be learned were not confined to the defendants alone. I felt that stories of violators being caught and convicted were valuable by-products of the judicial process and made people think twice about contravening the resource laws.

Game Wardens

One of the more colorful old-time game wardens was Lockwood "Locky" Freeman. Many stories about Locky fall into the well-known "I don't think I would have told that, if I were you" category. But there are kinder, gentler stories as well.

For as long as I can remember, Locky did his patrols in an eighteen-foot Glassmaster with a 140-horsepower engine. He customized his boat in the interest of comfort by installing an automobile bucket seat behind the steering wheel. Assigned to the boating division, he worked long hours and wrote lots of tickets. His chief focus was enforcing boating-safety laws, but he had no aversion to enforcing hunting and fishing regulations.

I could call him at any time of the day or night—even on his day off or holidays—and he would come without complaint or excuse if I needed him. I can still hear his gravelly voice calling for me over the radio, "Nine-two-five to B-four." Locky had the great good fortune to be able to take most of his cases to the long-serving East Cooper magistrate Paul Foster, his brother-in-law. Judge Foster would from time to time feel called upon to rap his gavel and scold Locky because he was wearing his cap in the courtroom. Locky would just sigh, give the judge his "twis mout" look (a local expression describing a grim countenance or appearance of consternation) and slowly remove his cap. The judge occasionally had to call Locky to task for providing loud commentary while a bench trial was taking place.

I remember patrolling the Rockville Regatta with Locky back in the early 1980s. We were each in his own patrol boat, and there was a huge amount of boating activity around the spectator fleet anchored in Bohicket

With South Carolina game warden Lockwood "Locky" Freeman, observing a logger-head turtle digging a hole for egg laying on Capers Island

Creek between the Sea Island Yacht Club dock and the sandbar just opposite it. It didn't take long to spot violations, and I began to issue a number of tickets. Word got over to Locky that the new game warden was writing practically everybody who came by. He eventually found me, took me aside, and cautioned me about being "too rough."

His philosophy was that the people were there to have a good time, and as long as they didn't do anything too blatantly stupid or dangerous, it was best just to keep an eye out for the really bad things. Unfortunately some years later the situation at the Rockville Regatta got so out of hand that the usual shenanigans could no longer be overlooked, and the officers of the Sea Island Yacht Club, of which I was a former commodore, asked the Wildlife Department for stricter enforcement on the larger and increasingly unruly crowds. The Rockville Regatta is perhaps now better known for its status as a floating cocktail party than for its challenging boat races.

From late May and into July, Locky and I periodically walked the beach at night on Capers Island to watch the loggerhead turtles come out of the surf and crawl up the beach to dig nests in which to deposit their eggs. It was a powerful sight, and it would be difficult to describe my feelings on seeing the reenactment of an event that has gone on for millions of years. Usually never lacking in his descriptive outbursts, Locky became totally speechless as we gazed on those marvelous spectacles of nature.

There was a persistent problem during the turtle-nesting season with poachers invading the deserted stretches of the barrier islands and gathering large numbers of freshly laid turtle eggs to supply a variety of exotic markets. Locky and I kept a close eye on boat traffic around the inlets during the nesting season. Other than their use in making moist cakes, the eggs had a reputation in some communities for improving a man's sexual prowess, and they were served as bar snacks at juke joints and "sweet shops" all along the coast. The wildlife department frequently employed African American officers as undercover agents to gain entrance to those establishments and ask if there were any turtle eggs they could have with their beer.

At one point the egg poaching seemed to be getting out of hand, and officers from inland districts all the way to the mountains were brought in to patrol the beaches during the nights of the peak nesting time. At first there was no lack of volunteers who thought that it would be wonderful duty to walk along the moonlit beaches in the coolness of the night. They thought that until they encountered the nightly clouds of hungry salt-marsh mosquitoes. They couldn't believe that we on the coast had to deal with these insects on a regular basis. The patrols went on for the duration of the nesting season and effectively put an end to the egg poaching.

I always appreciated Locky's willingness to assist on a search and rescue or a law-enforcement problem. He never made any excuses. During the cold winter months when we were patrolling in the wee hours of the morning in the upper reaches of the Cooper or Wando river looking for gill netters, he routinely pulled over to the bank of one or another small island, tied the boat off, and hopped out to build a campfire. Looking around on the ground with his flashlight, he gathered small sticks of wood and soon had a nice warming fire going. I worked with Locky a lot over the years, always enjoying his company and the stories of his adventures in the field.

Locky's father had been a Charleston County game warden for twenty years before Locky came on to take his place. When Locky retired in 1987 after forty-two years of service, he was one of the longest serving game wardens in the country. At a retirement reception for Locky hosted by East Cooper magistrate Jeanette Mullen Harper, among those present were two other long-serving wardens—one state, Mack Flood, and one federal, Bill

Lehman—who had worked with Locky from his earliest years in law enforcement. The combined service of the three men was calculated to be 122 years.

At this gathering Locky reminisced that, when he first came on, he made $150 a month plus $50 for gasoline. He said that a warden then had to furnish his own car, uniforms, and pistol. He added, "We even had to buy the badge provided by the Game Division. We had to pay two whole dollars for it."

The first time I ever met Locky was some years before I joined the Wildlife Department. I lived in an old 1880s-vintage house on Sullivan's Island with my wife, Anne, and my daughters, Melissa and Sarah. I had a homemade plywood bateau, which I named the *Putt Putt Maru* and kept in a small drain in the marsh behind my neighbor Lukie Lucas's house. When the tide was right, I often paddled out to the cove behind Sullivan's Island, to set my fifty-foot gill net. At the time I had a poultry pen behind our house containing many colors and sizes of chickens as well as two turkeys. Occasionally I took one of the chickens along for company in the boat while I fished the gill net.

I was out in the cove one day with a barred rock bantam rooster named "Cocky Locky" on board. I set the net and paddled over to the bank, where I could observe any bobbing of the corks on the net, which would indicate I was catching fish. I wasn't paying much attention to anything else, when I heard the sound of an engine approaching. Turning to face the sound, I saw the bow of a green boat operated by a game warden. When he asked to see my gill-net license, I instantly realized that I had neglected to bring it or any other sort of identification.

About that time Cocky Locky hopped from the bottom of my little craft onto one of the seats, flapped his wings, and crowed. The game warden, who I found out later, was Locky Freeman, seemed totally stunned by the presence of a crowing rooster in a boat. He asked me all sorts of questions about what I was doing out there carrying around a chicken and what was I was going to do with it. He was skeptical when I told him I had brought along the chicken just for the ride. Locky always had a word for people that he considered "not quite right," and that was *cracky*.

When he saw that crowing rooster in my boat, he had no doubts that I was "cracky" and told me that if I didn't have a gill-net license with me, I would have to take up the net and go to the "hill." I don't think he wanted to get close enough to me to give me a ticket, and he departed as quickly as he had arrived. I was glad old Cocky Locky was along though, because the fine would have been a major imposition on my meager funds. When I reminded Locky of that encounter years afterwards, he said repeatedly, "Ben, that was you?"

Late one Saturday evening Locky and I were patrolling the inlets around Capers and Dewees islands. We approached a large boat that was anchored in the middle of the channel and displaying no anchor light. As we pulled alongside, we saw a man sitting in a canvas chair on the fantail and holding a cold drink. As Locky was discussing the man's failure to display navigation lights, I noticed some movement near the stern, and glanced over to witness an attractive naked woman reclining in an enormous water-filled cooler. Locky spotted her about the same time I did and blurted out, "Great Gawd!" Noticing all this sudden attention, she stood up out of the water, stepped out of the cooler, sashayed across the deck right in front of us, and disappeared inside. She returned a few moments later wrapped in a towel and sat in a chair next to the man, acting as if nothing were out of the ordinary. By that time Locky was slack jawed and sputtering so badly he could barely manage a polite "good night" as we hastened to depart.

We had one other naked encounter, which this time involved men. One night we pulled close to a lengthy sailboat running without lights in the Intracoastal Waterway behind the Isle of Palms. We called over to the man at the wheel to slow down so we could come alongside. After I grabbed hold of their rail, Locky got up from his seat to interview the operator. When the man stood up, he was a little higher than Locky and without a stitch on. About that time another man emerged from below, and he too was unclothed. Locky was completely speechless. He returned to his seat and said in a low voice, "Let's get out here!" He told me later, "Ben, I just can't talk to somebody like that, right there in front of me." I told him that I understood, and we went looking for business elsewhere.

Locky fretted over what he was going to do when he retired. One day he said, "Ben, when people retire they ride around in boats and hang around in the woods. That's what I do for a living. I'm not going to be able to do that after I retire!" Being a game warden was his whole life, but he had to retire after he reached the mandatory retirement age of sixty-five. Locky did not live long after that, but memories of his personality and his stories live on.

Another colorful old-timer was Watson "Mack" McCaskill, a retired Charleston County policeman and a deputy Wildlife Conservation officer. He had also served with the Horry County Police. Mr. Mack had been hired in the early 1980s to be superintendent of Capers Island, a state Heritage Trust Preserve located between Dewees Island and Bull Island.

I had been patrolling that area of the coast for a number of years and had worked closely with the former superintendent. I was anxious to meet the new man because I had worked for his son, Dick McCaskill, when I was a stevedore on the Charleston waterfront, and I knew that if he was anything like Dick, Mr. Mack must be a pretty stalwart sort.

I was not disappointed. He was sturdier and more energetic than men half his age. Mr. Mack and I quickly became fast friends and spent a lot of time together riding the roads and the beaches, making improvements around the superintendent's camp, keeping the roads clear, and picking up trash off the inlets and beaches.

Mr. Mack was quite a storyteller and had plenty of tales to tell about his adventures on the Horry and Charleston County police forces with his friend Buck Taylor, who afterwards served for years as the Charleston County clerk of court. When he and Mr. Taylor would get together at the camp on Capers the stories would go on for hours.

Mr. Mack would frequently reminisce about the old rough-and-tumble days of law enforcement before Miranda warnings and other "professional courtesies" were observed. He said when a report of a cutting or killing came in, they would rush to the scene, round up anybody they could find, and give them a "scenic tour" of the Francis Marion National Forest. By the time they emerged from the piney woods, they would know who said what to whom, who did the cutting or shooting, and where the culprit was likely to be found.

Mr. Mack could whip up amazing quantities of good food in that tiny kitchen in the trailer at the superintendent's camp. His specialty was fried bream or bass caught in the pond by his home in Awendaw. That fare was served with his special coleslaw and hush puppies, but nothing was beyond his culinary reach.

He built fine, sturdy picnic tables, which he placed at several of the popular camping spots on either end of the island at Capers and Price inlets. He became annoyed when he discovered that some of the campers liked the tables so much they carried them home. After the thefts of several tables, he began keeping them near the road that ran through the middle of the island from the superintendent's camp to the beach. On weekends he dragged them, sledlike, behind his Jeep to the campsites of people he deemed trust-worthy. Over several years they developed a nicely sanded, rounded finish.

He was also generous in providing campers with firewood that he had cut from fallen tree limbs gathered from the interior roads. He said this eliminated the temptation for campers to chop up the picturesque sun-bleached trees strewn about the front beach, known as the "boneyard."

Capers Island was the locus of many biological studies, ranging from bird life to reptiles. Mr. Mack was frequently more knowledgeable than some of the biologists regarding the location and habits of the beasts they were looking for. He built observation blinds overlooking several of the big ponds near the west end of the island, and he always seemed completely at home in this wild, undeveloped landscape.

Mr. Mack and I shared a bad habit, which was chewing tobacco. We were driving around on the island one day, when I noticed that he didn't have his usual chew and offered him a pinch of mine. He replied, "Ben, I've quit. A couple of weeks ago, I was driving out on the beach. The wind was really blowing hard and when I leaned over to spit, the wind blew that quid right around my head into my left ear. I decided then and there that it was time to quit!"

Mr. Mack did a lot of work with children on the island. AmeriCorps groups and youngsters working off community-service time were given opportunities to clear paths, clean up litter, and make repairs around the compound. During the summer the temperature and humidity could be formidable. Mosquitoes, red bugs, and ticks were ever present, and the appearance of cottonmouth water moccasins was not uncommon. Most of the youngsters had not experienced nature that close before. It was not like *Nova* or *Animal Planet*. Some complained and found other forms of com-munity service, but Mr. Mack fed then well, and he was a hands-on super-visor with his shirt off, leading the way and outworking all of them. Mr. Mack was working until the last day of his life and was a good friend and a great asset to the department.

I frequently worked with agents of the U.S. Fish and Wildlife Service, the federal game wardens. Every time I felt burdened by the large territory I struggled to patrol, I remembered that just two federal agents were assigned to cover the entire state. I did a lot of work with Special Agent Garland Swain, a North Carolina native who had a reputation for being totally unrelenting in his mission to apprehend violators of federal game laws, most particularly the migratory-bird regulations.

Federal game warden Garland Swain with loggerhead turtle eggs seized from a poacher caught on Edisto Beach

There are many stories of Agent Swain materializing in the middle of a flooded rice field to apprehend men hunting ducks over bait. One hunter told me that on a brutally cold morning Agent Swain suddenly appeared out of the reeds not seventy-five feet in front of his blind and just as suddenly disappeared as he stepped into one of the deep quarter drains that intersected the field. All he could see was Swain's hat floating in the ripples. Continuing the story, the hunter said that Agent Swain emerged from the depths, walked in the knee-deep water straight over to his blind, identified himself as a federal agent, and asked to see his license. During the interview no mention was ever made of his mishap, nor did he appear to react to the discomfort of the freezing temperature. Agent Swain pulled one of the pink federal information forms from a canvas bag, took the necessary details, told the hunter that he would be receiving a federal summons on the charge of "taking migratory birds by aid of bait" in the mail, and departed, carrying two ducks he had seized. He retrieved his hat on the way out.

Another federal game warden was George Hines, who was the special agent in charge of the South Carolina district. A wonderful story is told about Agent Hines, who had for years been trying to catch a bunch of renegade duck hunters in Sparkleberry Swamp in Clarendon County. The word was out that the outlaws had built a number of hunting shacks high up in the gum and cypress trees. They used these tree houses as platforms from which to shoot ducks as they poured in to eat the bait that had been generously applied to the water beneath the trees.

Flying over the area in the fall when the leaves were off the trees, Hines found several of the arboreal structures and, using a chart, marked a compass route through the dense, flooded swamp. He was dropped off unseen at an obscure landing one Friday afternoon and paddled his small wooden Louisiana pirogue through the swamp until he found one of the houses. Hanging back long enough to determine no one was in the area, he threw out his bait scrape and found corn everywhere.

He then retreated some distance into the deep shadows of the tree line and waited. Just before dark, he heard the sound of an outboard engine echoing through the swamp. The boat stopped below the tree house, and he listened to two or three men engaging in a muffled conversation for more than forty-five minutes. He waited until all the noise had stopped and moved his pirogue in a little closer. He could see the light of Coleman lanterns through the windows of the shack. He heard movement and laughter from inside the shack until around eleven P.M.; then all the lights went out, and the night became silent and colder.

At five thirty the next morning, he saw light appear in the tree house windows. A few moments later, a man walked out onto the deck, hung out a lantern, and answered the call of nature over the rail. The man looked out into the darkness of the tree canopy for a few moments, took a swallow out of his steaming coffee cup, and called out, "George, George. You might as well come on over. I know it's freezing out there. Come on over and have a hot cup of coffee."

Hines, having no clue how they could have known he was there, paddled out of the darkness, climbed up the ladder to the deck, and was invited into the tree house. Once inside, he asked, "How in the world did you know I was out there?" The man replied, "Well George, we actually didn't know where you were, we go outside every morning and say that."

Marijuana,
Homegrown and Imported

ack in the 1970s and 1980s, marijuana smuggling was a common occurrence in the coastal waters of South Carolina. My first encounter with drug trafficking happened only a few years after I had joined the Charleston unit. I was in Mount Pleasant checking seafood dealers when I got a call on the radio for me to proceed immediately to Steamboat Landing on Edisto Island, where a major drug bust was going down.

I drove as fast as my old Plymouth would go. By the time I got there, the needle on the temperature gauge was out of sight. A sizeable contingent of Charleston County policemen was already there, and a large tractor-trailer truck was parked on the edge of the landing. Several handcuffed culprits were already in custody. Other officers had fanned out in the wooded area around the landing looking for other suspects.

The back of the trailer was open and appeared to be fully loaded with small rectangular bales of marijuana packed in black plastic trash bags and bound with duct tape. Everybody was in a state of great excitement. Radios were blaring, and various officers were giving rapid-fire orders. In the midst of the flurry of activity around the parking lot, came the roar and screeching siren of a rapidly approaching vehicle.

Around the curve careened a game-warden car, which came to a grinding stop in a cloud of dust and gravel in the middle of the parking lot. As the dust settled, a dead chicken dropped to the pavement from the shattered grill of the car, and another could be seen deeply imbedded in the grillwork of the radiator. Officer Wiley Knight, then a corporal, exited the smoking patrol car and came over to where the group of officers was standing, to find out what was going on.

As he approached the knot of officers, he noticed that they were all staring at his car. He turned and saw the objects of their attention, the dead chickens in and around his front bumper. He said he had noticed a flock of chickens crossing the road as he came through and explained that he thought they had all made it.

A short time later one of the county officers came over with a large piece of chalk and drew a circle around the chicken "crime scene" as well as an outline around the "body." Everyone present was getting a lot of laughs over that little spectacle and hardly noticed when an old rusty red pickup slowly pulled into the parking lot and stopped near Officer Knight's car.

A gray-bearded man emerged, walked over to the "crime scene," and stood there gazing at the dead chickens. Officer Knight walked over to inquire about his interest in the mangled corpses. The old man said that he wanted to know who killed those chickens. Officer Knight replied that he had done so and that he was conducting an investigation on exactly who owned those chickens, which had been turned loose on the public roads and had caused such great damage to state property.

The old gentleman quickly stated that he didn't know anything about who owned those chickens. He said that he was just curious about who had killed them, and he slowly crossed the lot back to his truck and drove away.

Not all the marijuana coming into the state was imported. A substantial quantity of it was homegrown. Once while I was patrolling landings north of Mount Pleasant, I heard District Five sergeant Edwin Mitchum come up on the radio and ask if I could give him a hand. He said that the day before he had spotted a car parked on a side road in the Francis Marion National Forest. When he pulled up behind it, a man jumped out and fled into a section known as Button Bush Bay. Earlier in the morning a group of deer hunters heard someone shouting for help, and Officer Mitchum figured it was the person who had run on him.

After the man had run away, Mitchum had followed a small track through the woods not far from where the man's car was parked and discovered a half-acre patch of cultivated marijuana plants. Officer Mitchum had called in the Charleston Metro Narcotics Unit, which had come the day before, cut down all the plants, and hauled them away.

I met Officer Mitchum at his house at Green Bay in Berkeley County, and we drove over to where he had seen the man run into the woods.

Mitchum said he never thought the man would get too far because that area was so thick that even a deer could hardly get through it.

Soon joining us was another District Five warden, Officer Victor Lincoln, who lived at Honey Hill in the middle of the Francis Marion National Forest. His reputation for tracking was legendary. His tracking skills were said to be so keen that he could track a snake across a paved parking lot. Officer Mitchum, who was considerably older than Lincoln, was no slouch in the tracking department either. Both officers were well known by Hell Hole Swamp deer-hunting crowd.

Officer Lincoln headed straight away into the dense brush and was quickly lost from sight. Carrying only his service revolver and a hand-held radio, he reported from time to time that he was on the man's trail and that he could periodically hear someone cry out in the distance.

After about an hour and a half, Officer Lincoln reported that he had found the man and that he was unarmed. He had been snakebitten, was covered with insect bites and scratches, and had had most of his clothes torn off. Reporting that the man was too weak to walk, Lincoln didn't see how he could carry him out.

Officer Mitchum immediately thought of several solutions. The first was to call the U.S. Forest Service to come with one of the heavy turn plows they used to cut fire breaks and bulldoze their way to him. He had already contacted the county police, and a few of their officers were beginning to arrive. One of the county officers suggested getting a helicopter.

Several calls from the county-police headquarters secured the services of a helicopter from the McEntire Air National Guard Base, near Columbia, which had "vertical extraction capability," the military moniker for a basket at the end of a rope.

By the time the helicopter arrived, there must have been twenty law-enforcement vehicles parked around the area, as well as an EMS truck, the Forest Service bulldozer, and several television-news vehicles. The "vertical extraction" was expertly performed. Officer Lincoln sent the exhausted and tattered fugitive out first. The man was probably glad at that point to be taken into custody and have his many maladies attended to. Officer Lincoln came out next, also muddy and scratched up, and he descended in the basket amid much celebration and fanfare.

There were stories from time to time about "square grouper" found floating far offshore, or washed up on the beaches of the barrier islands. There were also tales of large stashes of those marijuana bales having been offloaded on remote islands and hidden in the dunes under coverings of canvas and sand. Many of those involved were the grandsons of men who helped smuggle Canadian whiskey through the same beaches and marshes during Prohibition and who transported the legendary Hell Hole moonshine from the nether regions of Berkeley County to the "Blind Tigers" throughout Charleston. "Blind Tigers" were establishments where illegal whiskey was sold. Back then South Carolina was known as the "Iodine State," and the motto of Berkeley County was "There ain't a goiter in a gallon" because of the corn grown in its iodine-rich soil.

One afternoon I was patrolling in Price Inlet and spotted a sailboat awash in the surf about halfway down the Capers Island beach. I pulled my boat up on the point of Capers, set out my anchor on the sand, and walked down toward the boat, which was lying on its side being battered by the breakers.

At some distance ahead of me I noticed two boys walking in my direction. They were wearing bathing suits and carrying something between them on a long board. When they got close enough to recognize my uniform,

Examining a marijuana smuggler's sailboat that washed up on the Capers Island beach. Beached and sunken drug boats were not uncommon in the late 1970s and early 1980s.

they turned and walked over to the ridge of sand dunes, where they quickly disappeared from view, appearing empty-handed only moments later.

As they neared, I introduced myself and asked what they had been carrying. "Nothing," was their reply. On a sand beach it is not difficult to follow footprints, so I traced their tracks over the dunes and came upon a long board with a beach towel covering several black garbage bags. I untied one of the bags and could clearly see that it contained some rather soggy marijuana.

I waited for the boys to get into their boat, where I could reasonably expect to see some identification. I explained to them what I had found and that their foot tracks provided a steady trail along the beach to where it had been left. They quickly denied ownership of the bags and claimed that they had found them in the surf near the abandoned sailboat and were "just cleaning up the beach."

It was clear to me that they were not the smugglers and that they had just picked a bad time to take advantage of what they saw as a good opportunity. I took down their names, addresses, and phone numbers in case I needed to talk with them later and headed back down the beach to the stranded boat. I walked out to it and found no identifying numbers. There was already a lot of sand in the cockpit, and I saw no additional evidence of contraband in any of the compartments.

Further up the beach I picked up two more garbage bags containing marijuana. They were heavily waterlogged, as were the two bags left in the dunes. I threw all of them over my shoulder, carried them back to the inlet, and flung them in the bow of my boat. On the way back to the waterway, I saw several trawlers tied up at the dock on Little Bull Island and stopped by for a little "show and tell." A contingent of the Shem Creek commercial fishing crowd had arrived for some weekend festivities. When I brought one of the bags of marijuana up, they all howled. They begged me to go inside the house for a little bite to eat, saying they would "watch out" for that bag until I came back out.

Their entreaties were to no avail, and I left a much-disappointed crowd sitting mournfully on the front steps of the Magwood House. A member of the Charleston Metro Narcotics Unit met me the Isle of Palms Marina and retrieved the contraband. The sailboat was later salvaged by a shrimp trawler and sold.

Off and Running

I n a flurry of decision making, I resolved to retire and leave the field to the younger generation of game wardens. The department made my decision easier by offering a voluntary separation incentive, a new statewide policy designed to ease out to pasture some of us who had grown long in the tooth. It was part of the department's efforts to preserve dwindling operating funds during a period of severe state-budget cuts.

I picked the time of my retirement to coincide with the final moment of the 2001–2 duck season, which was at sunset, 5:45 P.M., on January twentieth. I launched my johnboat on a gravel ramp at the Edisto River end of the airplane runway on Pon Pon, a three-thousand-acre plantation managed for hunting. Before the curtain fell on my career, Belle and I had patrolled for fourteen hours on the Edisto River between Jehossee Island and the Prospect Hill impoundment, issuing nine warning tickets for waterfowl violations.

Remembering my first days as a game warden when I earned the moniker "Mudflat Moïse," I thought it seemed appropriate when the car bogged down to the frame at the bottom of the ramp as I was attempting to pull my boat out of the water at the end of the patrol. To get help I had to walk more than a mile in the mounting darkness to the far end of the runway, to intercept gunners leaving the "Temple of the Hunt," George Dean Johnson's Pon Pon hunt camp. Tadpole Baldwin, the plantation manager, and an entourage of curious hunters, returned to the ramp in a train of pickups

Patrolling the area offshore of Sullivan's Island on August 8, 2000, during the raising of the Confederate submarine Hunley

and assisted me with the task of removing my car and boat from the primordial ooze.

By the time they were dragged over the crest of the ramp, the car and boat were covered with a thick layer of mud, spun out from my car wheels and the truck doing the towing. I contemplated that turn of events on the drive back to Charleston and started laughing. I hooted and cackled all the way back home at the thought that the first minutes of my retirement were spent digging myself out of the mud, an event in many ways typical of some of my more memorable days as a game warden.

When I parked my muddy rig at the Fort Johnson law-enforcement office the next morning and turned in my badge, gun, and uniform, I left a job whose responsibilities had changed considerably since my initial trip to that office more than two decades before. When I became a game warden in 1978, we were under the leadership of Dr. James A. Timmerman, only the fourth director since James Henry Rice was appointed to that position in 1910. The modern Department of Natural Resources grew out of what was essentially a warden force. The ensuing years brought dramatic growth and change, as the introduction of state hunting and fishing licenses and federal aid programs made it possible to increase the breadth of services beyond mere law enforcement.

When I first donned the uniform, college degrees were not considered an important requisite for being hired. The idea of issuing twin-engine speedboats, automatic pistols, and global-positioning systems to officers was unthinkable. State duck stamps and saltwater-fishing licenses were nonexistent. There were no size or creel limits on saltwater fish either.

It was not uncommon to see fishermen returning from trips standing knee deep in fish piled on the decks of their boats. Sometimes there were so many fish that there was no more room for them inside the fishermen's coolers. Many of the fish lying about the deck were curled up and dried out by the sun. On weekends the trash bins and waters around every marina and landing used to stink from the rotting sailfish and marlin that had been brought back to the dock and thrown away once the bragging and picture taking was done. Conscientious sports fishermen, who saw increasingly depleted stocks of the more popular inshore fish such as spottail bass, trout, and flounder, and marlin and sailfish offshore, came to understand the effects of the excesses.

The laws regulating saltwater sports fishing, as well as the requirement for a saltwater recreational-fishing license came as a result of the initiatives of the sports fishermen themselves. They lobbied the Wildlife Department and the members of the General Assembly to enact regulations on size limits and catch limits. As a result of their public-information efforts, regulations were enacted that in time greatly improved the quality of coastal fishing.

The new responsibilities had come in addition to ones traditionally associated with the job. Boating-safety patrols enforcing newly enacted boating-under-the-influence laws became a core responsibility, and a cooperative agreement with National Marine Fisheries required state officers to regularly patrol far offshore, enforcing federal regulations on pelagic fish. Following the 2001 terrorist attack on the World Trade Center, coastal game wardens had become a key component in maintaining homeland security in the state's busy ports and along the coast.

Back in the old days newly hired game wardens were issued a badge, a law manual, and a ticket book and sent forth to apprehend violators. On the cover of the 1932 *Game and Fish Law Manual,* Chief Game Warden Alfred Aldrich Richardson boldly printed an admonition: "Thoroughly familiarize yourself with these laws and save useless correspondence with the office as to the laws. The law is plain." That manual was printed on fifty-seven pages. Now it requires twice that many pages to cover only the marine fisheries regulations, which are in addition to the fish, game, and boating laws.

Other than having the requisite local political connections, most of the old wardens were hired because they possessed some knowledge of the woods and waters in their counties. At one time it was widely believed that some of the most notorious violators were hired as wardens just to get them on the side of the law. Since that time woods skills have become secondary to education and "professional" law-enforcement training. As a consequence game wardens have evolved into "conservation officers" and, more recently, to "law-enforcement officers." I always preferred the time-honored title of "game warden," which, once said, required no further explanation.

The new requirements of resource enforcement often required advanced technical expertise, involving training in the functions of various types of equipment or in identifying the expanded number of regulated fish. Officers now are far better informed and technologically savvy than we were twenty years ago. Aside from the remote threat of an encounter with a terrorist, officers still face the traditional dangers of working in an environment with neophyte boat operators, inexperienced hunters, and all-too-numerous folks inclined to display an aggressive, in-your-face attitude. They are now better trained and equipped to deal with it.

Even with their heavy load of duties, some officers find the time to become involved with conservation organizations or carry the message of conservation to various civic groups. Some officers are more comfortable on a podium behind a microphone than others. It always scared the hell out of me, but I designed ways to get through it because I believed that an informed public was a valuable ally to law enforcement.

So far mine has not been an idle retirement. Even after five years I still field a lot of phone calls on resource issues. My bride, Anne, and I have traveled to China and twice to South Africa. We have attended to the marriage of our younger daughter, Sarah, to Simons Young. We have also welcomed the birth, four years apart, of our two granddaughters, Margaret Anne and Sarah Elizabeth, to our older daughter, Melissa, and her husband, Boyd McLeod, of St. Matthews. After Anne retired from the South Carolina State Ports Authority, we undertook a major renovation effort on our circa 1844 home in downtown Charleston, where we have lived for almost thirty years.

I continue to write book reviews for the *Charleston Post and Courier,* which I have done for more than twenty-five years. I also write stories on outdoor topics for another newspaper, the *Charleston Mercury,* and other publications. I like to think that I follow the tradition of an illustrious array of native writers whose observations and prose were inspired by their enjoyment of the woods and waters of South Carolina.

Those writers shared their individual perspectives and particular concerns about the portion of the natural world they frequented. My take on the natural scene—aside from a few vignettes of personal hunting experiences—comes from a completely different angle. Writers such as William Elliott, Archibald Rutledge, Henry E. Davis, Harry Hampton, and Havilah Babcock wrote stories of their own hunting adventures or stories about hunting or fishing in general. The focus of Mr. Davis's book is on the eastern wild turkey; Dr. Babcock's books center around the bobwhite quail. My book centers on violators.

Mr. Rutledge and Mr. Hampton wrote elegantly of their experiences afield with a keen eye for detail. Their writings reveal that for them the seeking was perhaps even more important than the taking. Their writings also reflect their strong sense of stewardship, a deep-seated regard for the land, and they had a wonderful facility for connecting the reader with their sentiments. That sort of ecological consciousness is also apparent in much of Mr. Rutledge's poetry. I can understand how he, and other authors, could be moved to express in prose or poetry the many delights of the outdoor experience, for I too have been similarly affected.

My friend John LaRoche and I remain involved in conservation causes, but in a different way: by either doing or donating for auction or by hosting oyster roasts for such organizations as the Sewee Environmental Education Center, the Keepers of the Wild, the Lowcountry Open Land Trust, the Harry Hampton Memorial Wildlife Fund, and Ducks Unlimited—to name only a few. We feel good that our efforts have proven to be effective and productive fund-raisers for those organizations, whose special concern is protecting and preserving the natural resources of our state.

Enough cannot be said of the value of those organizations' mission and the hard work of their staff and volunteers. It has been largely through their efforts—in league with the South Carolina Department of Natural Resources—that environmental awareness has been heightened among the general public as well as politicians. Taxes have been earmarked to acquire and maintain open spaces. Conservation zoning has been enacted, and property owners have been afforded opportunities for property-tax abatement if they place land in protective easements.

Those measures will not halt the sprawl that appears to be engulfing the lowcountry, but they should serve to steer development in the right direction and help to minimize its impact. I have witnessed the burgeoning pressure on the lowcountry landscape, gradual at first, then with a headlong rush to fill every vacant gap in what used to be long stretches of unbroken tree lines.

It has been alarming to see the erosion of the commercial fishing infrastructure as waterfront land values have dramatically increased and steadily moved out the fishermen. Rows of private docks now intrude into oyster grounds; hotels and restaurants stand where packinghouses and ice plants once existed; and houses have supplanted boat-repair yards and shrimp-boat docks.

As the lowcountry becomes more populous, the pressures of competition for public spaces will increase. Areas that once were considered remote, offering respite from the noise and bustle of urban life, are now scenes of parades of boats and throngs of people enjoying the country life.

There are now more people afield in the woods and waters who are completely reliant on the new technology rather than on knowledge of nature gained through personal experience. Technological improvements have become a dominant force in hunting and fishing, with better navigational devices, powerful boats, new firearms and cartridges, and catalogs full of items that improve the edge of the hunter or fisherman over his quarry.

People now tend to be in too much of a hurry and less inclined to take the time to savor their outdoor experiences fully. There is more talk about getting a limit as a measure of the hunter's success as opposed to the broader sense of enjoying the experience of being in the woods or on the water. The lack of restraint and being in a hurry are probably the chief causes of violations, apart from motives of pure greed. The Department of Natural Resources will likely face regulatory challenges that spring from aggressive self-interest and the increasing intrusion of outdoor technology.

Aldo Leopold wrote in his *Sand County Almanac* (1949) that there is value in any experience that exercises those ethical restraints collectively known as "sportsmanship." He called them "split rail values," a viscerally felt land ethic and ethos of sport formerly instilled in impressionable neophytes at a father, grandfather, or uncle's knee. There are no substitutes for such parental or avuncular lessons, for the novice pays heed because his teacher, a person he respects, has considered the instructions important enough to share and because the lessons usually arise from a common experience as opposed to a gratuitous dispensation of advice.

The lowcountry has a long tradition of considering sportsmanship afield as one of the distinguishing characteristics of gentlemanly conduct. Along with observing the normal courtesies such as practicing gun safety, obeying the game laws, and thanking the host, a well-rounded sportsman is expected to have an understanding and appreciation of his quarry as well as a knowledge of the flora and fauna of the surrounding terrain.

Along with the visible impacts of urbanization on the land, the biology of the lowcountry is also undergoing dramatic shifts. Nonmigratory Canada geese, coyotes, armadillos, green mussels, Pacific barnacles, and phragmites —an aggressive reed, seldom, if ever, seen twenty-five years ago—are non-indigenous animals and plants that have taken up residency in the low-country and compete for food and space with native fauna and flora.

Twenty-five years ago, alligators and the eastern brown pelican were categorized as threatened species in South Carolina. Alligators have since become so numerous that a limited harvest is permitted, and pelicans have experienced a resurgent population growth, largely through strict regulations on the application of agricultural insecticides. Invasive and endangered species will continue to occupy the agenda and tax the ingenuity of our wildlife department. I am confident that all those issues are being addressed and that reasonable solutions are in the works.

I continue to savor my own hunting experiences and plan to learn how to fly fish one of these days. Duck and turkey hunting remain two of my greatest passions, and I have been fortunate to be a guest at places as remarkable for their scenic qualities and opportunities for socializing as for their abundance of game. Some of my recent hunting experiences have involved traveling to places such as South Africa for big game, Arkansas and Canada for ducks, and Texas for turkeys. The spring and the fall still retain their magic for me, full of the excitement of pure opportunity.

I have promised myself that I am going to spend more time on my favorite place in the world, Moïse Island, a less-than-quarter-acre hummock in the marsh on the Intracoastal Waterway near the Cape Romain Refuge and Capers Island. For some odd reason, I seemed to have had more "organized" free time when I was working than I do in retirement, and of late my sojourns there have been few and far between.

I acquired the island in 1985 from my friends Gene and Sue Drew of nearby Driftwood Plantation in Awendaw. With the help of countless friends, I built a small cabin, an open cook shed, and a dock leading to a deep-water creek. The campfire, formed by stones brought by friends from every part of the globe, is the nerve center of the island, and the warmth and spirit of camaraderie it imparts has encouraged me to tell many of the stories you have just read.

About the Author

BEN McC. MOÏSE was a conservation officer with the South Carolina Department of Natural Resources from 1978 to 2002, working primarily in the marshes and coastal waters of the Palmetto State. In recognition of his achievements in law enforcement, he was presented the Guy Bradley Award in 1990 by the North American Fish and Wildlife Foundation and the Order of the Palmetto in 1994 by South Carolina governor Carroll Campbell. In retirement Moïse is a freelance contributor to the *Charleston Post and Courier, Charleston Mercury,* and other regional publications. He lives in Charleston with his wife, Anne, and their Boykin spaniel, Belle.